Controls From Within

CONTROLS FROM WITHIN

Techniques for the Treatment of the
AGGRESSIVE CHILD

by

FRITZ REDL

and

DAVID WINEMAN

THE FREE PRESS, *New York*
COLLIER–MACMILLAN LIMITED, *London*

Collier-Macmillan Canada, Ltd., Toronto, Ontario

Library of Congress Catalog Card Number: 52–8161

FIRST FREE PRESS PAPERBACK EDITION 1965

Third printing November 1966

To Our Wonderful Staff

PREFACE

IN *Children Who Hate* [1] we tried to describe what the situation looks like if Behavioral Controls suffer a severe breakdown, and just what the various ways are in which children's "egos" and their "consciences" may be disturbed. We based most of our descriptions on our own observations within the framework of three projects which had given us such a wonderful chance to observe at close range, in actual group life with children, what otherwise is hardly accessible to such minute study: *The Detroit Group Project,* its *Summer Camp,* and *Pioneer House.* We had tried to center most of our illustrations around the group of children with whom we lived at Pioneer House, mainly because we felt it would help the reader to catch the intangibles of daily behavior and group atmosphere if we kept a relatively small group of youngsters constantly before his eyes over a considerable stretch of time.

We concentrated, so to speak, on describing the control-breakdown of the children who hate. We hoped, however, that the light which the study of their more extreme pathology is likely to throw on basic personality functions might also show us more than we have been able to see before about the specific functions of the normal ego and the normal conscience of the average child in their daily job.

This book tries to fill in the other side of the story, the one of

[1] Fritz Redl and David Wineman, *Children Who Hate* (Glencoe, Illinois: Free Press, 1951).

[7]

even greater importance, for the purpose of which everything else, no matter how fascinating, is but a prelude. For, how would it help us to know how disturbed children act and why they act that way unless we would also search for ways of *prevention and cure?* This book attempts to draw in bold lines the pattern for a new treatment design for the ego disturbances of the extremely aggressive child. From a general awareness that these children need more comprehensive treatment approaches than the individual interview of the usual therapy session is able to provide, we try to lead into much more concrete and specific suggestions of just what needs to be done, step by step, and what tools the clinician has to make available for combat with their peculiar disease. Just as in the other book, though, we are also eager to lead the reader into a much more specific inspection of just what constitutes wise handling of behavior in the daily life of the normal child, a question which every teacher, group leader, and parent is vitally interested in. Again, we are going to depict what we are trying to suggest primarily in relation to the behavioral productions of our Pioneers. In the struggle of finding ways of treatment for them, a number of tools become more sharply perceivable which are just as important for the educational scene of normal daily life in home and school.

Our emphasis on the importance of the "control system" in the human personality has led to the title of this book. For one of the ultimate goals of the educator as well as of the clinician is to secure adequate "controls from within." The reader will notice that our story shows that the way to controls from within is amply paved with abundant incidents of "controls from without." This must not be misunderstood as suggesting the belief that controls from within are the automatic result of a system of outside interferences. On the contrary, this book is especially eager to show the complexity of design that is needed in order to secure the growth of really well-internalized behavioral controls, even in such moments when, for reality reasons, outside interference seems to dominate the temporary scene. We also hope to describe, in part at least, the very process of internalization itself, without which any temporarily achieved behavioral control would remain educationally and clinically sterile.

For those who open this book without having read *Children Who Hate*, a few special notes are in order. It was unwise to repeat nearly all the essentials of the description of our children, their background, and so forth, or of the design of the treatment projects on which these pages are based. Some of these details will naturally emerge as we unfold our treatment strategy before your eyes. Other details might better be looked up right away. For this purpose we added a condensed description of some of the data needed in order to put our illustrations into the right perspective. It can be found on page 321 in the Appendix of this book.

The illustrations used in this book are, again, of two different types: Some of them are drawn literally and mostly verbatim from our recordings and are marked, at the end, by the notation "Entry." Those illustrations not marked "entry" are also taken either from the recorded materials or from the recollection of incidents by the staff. They frequently represent excerpts from episodes, the detailed verbatim reproduction of which would have been too clumsy for the purpose of illustrating the point for which they were used.

Most important of all, however, seems to us the recognition of the need for caution in the evaluation of the material offered in this book. We do not pretend to come out with a blueprint for the way children should be treated, nor do we imply that the way Pioneer House was set up should be considered as exemplary and ideal. Far from it. We ourselves would not repeat the design without considerable changes if we had a chance to start all over again. We also realize how many modifications and variations of anything we are going to say the specific background, age, disturbance type of similar but not identical children would demand, and what serious modifications of all this would be necessary, were it translated into socio-economically and culturally very different settings. By the way, we are not apologetic about the imperfections of our own design either. Only actual tryout and thoroughly recorded experiences can lead to eventual answers, and one always has to start such a tryout with some design in order to get enough new questions raised on the basis of which further research can proceed.

We do imply, however, irrespective of how many adaptations and changes in details may be needed for an "improved design" for any specific treatment home, that the basic issues involved in clinical treatment of the ego-disturbed child will remain constant to a considerable degree. We think that what we went through and learned at Pioneer House is important enough to be conveyed to other practitioners, and specific enough to form the basis for new and much more extensive research on a much more organized and a larger scale.

Besides the special task which we set ourselves in conveying this material for the sake of what may be its intrinsic value, we also hope that this book will stimulate a more thoughtful approach to the handling of child behavior by parents and teachers, that it will lead to a clearer concept of "treatment" and to revision in design for many children's institutions, reformatories, and detention homes. We also want to induce enlightened communities to create new and badly needed facilities for preventive treatment, to create adequate projects for further research into new treatment techniques, and to stir the average citizen out of his amazing apathy toward the inexcusable and unfortunate amount of avoidable human waste.[2]

[2] No one has focused on this problem so poignantly and vividly as Albert Deutsch in his book, *Our Rejected Children* (Boston: Little, Brown & Co., 1950).

CONTENTS

The Challenge of the Children Who Hate

WHAT is so special about the "children who hate"? Is it not well known enough by now that all children develop negative feelings even toward those they trust and love? Of course it is, and many wonderful studies have pictured the story of childhood aggression in great detail. The children we are going to describe are sharply marked off from their less disturbed contemporaries by two characteristics. They are the children who cannot meet the challenge of the tasks of everyday life without becoming a helpless bundle of drives. And, among the variegated impulses which they cannot curb and master, most vivid, most starkly sketched against whatever social backdrop forms the canvas of their life scene are the strivings and urges we have come to identify under the concept of *Hate*. Out of their failure to meet this challenge for the synthesis of their inner strivings with some kind of value- and reality-scheme of things is born their challenge to us. Who, now, is *"Us?"* Us is whoever lives with them, educates them, raises them, tries to pattern them. *Us* is also the clinician who tries to help them overcome their disturbances, the settlement worker and playground leader who plan their recreation, and the many other adults who play more than marginal roles in their everyday lives.

In our own work with these youngsters we found that it is not only hate that they cannot master. Let's make no mistake about

it—they have plenty of hate: whirlpools and rivers and oceans of it
flooding, unchecked and uncheckable, the terrain of their everyday
lives. But, since in order even to begin to help them we had to
devote ourselves to a most intensive scrutiny of how they looked
in their moments of breakdown, we found that what psychiatry
calls their ego is afflicted in many areas of functioning with a severe
performance weakness. By ego, incidentally, we mean that part of
the personality which is charged with keeping us in touch with
"reality" and with helping us to regulate our impulse expression
so that it is within the bounds which such a reality dictates. Imagine
a man on the way to a party, a little late, and anxious to get there,
in order not to miss any more good fun than he has to. Approaching
a railroad crossing, he sees the red danger lights blinking off and
on and hears in the distance the increasingly loud wail of the approaching train. Maybe he can beat it—and maybe he can't. Does
he try? His ego makes the decision as to how he meets his impulse
need to get to that party in the face of the threat of physical danger
from the train bearing down upon him. Where the issue is complicated by value demands—is a given act right or wrong?—the case
is the same but only more complicated by the relationship between
the conscience and the ego and between both of these and the impulses. In *Children Who Hate* we have dealt in much more detail
with the total complexities of ego function and the ego's relation to
other parts of the personality. However, we think that this précis
may enable the reader to approach on some common ground with
us the problem of the breakdown of ego functioning in children
whom we studied.

We were able to construct a kind of *crude task chart of everyday
challenges to the ego* in which these children were seriously deficient. Ironically enough, however, as though to add to their enormous problem in coping with their hate-corroded inner selves, in
the breakdown of their ability to meet these varied tasks there was
one major catch-all and end-all reaction: Hate. Thus we saw hate
expressed as a primary, basic striving far beyond what can be even
remotely construed as average or normal, and hate, too, as a secondary reaction to failure in task challenges which have, by their nature, not so much to do with it. Consequently, the surface of their
behavioral picture is full of hate coming from either or both of these
sources.

For example, such children are not able to face up to fear, anxiety, or insecurity of any kind without breakdown into disorganized aggression. They cannot cope with guilt feelings produced by what they do without again becoming full of aggression (because they feel guilty) and repeating the same acts which initiate this guilt in the first place. Faced with the prospect of a pleasure-filled activity (from the point of view of most children), they cannot see the inherent implications of fun and escape into impulsive destructive behavior rather than investigate such new chances to learn other ways of recreational gratification. Should the adult have succeeded, by dint of great effort and detailed planning, in pulling them through a pleasurable activity, they just can't seem to store up enough of a memory image of it to remember how much fun it was. So in moments of boredom, instead of having saved up something to fall back upon and use, they again break out into wild, disruptive, and impulsive behavior. Then, too, they can't wait for anything: whatever they want has to be granted RIGHT NOW, and, if it isn't, they again break down into seething hostility. As for realizing what their own behavior contributes to a situation, how they provoke someone else or how they play into circumstances which are often to their own detriment—in this they are notoriously deficient. Whatever momentary awareness they may have evaporates so quickly that, if one asks them thirty minutes later what happened, it is always some other person or some trick of destiny, as they see it, that is to blame for their plight. And if one is nice to them, if one surrounds them with affection and toys and good food and adults who want to help them—they seem to feel that whatever shred of reasonableness they may have maintained can now be thrown to the four winds: now they can ask for anything and everything beyond what any reasonable adult can or should ever grant. If the adult does not come through—the inevitable explosion of hate. Another fascinating and peculiar problem of the children who hate is this: they don't know when to ask for help from the adult, or the outside world in general. Lest our reader think, "Oh, well, tough kids, what do they expect, they would never make themselves dependent on the adult," let us assure him that it is not a matter of pride. Our children were not too proud to make the most infantile bids for close attention in dressing them, such as in helping them put on their boots. But the number of situations in which they had a real clear-cut realization, "Here I need help," was pitifully low. And, of course, it can easily be imagined how from this weakness sprang the release of massive amounts of hostility because of the confusion and frustration produced in the many situations they could not handle by themselves. Even a cursory list of their troubles would be incomplete if we did not mention their extreme problems in the face of failure and mistakes, and yes, even of success. Any failure produced in them torrents of aggression against their surroundings or sullen withdrawal; mistakes too were experienced as the machinations of a hostile world against them to which they had to reply with counterhatred or severe, hostility-soaked sulk. As for occasional success, it produced irritating (to other children, especially) "crowing," and bragging, and fed delusions of greatness.

Indeed we could go on in much exhaustive detail, as we did in *Children Who Hate,* multiplying instances of task failure from the point of view of the ego-functioning of these youngsters. And each and every one of these performance failures would show our children again helplessly caught up in the uncontrolled discharge of aggressive drives and impulse energies. This, then—this very withering away, or failure in the development, of adequate patterns of impulse control—is of nuclear significance in the psychology of the children who hate.

Yet the challenge of the children who hate would be vastly simplified if this puniness of their ego functioning were the whole story. What is so strange and paradoxical is that side by side with it lies an enigmatic and unexpected power, a vigilance and ingenuity in the use of psychic energies that one would never expect if these children were only seen in moments of "task failure." Only, this power is in the service of the wrong master, namely, of the very impulsivity, hatred, and destructiveness that pour so torrentially and triumphantly across the shattered controls. Or, let us state it more aptly, the selfsame ego, so unable to cope with the impulses themselves, suddenly, with an exasperating and amazing efficiency, performs superhuman tasks in defending impulse gratification at all costs. Instead of performing its task of looking for synthesis between desires, reality demands, and the impact of social values, the ego is, in these moments, totally on the side of impulsivity. With fanatic and frantic dedication, the egos of the children who hate battle on many fronts in the task of making impulse gratification possible. To examine their battle behavior in its full array would take us far afield from the scope and purpose of an introductory chapter. But, at least—like visiting "brass"—let us tour swiftly from front to front so that we can get a bird's-eye view of some of their incredible feats of strength and strategy. They fight a battle on four fronts, as it were:

First is *the battle with their own conscience,* the inner enemy of impulse license, of the kind of freedom for hatred and destruction which they treasure. The strength of the conscience may vary from child to child but we have never seen a child in whom it is totally absent. The children who hate, for example, discover ways of repressing the intent that may lie behind an unacceptable act. "Sure I stole the stuff but I really needed it. It wasn't to be mean," they may say when confronted with a stealing incident. Untaxed by guilt, embarrassment, or shame because their argumentation with the internal "guilt assessors and collectors" becomes so skillful, impulse freedom is guaranteed.

The second battlefront is not a real one in the sense of warfare. It is rather a campaign for supplies in the form of *search for delinquency support*. Just as a major campaign in the field has to be supported by certain home front and civilian activities, the delinquent warrior, too, has to acquire a sense of logistics, to keep the ammunition rolling. Thus special diagnostic skills in recognizing other children with similar ideologies are developed. Or, even looking into one's own personality to find parts of the self that can best be exploited for this purpose is developed into such a skill of inner perception as one would never think possible for these otherwise insight-blocked egos. "Gosh, how could I help hitting that guy—you know what a bad temper I've got?" Such exploitation of one's own moods and psychic frailties which are otherwise bitterly denied (because they might lead to tampering and improvement at the hands of the caseworker or psychiatrist) to support primitive and brutal impulses is only one of a number of pernicious and efficient weapons in the arsenal of "freedom for impulse expression."

Returning now to the field of action, we come to the third front: now we see the ego in *direct defense against change*. It has been impressive to watch psychological warfare still the voice of conscience; it has been fascinating to see the diligence and persevering skill involved in building up the arsenal of delinquency supplies in the "fight for impulse freedom." But on neither of these two fronts have we seen the pyrotechnics, the deadly and tireless warfare, of which the egos of the children who hate are capable until we see them defending themselves against situations which directly imply change. Especially when a full frontal attack is made on their defenses in some kind of treatment design. Here they really fight for their very existence. For example, watch such a youngster when he is "caught with the goods" after a stealing incident. The "loot" is fairly hanging out of his pocket. He knows that we know what he has done. Will he own up to it? No. He suddenly develops "confessional constipation": he "clams up," he cannot talk. And he really cannot. This sudden language block which he experiences here is not conscious but there is a plan behind it, an unconscious design: "I'll make them search me, make them make me mad. Why should I give them a chance to prove how nice they are, how fair, to live up to their promise that they won't punish me? I'll make them act like those bastard cops who always search me. Then I can keep hating their guts. Then I'm safe against giving in." Other front-line practices prevail: going over to the enemy is punishable by death—*social death*. The kid who reforms is ruthlessly ostracized by his group, even though in some ways he wants to remain friendly. In addition and closely allied to this is the dictum of all armies to their men: no fraternization with the enemy peoples. Applied to our children this means: avoid "nice" kids who like adults and are "good." They may corrupt you. You may get to like them and want to act as they do.

And now to our last and final visit "up front": our fourth battle zone. Here we see a front-guard action. For the ego that pretends really to cope with the threat against change, it is not enough to know how to cope with situations. Skills in handling the personnel who may *create* such situations must be perfected. Here then we observe *mechanized warfare against change agents*: the brilliant deployment of a whole arsenal of direct defense techniques. How fascinating to observe here the ego, which seems to be so stupid in its perception of social reality, so "socially blind," operate with a diagnostic acuity about the feelings and attitudes of the adult. It knows, for example, how "mad" the adult is at any given moment and therefore how safe it is to goad and provoke just a little more before it becomes unsafe. Yet this same ego does not seem to be really able to tell when the adult loves, when he is fair and reasonable in other less battle-relevant moments. How baffling it is to see children who can't learn, who are confused not infrequently as to questions of time and place (some of them can't even learn to tell time), defend themselves with as full an arsenal of tricks as a courtroom lawyer has when they are "on the spot." For example, they pretend that any attempt we may make to talk with them about a theft is an accusation. Thus, while it is customary to talk to everyone in a cabin group if something is stolen from one of them, the youngster who is really the culprit will react to this as though it is in itself an accusation and then proceed to accuse us of "blaming me just because I'm a crook," which makes us out to be illogical, stupid, and mean. Or they demonstrate a sharp sophistication in the rules of evidence. Thus, before any admission of misdeed (whether it be stealing, brutality, destructiveness, or what not) on their side occurs, the incident has to be conclusively proved, step by step.

And now, behind the lines once more with our reader, let us remind him that this nutshell tour has really failed to do justice to the total combat skills of the egos of the children who hate. But, if he understands what we mean now when we talk about "defense against change," we are satisfied.

We are still more ambitious for our reader, at this point. We want him to perceive more than merely how weakness and strength are blended in such strange and baffling proportions in the children who hate. We want him to try to think with us about the uniqueness and power of the challenge they hurl out at the world around them. What *can* we do with them or for them? What tools *are* there to use?

Quite naturally we think of child psychiatry, of the *psychiatric interview method*. Aren't many children with problems seen and helped by child analysis, in child guidance clinics, family service agencies, by visiting teachers and other special consultants? [1] What about these tools in relation to the problems of our children? Well, for many children the use of these has indeed proved a wonderfully productive approach. It is, however, dependent upon certain minimum conditions without which it appears to be ineffectual. *Treatment rapport, adequacy of communication channels, and protection of the interview from excess hyperaggressive and destructive behavior* must be guaranteed, else the interview approach falls seriously by the wayside. With the children who hate, these minimum conditions are not given.[2] The amount and intensity of restlessness and hostility they are capable of displaying are clearly beyond the resources of the interviewer or interview situations to cope with, and, inevitably, they force the therapist into acts of interference long before anything like a "transference neurosis" or relationship can be established.[3] Most importantly, too, the separation between the therapist's role and the rest of their lives constitutes a tremendous advantage to their defenses against change. In

---

[1] For a lucid analysis of the pros and cons of child analysis as a therapeutic approach to different types of problem situations, see "Child Analysis" by Dr. Margaret Shoenberger Mahler, in D. C. Lewis, M.D., and Bernard L. Pacella, M.D., Editors, *Modern Trends in Child Psychiatry* (New York: International Univ. Press, 1945).

[2] In Hyman S. Lippman, "Treatment of Juvenile Delinquents," *Nat. Conf. Social Work, Proceedings*, 1945, pp. 314-323, some of the trials and tribulations of the traditional treatment of "children who hate" are presented.

[3] For a thorough treatment of the application of traditional psychoanalytic techniques to the problems of children with disturbances of the kind we deal with here, see Kate Friedlander, *The Psychoanalytic Approach to Juvenile Delinquency* (New York: International Universities Press, 1947). S. Lorand's article, "Psychoanalytic Contribution to Treatment of Behavior Problems in Children," *Am. J. Psychiat.*, 105, Nov. 1948, pp. 357-360, is also of interest in this connection.

fact, this is such a serious strategic disadvantage in the face of our attempts to offer such children interview therapy that there is virtually no way out. To be sure, there may be intervals of "positive rapport," although these are rare with such children as we are describing, when they produce "significant" material. The chance, however, that any of this can be utilized by the therapist to influence their behavior in the "civilian life" scene is exceedingly slim. Their egos are so poorly equipped to meet their daily life tasks that they simply are unable to carry over some temporary gain in insight either into their own mechanisms or the social reality of their surroundings. They are so impoverished in the ability to find adequate channels for achieving satisfactions that they inevitably resort to primitive, impulse-dominated behavior which arouses punitive counterwarfare from all kinds of personnel on their daily life scene who cannot be controlled by the therapist who is so remotely connected with these happenings. We mean the parents, teachers, playground recreation leaders, neighbors, even playmates, who are so intimately and innately a part of the emotional environment of every child. There is no doubt that, while we may find here and there a parent or teacher who is "sympathetic" to therapy, the majority of persons with whom the aggressively disturbed child comes into contact every day are either not interested in him at all or, even worse, are negatively oriented toward him because of the disruptive and hostile way in which he approaches his world. Thus, the children who hate can and do produce such problems on the scene of their lives that the interview therapist is powerless to cope with the aftermath.[4]

If psychiatry, in the sense of the formal interview method, is not applicable to the children who hate, what does "education" offer in the way of a ray of hope? If the children are too disorganized to be reached through the interview which is too detached from the reality scene, what would happen if they were exposed to a good educational setting and surrounded by benign adults who handled them with wisdom and affection? More specifically, let us assume that, because they are so disturbed, the educator really tries to provide them with rich recreational opportunities and sufficient channels for "constructive fun." If the door is open, they should step

[4] The social casework approach to children's disturbances is well depicted in *Child Therapy—A Casework Symposium*, Eleanor Clifton and Florence Hollis, Editors (New York: Family Service Association of America, 1948).

through, theoretically, and leave behind their peculiar addiction to mischief, destruction, and many varieties of hostile vandalism. As a further step, the educators will try to combat their chronic irritability and hatefulness through teaching them ways and means for successful achievement and mastery, for, as educators, they are mindful of the basic, destructive frustration that failure alone can produce in children. They will do this through surrounding them with experiences that "fascinate and challenge them." And, too, they will try to see to it that the group life of the child who hates is regulated so that he is surrounded by happier children, not so disturbed as he. The sight of his companions, positively and happily engaged, may make the "bad child" eager to change because he sees that there are pleasure and tension release in other modes of behavior. In so doing, the educator hopes to reverse the ancient incantation, "One bad apple can spoil the barrel"; he aspires to array the rest of the barrel against the one bad apple. He assumes, further, that the law of "learning from experience" will work in his behalf and that, if the children who hate observe that they can gain love and approval from positive behavior, they will develop accordingly. And, it goes without saying, he will never confront them with the cruelty, abuse, insult, and embarrassment which they have experienced in their previous contacts with adults, and this too will accelerate their metamorphosis into secure, happy children. To complete this sketch of what a "good educational setting" is prepared to offer such children, let us say that educators are not naive enough to believe that simple exposure to their design will be enough. Every child needs certain "booster shots" for his motivational system to catch hold and work the way it should. For this the educator turns to his reservoir of "educational techniques." Such tools as friendly punishment, kind criticism, special rewards, promises, encouragement, will create additional "incentive" to motivate desirable behavior. In the educator's mind, this is a good "educational diet," and, when it is combined with his deep and friendly interest in children, he can really look to it to accomplish the growth-producing wonders that he expects of it.

The simple truth is that in the cases of thousands of children such an educational design suffices beautifully. Only—the children who hate are painful exceptions. In order to be effective such an educational attempt presupposes certain potentials for response, which, in the case of the children who hate, are not to be found. Let us try to review some of these in summary form.

In order to enjoy a constructive or challenging activity, a child must be capable of a high level of frustration tolerance, must be prepared to achieve fun out of sublimated rather than primitive channels of drive satisfaction, must be ready to sacrifice the impulse of the moment for future gain. Yet the children who hate are notoriously short of *frustration tolerance, sublimation capacity,* or *ability to postpone immediate impulse satisfaction.*

In order to be "challenged by fascinating life tasks or learning situations," a child must have some image of his own future, must be able to take the fear of failure without a breakdown, the victory over an opponent without triumphant hate. Yet the children who hate *cannot establish adequate relations to future experience and are pitifully ill-prepared to cope with the implications of failure without primitive rage and disappointment, and with success without grandiosity and irritating bragging.*

In order to be motivated by friendly adult behavior, a child must have developed a real need for adult love and must be able to recognize adults as basically fun-loving even at times when they temporarily interfere in fun. *Instead, the children who hate have extremely weak, distorted, and confused wishes for object relationships with adults and interpret necessary and mild limitations as deep rejection on the side of the adult.*

In order for criticism, punishment, reward or praise, promise or threat to work at all, a child must be aware of his own guilt at the very moment when someone else interferes in his life, must understand the connection between his own effort and what he has achieved, must have learned from previous experiences how to cope with temptation challenges toward unacceptable behavior. *Yet the children who hate have severe disturbances in their ego-superego relations, frequently feel guilt in the sense of too late or too little, have only a dim, if even existent, insight into their own responsibility for what happens to them and the weakest possible resistance in the face of temptation.*

These are just a few of the clinical complications preventing what we might call a good educational approach from being effective with the children who hate. Practically none of the personality ingredients which are necessary for even so well-designed an educational program to work exist at all in these children. They simply do not react as we would want them to and some of them even get worse because something about the very attempt to lure them out of their pathology makes their defenses "work overtime."

Thus, we are driven to the conclusion that good education is not curative enough for the children who hate. Really, the reverse is truer: in order for a good educational diet to work, considerable repair must first be done on their basic personality weaknesses. If psychiatry and education are equally baffled, it is obvious that a new design must be invented to cope with the problems these children present. It must offer a strategic approach of somewhat different dimensions than that of either good education or formal psychiatry, although certainly taking full advantage of certain insights and techniques which both of these disciplines have developed. The basic innovation which such a new design would stress is the concept of the treatment or residential home as offering the best potentialities for an effective strategy for coping with the problems of such children. It is obvious that, if the psychiatric interview in the formal office setting is too reality-detached from the real life scene of the child, if his community milieu is too unsympathetic or aggravated into hostility by his depredations, then no strategy will reach him as long as these conditions pertain. Mere living together with the child, however, is just the beginning. The clinical complexity of the children who hate, the almost unbridgeable alternatives that one has to bring together in the attempt to help them, will haunt the residential therapist just as they have the benign educator or psychiatrist. The exhausting and endless battle with surface behavior in the midst of the search for the key to their basic pathologies will combine the nightmares of the educator and psychiatrist into one. Finding clinically useful activities which at the same time permit impulse and affect ventilation and develop new skills in ego functioning will occupy much time, as will the management problems with respect to behavior and the weighty issues of causation and cure of pathology which stare us in the face. Residential therapy with the children who hate is an ordeal with chaos. The following chapters of this book are an analysis of the clinical philosophy and strategy which such experimentation seems to require.

Tool Vacuum on the Educational Scene

There is one thing all children have in common, irrespective of age, background, and neighborhood. Many times during a twenty-four-hour day, their ego is confronted with the task of *behavioral control*. This is as true of the most normal and healthy youngster as of the severely disturbed one. For not only distorted or "sick" desires and fantasies need to be blocked from being acted out; even the most understandable and normal urges of childhood quite often need to be cut off from behavioral expression, or must at least be stopped for the time being and postponed for a future chance. For instance, a boy or girl skipping through the toy floor of a department store doesn't have to be a kleptomaniac to be assailed by desires, wishes, impulses, and fantasies of owning and using some of the seductively displayed gadgets on the counters. There is nothing abnormal in intensive yearnings to have them, and even a not too impulsive child may literally drool at the mouth with greed when exposed to such an alluring display of gratification potentials. In fact, we would even grant as perfectly normal some "substitute" fantasy produced by the child's ego in a flash and designed to keep the mounting frustration and disappointment from breaking down his morale. The most wonderful and nondelinquent youngster might, exposed to such torture, easily have a short daydream in which a stranger suddenly approaches him, and, with the explanation that he is too old to enjoy such pleasures himself, happily buys the child that bicycle to take away for keeps right now. Or, if temptational challenges are too heavy to be totally repressed, a daydream might weave them into the following spur-of-the-moment design: the child might visualize himself riding off on this bicycle, with greater and greater temptation of taking it with him, and then deciding, at the last moment, to take it back. The floorwalker, who had already begun to suspect him, is touched by his honesty of confession and final self-control to such a degree that he makes an exception and lets the youngster have the trophy as a reward for being such a sincere and repenting child. A wide leeway of such "temptation daydreams" must be considered perfectly normal, and, as long as the child is able to block his desires from cutting into the scene of open behavior, and as long as these supportive daydreams do not assume too pathological a design, everything is all right. But it is clear that the naturalness and legitimacy of the child's desires and impulses themselves do not solve the problem entirely. His ego is still saddled with the task of *behavioral control*. In short, this task of behavioral control hits not only the child with an unusual amount of greed or with special distortions and perversions in his impulse system, but is *part of the daily job of the ego of the most normal child in the pursuit of everyday life.*

Our life with the children who hate has shown us just what happens if an ego is totally unable to fulfill this task. But, let us forget for a moment the children who hate. For, the trouble they have is only a magnified and intensified picture of some of the troubles every child has to go through in his attempt at self-control. And here is where the most important challenge of the ego disturbances observed in our Pioneers hits the educator and parent at large: The fact that your child's ego is basically "normal" and your youngster is a "wonderful kid" does not mean that his ego is expected to succeed in its task at behavioral control under all circumstances. On the contrary, we can make two statements with great assurance: first, all egos of children, even those of the most normal and wonderful ones, develop gradually over a long stretch of time, and in the meantime need a good deal of "support from the outside"; and, second, even the best ego is meant to fulfill this task of behavioral control *only within a certain limit of complexity.* If circumstances pile up on a child, or if an unusual pressure of impulsivity hits a youngster at a certain time, or if a variety of other things go wrong in the picture, even the normal and most well-developed ego is not expected to manage the task of behavioral control *all by itself.* It is in need of support in order to accomplish its job. In short, the difference between the normal and the severely disturbed child is not that the disturbed child cannot handle the task of self-control by himself while the normal one can. The difference is that the normal child can handle the task of behavioral control even under adverse circumstances *if given adequate ego support,* while the really sick one *cannot even make use of* valid ego support which it is being offered.

This, then, makes it obvious that the search for effective ways of ego support is not an exclusive task of the clinician who tries to survive with children as severely disturbed as the ones described in these books, but that it is an equally important pursuit for the

parent and teacher of any child. To be sure that this is well understood in spite of the general confusion of public opinion on this
issue, let us leave out the children who hate for a few moments and
illustrate our point by a life incident involving an entirely different
child.

Ken is nine years old. He is a lucky child. His arrival in a family
of modest means but quite comfortable middle-class living standards had been anticipated with joy, and he has been raised by unusually intelligent, sensitive, but also sensible parents. We might
fill in the details of his life conditions and history as positively as
we want to, as long as we avoid becoming unrealistic and are sure
to grant that Ken's life must also have been hit by a variety of the
usual mild complications that befall all children. We expect that
the basically desirable and pleasant school life has been punctured
at times by a stupid or mean teacher or two, that his neighborhood
play was not void of occasional panic about being bullied by a
stronger and hostile child, that the usual run of childhood diseases
must have exposed Ken to the accompanying traumas of convales-
cence or surgical interference, and we may even grant that his wise
and loving parents do not always hit the educational nail on the
head with perfect precision, but commit many a minor mistake, or
allow themselves the occasional weakness of reacting to his behavior
with their own emotion or mood rather than with their usual wisdom of educational restraint. To all this, we add that Ken is, of
course, far from being a mama's baby or model child, even though
we have to admit that wise handling will usually find him rather
amenable toward mending his ways, and that what mischief he
dreams up and perpetrates is free of the extremeness of unreason
and pathology which we have described in connection with our
children elsewhere in this book. In short, Ken is depicted as a perfectly "normal," in fact a rather wonderful, youngster, in an unusually favorable life setting.

To watch his ego at work, let us confront him now with two complications in his youthful existence. Nothing serious, just enough
to constitute a somewhat more "complicated" situation than he usually finds himself in. The first of the two experiences happened this
afternoon. Ken was playing with his neighborhood gang when all
of a sudden Mr. N, the father of one of his chums, turned up on
the scene in an obviously uncontrolled rage. He berated Ken's pal
for some minor issue of domestic disorder with great vehemence,

but the worst of it was that he really shamed the boy in the most tactless manner in front of his group. Since the child in question was anything but a rebel, his exit from the scene of neighborhood group life was the most shaming spectacle of ignominious defeat. The gang was cowed into silence by Mr. N's vehemence, and Ken suffered the tortures of a coward who abandons his pal in battle. His vicarious identification with his buddy made him seethe with impotent fury, and never before had he openly felt like hitting an adult, a sensation which in itself sent panic up his spine. The most gnawing feeling left in all of them, however, was the typical pre-adolescent shame about being made as ridiculous as "little babies," about being powerless to do anything about it, except through fantasy correction of the real-life scene, or through displaced "small stuff" rebellion and mischief in areas where it is safe.

The other complication in Ken's life is happening right now, the evening of the same day. For his parents have planned a party for today. And this one is somewhat unusual. Personal friends as well as business acquaintances have been invited, and the impression the family leaves on some of the business guests is perceived as being rather important for the future career and prosperity of the family in the neighborhood to which they moved not too long ago. Ken has been told that he may stay with the party for a while, passing around refreshments and emptying ashtrays, which he seems to enjoy so much, but it has been made quite clear to him that the deal would be as usual: 8:30 is the time for him to remove himself from the adult operations, to go up to his room and to do so without any fuss or embarrassment to his parents. This point was rubbed in with increased emphasis tonight.

Well, the party starts off in the usual fashion. That is, the adults use the child as a gadget to help them over their own first stiffness of social relationships, and the easily embarrassing pauses in conversation are happily filled with the fuss that is made over the youngster. He becomes quite clearly the center of the scene and can bathe in the many complimentary remarks or glances even though these are meant for parental consumption only. Let us add a few guests who really have a way with children, so that Ken will soon find himself personally stimulated by the interest they show in him, the chance they give him to tell them what he really enjoys talking about, or just by the friendly tussle and roughhouse that so often relievingly replaces the need for verbal patter between the adult and the child. In short, Ken will soon find the experience more rewarding than he even hoped for, and, caught by the general party atmosphere and the personal attention he receives, will get quite "excited" and even overstimulated by the occasion.

By the time 8:30 comes around, Ken's ego will be in a jam. Even if it tries to stick up for reason and decency, in view of the fairness of the parental deal, two forces will make it hard to decide. On the one hand, the desire to stay around has by now increased; the gratification from adult attention and the boost to his morale by being treated "like a grown-up" have made his wish to stay around a while longer much more intensive than it usually is. At the same time, the incident of this afternoon throws its shadow over an issue which, without it, would have been quite clear. In view of what happened this afternoon, the gesture of Ken's father who points at the clock may not be experienced as a simple "reminder of a previous deal." Today his father, gesturing at the clock and the staircase, suddenly becomes one of those adults "who always spoil your fun," and the visualization of himself walking up the steps suddenly assumes a frightening similarity to the scene this afternoon of his pal creeping away like a whipped dog, obediently surrendering the pride of preadolescent independence in favor of blind obedience, under a cloud of group derision and shame.

Let us leave Ken suspended for a moment in his predicament. The task his ego has now to perform really falls into two categories: (1) *It has to decide on which side to throw its weight to begin with.* For, theoretically, it may want to support the forces of reason and "fair deal" decency, and forfeit the gratification of onrushing needs in spite of it all. It may also decide to "give" and to swing its support to the side of what may seem a quite "justified" desire for continued "fun which doesn't harm anybody," and may therefore be ready to look for techniques of guaranteeing such fun against parental interruption attempts, and to find ways and means to get to stay for yet a while. (2) No matter which way it decides, Ken's ego will also have a second job to do. We might call it *mop-up of secondary feelings.* For decisions are rarely so "clean-cut" that they leave no loose ends tangling. Most of the time, something remains to be handled, and feelings around the decision struggle itself may have to be taken care of. In Ken's case, for instance, we can expect that complications may set in no matter how he decides. If he decides in favor of staying, his ego will have to do something with the feelings of guilt which will rise sooner or later for having gone back on the deal with the parents. If he decides to obey and go to his room, his ego has his "shame at surrender to an infantilizing demand" to deal with, and maybe also feelings of loneliness, resentment, and excludedness once he stews over it all in the seclusion of his room.

The point we are trying to make is that Ken's ego, quite capable of handling either issue under its own steam, may need *outside support* on both of them today. Just which forms this "ego support" should take can, of course, not be prescribed in general terms. But it can easily be planned on the basis of just which form his predicament assumes or just which techniques he uses to prolong his stay, and a wide variety of channels are open to him along that line. He may simply try to stall for time, by being inconspicuous whenever a watchful adult might remember the bedtime issue. He may try to coax, cajole, or divert the going to bed battle through "cute" behavior long enough until it is forgotten for a while again. Or, he may try to plead a need for his prolonged help in serving refreshments and emptying ashtrays, acting so efficiently on his job that the adults will hardly have the heart to remind somebody so useful of as civilian and inglorious a matter as bedtime. He may, on the other hand, make a play for the sympathy of the adult group, or he may try to wheedle one especially child-favorable friend among the guests into open collusion in support of permission for prolonged stay. On the other hand, hit heavily by this afternoon's incident, the otherwise compliant Ken may really start some more open rebellion, or may try to embarrass his parents through an impending scene into temporary surrender. Or, as a last resort, even when giving in to parental demands he may easily make such a show of being sent upstairs that he wins by a triumphant exit even though he loses the original point at stake.

Giving Ken "ego support" in his decision will assume different forms, depending on which of these techniques he will choose. If all he does is stall for time, a more direct "aside" by his mother or father, accompanied by reassuring affection but not lacking in clarity of reminder of the original deal, will do the job. If "cute antics" are chosen as a way out, the parents will wisely let him have a fill of some of this triumph and laugh with him rather than become angry, but will wisely terminate such a technique after a while, will get him into another room, by all means away from the

immediate scene of potential loss of face, and will have a more
serious chat with him about the importance of going up right now,
even though the parents understand his desire to stay on, and the
reasons for such decision. If job efficiency is chosen, the termination
of one phase in that job, such as serving refreshments, or the use
of the maid or a guest for his helper at first, for his substitute later,
will offer a nice "structure" to limit his stay quite reasonably.
If he openly plays for the sympathy of a special friend among the
guests, it will be this friend's task to give him the ego support he
needs. This may well take the form of this guest saying to him
something like this: "Listen, Ken, this I can't do. You told me yourself you had promised your mother you wouldn't give her a hard
time about bedtime tonight. This really wouldn't be fair to her.
But I'll tell you what. How about my asking her if she'll permit
me to go up to your room with you? You could show me that sail-
boat you just told me about, and we could be together for a while.
But after that, no fuss when I have to leave. O.K.?" With that
much "rub-in" of the real issue and that much actual "support" in
going through with a painful decision, Ken can manage beautifully. If Ken becomes more rebellious, a wide variety of ways is
open; among them an aside by his mother to the effect that he really
wouldn't want to embarrass her at this special party may be the
most effective one. Or maybe, if the waves of excitement have become very high, his father may have to get a little tough about
going up, after having left him a face-saving margin of sand-
wiched-in disobedience for a while, and have it out more in detail
upstairs or tomorrow morning, when Ken is his old sweet self again.
If he makes a real scene on the way out, planned ignoring with
later follow-up is the obvious ego-supportive technique to be advised.

However, let's assume Ken goes upstairs either right away or soon
after some stalling. His ego will still have the task of "mop-up of
secondary feeling." And he may need some help on that, too. For
Ken is only preadolescent; that means that his somewhat sturdy
self-assertion in the face of adult obedience demands is not yet
coupled with an openly enjoyed emancipation battle, as it would
in a child more advanced in his puberty. To Ken the sight of his
room with the laid-out pajamas is still remindful of a motherly
tuck-in, of some fussing over his clothes or cleanliness, and even
though he left downstairs in revolt, the absence of the comforting

parent before going to bed would be hard to take. Or else, the shame of ignominious surrender remembered from the afternoon scene may have made his voluntary going upstairs much more face-losing than it otherwise would be, for with preadolescents some-times the whole gang is looking over their shoulder, even though they act in lonely seclusion. In that case, Ken's ego may be flooded with daydreams of revenge and fury, or with recollections of weak-ness and shame, and both may leave him either crying or sulking, or helpless and panic-stricken in the dark room. Therefore, Ken's ego needs the adult's support on this "mop-up of secondary feelings" job, too. A wise mother may, for instance, drift up after a while—not too soon, so that supervisory suspicions are not ascribed to her action—and then may behave casually, not mentioning a thing about the previous trouble, nor nagging about Ken's slowness about undressing or bathing, but assuring him of her affection through just such understanding omissions, or maybe reminding him of the fun he had downstairs, or whatever modification the details of a speci-fic situation may imply. Both parents would, of course, also realize, if they knew anything about the afternoon incident, that Ken's handling downstairs as well as upstairs needs, today, a very wide leeway for tolerance. For he must have a chance to rebel a little, at least in the way in which he obeys, unless they put his ego into too difficult a conflict with his natural preadolescent pride. So, both parents will give concomitant ego support even while they try to get him to oblige, by avoiding anything too face-losing or embar-rassing or anything that smacks too much of the "send the child up to bed" instructions of earlier infancy years.

By the way, not all ego support to help Ken with his problem of behavioral control need come from the direct handling by the adults who are with him. We can easily see, especially if we compare Ken with less fortunate children, how the very arrangement of a child's life space may have something to do with the question of whether his ego has its task made easier or more difficult. Let us assume that Ken's parents were less affluent. Then he might have had to go to bed in an improvised place near the room where the party goes on. Lying in bed, listening to every detail of the increasedly hilari-ous party, Ken might easily have suffered an increase in his hostil-ity toward adults who kick him out but keep him disturbed after-wards. His resentment against the parents who so audibly have a good time with all these strangers instead of caring for him might have become much more hysterical in content and intensity, and the friendly guest who was so nice to him might now appear like a traitor, who didn't help him in his predicament at all and obviously doesn't miss his presence as the loud guffaws just now audible all too clearly prove. In short, in Ken's life as described before, the very arrangements of room distribution, the very factors of housing, comfort, and facilities constitute an element of ego support. Beyond this, we might wonder what difference it would make for Ken whether he was sent to bed after participating in a clear-cut program structure or with just an abrupt reminder of previously entered upon obligations. If Ken, for instance, had been engaged by his adult friend in looking at his stamp album, and mother just then would have reminded him that this was the last thing he could show tonight—"after this you'll have to go up"—then such clearly terminated activity would make the transition toward upstairs much easier for the child. If he had suddenly been sent up in the middle of an unstructured milling about while everybody became more and more loud and excited, his send-off to bed would much more resemble a willful "bouncing" or a sending to bed of the little infant than a deal made with a reasonable and older child. In short, the very design of an activity, our policies of timing and sequence, may itself constitute an element of ego support. Needless to say, the question of whether Ken can go to bed gracefully or not is not only defined by what happens right now, but also by things which went on before, and by how Ken perceives the "underlying feeling tone" of the whole issue in his own mind. Thus, with parents who wouldn't know how to handle a preadolescent with tact, and would rub in Ken's "youngness" as a main reason for being sent to bed, any bedtime issue would necessarily become a severe battle, no matter how much "reason" such a demand might have. Or, if Ken's parents were in the habit of protecting their comfort primarily, so that they would sometimes send him to bed early for the sake of convenience and at other times keep him up for errands they need him for, a much more hysterical reaction to any bedtime routine would have to be taken for granted. For the *total strategy* with which a youngster's life experiences are being handled and the basic "atmosphere" in which people live together belong to the most important factors of ego support.

In summary, we can say that even if Ken has trouble today in making the right decision quickly, with adequate ego support from his total surroundings he will manage pretty well, while without it, or with an unfavorable life design or poor adult handling, he and his life would be in bad shape. This also implies that the question of just how much ego support a child is given when he needs it becomes of great importance, not only on the clinical scene of life with disturbed children, but in the daily life of the most normal, even most wonderful, child.

This is where the greatest shock hit us, when we were scrambling so frantically for techniques to survive with the children who hate. Even though our children were obviously seriously disturbed, we thought that maybe as far as the handling of daily behavior and the offering of ego support were concerned we might learn something from the way in which we would give ego support to the normal child. We soon had to see how desperately wrong we were in this assumption. For, we don't know how to give ego support to the normal child either. Far from learning from "education" how to handle the clinical task with the disturbed child, it seems that we have to collect our clinical findings in order to create even the rudiments of a science of ego support for the normal child, to be applied by the teacher and parent in their daily tasks.

For a while, we didn't trust our eyes. We thought it couldn't be as bad as that. Only, it is. With all the libraries full of books in which people quarrel about principles of education, values, and ways to "inculcate them" into children, the parent who looks for leads to a question as simple as, "How do I get Johnny upstairs to bed without making a mess of things in other places?" will still vainly look for concrete and scientifically sincere guidance. He will find plenty of suggestions as to how to help the neurotic child over nightmares (after somebody got him into bed) or how to "discipline" the recalcitrant child into more obedience (without reference to the conflict produced in other places by force techniques). He will have no trouble finding hundreds of studies as to why children would like to stay up longer, or why they would avoid transition from the waking state into the land of their dreams. The question of actual support to the ego of the normal child in moments of ego confusion is still left either to philosophical beliefs "in general," or to repetition or compulsive avoidance of whatever techniques the adult had used on him as a child, or to general preferences for child care styles, or to issues of personal comfort and taste.

This same vacuum in the area of specific educational tools is equally painful in many school and home situations which are much more serious than bedtime on a party evening. In fact, all questions pertaining to techniques like punishment and rewards, praise or criticism, permission or Verbot, indulgence or authority, encouragement or scolding, and the whole gamut of problems around the setting of limits and of what to do if they are trespassed are still a No Man's Land in which anybody can believe what he wants to, quite similar to the state of affairs in which our concepts of body health, eating habits, etc., were about one hundred years ago. "What tastes well can't hurt me," "This did me a lot of good when I was a child, so it ought to be good enough for those youngsters of today," "Our grandparents had been brought up this way, too, and they were respectable folks," and other stereotypes seem to govern the scene of daily educational practice, no matter how fancy our philosophical speculation about its basic goals and values have become.[5] People who never would send their child to a dentist just because he used the "good old tools" which their grandparents knew will raise an argument on just such a primitive level when an issue of physical punishment is concerned. People who read the most complicated psychiatric books on unconscious motivation may still insist that a temper tantrum they afforded around a misbehavior of their child is bound to "teach him."

It doesn't do to continue in our ignorance much longer, for, in the long run, collective ignorance never pays. And further, parents and teachers of the normal child have become more and more outspoken in their demand for "concrete" answers to questions like "Just what do I do when he acts like that?" Over and above the very valuable "deeper" insights in the motivations for child behavior which they already have received, it is time to start on an organized *"instrumentology of behavioral control,"* as part of a larger system of "techniques of ego support."

This book is only a beginning in that line. As in *Children Who Hate,* we are using the things we learned in order to help the children with extreme ego disturbances to find out what techniques we have for the support of ego control to begin with. We can present only a fraction of our materials on this issue here and must leave it to the reader, while looking at our struggle with the behavioral control of our Pioneers, to draw analogies and yet respect differences sufficiently so as to see the impact of all this for the support of ego functions in the normal child.

As the reader might suspect from our analysis of Ken's conflict, we expect the main inventory of techniques for ego support to be so rich in number and variety that they may still resist classification. We do suggest, for the first attempt, that we store them in four tiers, so to speak: (1) *The ego support by the impact of the design of the total environment*, with special emphasis on physical arrangements and atmospheric implications of policies of life in a given place, (2) *The ego-supportive role of activity and program structures*, of toys, tools, gadgets, and of the emotional undertone with which they are offered, (3) *The specific instrumentology of techniques to handle surface behavior*, or, in other words, ego support through the way in which we interfere with what children want to do, and (4) *The ego-supportive impact of the whole strategy of handling their own life experiences* so that they learn from what they do, learn from what they couldn't do, and become able to receive from one well-handled life conflict benefit for increased self-control and increased wisdom of approach to the next.

The chapters in which we show what all this looks like when applied to children with severe ego disturbances are arranged in this very same sequence. The task of applying in his own mind what all this suggests to life with the less disturbed child must be left as a challenge for the reader's own creative reaction to this book. We hope that the future may make it possible to start the research that would actually be needed to change this very rudimentary material into a design of really organized and thorough, but also practitioner-geared, research on the techniques for Ego Support. In this respect, this book about the treatment techniques for the children who hate is also meant to be a prelude to a scientific instrumentology of Ego Support as such.

⁵ In Edith Buxbaum, *Your Child Makes Sense* (New York: International Universities Press, Inc., 1949), a notable attempt is made to stimulate parents to think strategically about their children. See also Dorothy W. Baruch, *Parents and Children Go to School* (Chicago: Scott, Foresman, 1939).

I
STRUCTURE AND STRATEGY
OF A TREATMENT HOME

THE *"individual treatment process,"* as it was developed after the original classical model of child analysis, is built around two major areas of concern: the establishment and manipulation of a treatment-favorable personal rapport and techniques for the handling of fantasy material and behavior which are produced during the treatment process. It is true, of course, that, over and above these two focal areas of concern, every good therapist will be interested in the influence of the environment in which the youngster lives while in treatment. He will often be forced to perform a certain amount of "environmental manipulation," and may have to handle the relationships of other personnel to the youngster in treatment and to the treatment process itself. The major "power" of therapy, though, is traditionally ascribed to the two factors mentioned above.

As soon as we step into a situation where the children live in the same institution in which the treating psychiatrist or case worker operates, we have a whole host of new variables crowding us with much more vehemence than before.[1] For it is obvious that, even if our main effect is still expected from the "individual treatment" the youngster receives in our "sessions" with him, everything else that happens to him while living in this institution may have a drastic effect upon him. Especially when things go wrong, we are ready to

[1] See Irene M. Josselyn, "Treatment of the Emotionally Immature Child in an Institutional Framework," *Amer. J. Orthopsychiat.*, Vol. 20, 1950, pp. 397-409, for a picture of the psychiatric interview process in an institution.

emphasize our respect for the power of those life factors which are not within our immediate reach. No matter what geniuses we may be and what flawless job we may have performed in the treatment of a child's anxiety neurosis in our sessions, how can we get any place if the same child spends twenty-three out of the twenty-four hours of his waking and sleeping day in a framework which is so full of traumatic situations? How can we help a child if, soon after his meeting with us, he steps into a world regimented by the compulsive picayunishness of suppressive rules and routines, narrowed by a programless exposure to boredom, sprinkled with the overstimulations coming from seductive contagion-initiators in his group, peppered with the scenes of sadistic punishment and sentimental teacher-pet cultivation, and punctured by nothing but wordy speeches and lectures from child-disinterested representatives of societal demands? It is clear that any children's institution or home which claims that individual treatment is being carried on within its walls will need to take seriously the impact of "institutional hygiene." By this is meant the demand that every part of institutional life be so designed as to support the basic trends of the treatment goal and be carried out in such a way that it at least does not do damage to the treatment process.

Historically, most institutions or homes which now undertake to do a "treatment job" with their children did not start out with such a favorable design.[2] The usual course of events is that institutions or children's homes have developed their programs, their housing facilities, their policies of hiring and firing staff, their rules and regulations, as well as their policies of dealing with those who impinge upon them, long before "criteria for clinical antisepsis" had even been thought of. Individual treatment services usually were "built" as an additional appendix much later and then had to face the enormous problem of conflict with and adaptation to what was originally an undisputed system of "institutional life." Needless to add, the efficiency of even the best-staffed individual treatment service built into an institution is highly dependent on the degree to which we succeed in harmonizing the original institutional de-

[2] Ruth Topping, in "The Treatment of the Pseudosocial Boy," *Amer. J. Orthopsychiat.*, April, 1943, pp. 353-360, describes some of the peculiar treatment challenges of juvenile offenders within a large institutional framework. Clearly implicit in the article is a plea for reshuffling traditional institutional design in order that suitable channels for efficient therapeutic contact be established.

sign with the new treatment goal and in "cleansing" the whole institutional life of anything that is clearly not "clinically pure."

As soon as we step from such a concept of "a children's home with good treatment services built in" to the concept of what we would call a *genuine treatment home,* this principle of clinical antisepsis is pushed into a total priority position.[3] And this is exactly what we have in mind here. We are convinced that for the "children who hate" a good institution with built-in psychiatric services is not enough. We are fascinated with the development of an entirely new design. We might call it "residential setting with a total treatment design"—by which we mean that *every phase of it* must not only be "supportive" of the basic treatment we take on but must become an integral part of it. To make a drastic distinction between this concept of a total treatment design and the customary lip service which is given to the "importance of every person in an institution to the treatment plan," let us use a simple example: In a good treatment home with individual therapy built in, it will be recognized that it is important whether the cook yells at the children when they get in her way or whether she is a kindly, warm person, and that the relationship which a good arts and crafts teacher or recreation leader develops between himself and the children is an essential ingredient without which the psychiatrist couldn't work his miracles quite so well. It is still taken for granted, though, that the "real treatment" happens during that hour in which Johnny is in the psychiatrist's office. We may step on toes when we say this, but we cannot help it: Our concept of "total treatment design" does not agree with this. We really think that the question of just how the cook acts when Johnny steals a second dessert is as much part of a "treatment process" as what the psychiatrist may have said in an interview, that the question of which arts and crafts materials are picked and how the workshop is being handled can be as much actual "treatment" as the "talk" we had with the children the other day. We go even further than that—we are convinced that the very way the house is laid out, the very policies of housekeeping that are in vogue, in short everything that happens during a day and night may be made part of the most essential treatment plan and may assume top priority of treatment relevance at any

[3] The pioneer attempt to create a residential treatment milieu was made by August Aichhorn and is described in his book, *Wayward Youth* (New York: The Viking Press, Inc., 1935).

one time. The institution which, in our judgment, has to date taken this concept of total residential design most seriously and has followed it through into the details of everyday life with the children more than any other we know of is the Orthogenic School of the University of Chicago. Bruno Bettelheim's child population differs considerably from ours, in that his youngsters come from much more middle-class backgrounds and, on the whole, are still backed up by families who are at least ready and able to spend considerable sums of money for their repair. Some of the implications of a total treatment approach and the designs of a residential treatment home, however, have been so well described in his book *Love Is Not Enough* that it becomes unnecessary for us to give this question the space which would otherwise have been necessary. Rather, we can happily summarize what is implied in Bettelheim's approach, translate it into the specific forms of life which the nature of our youngsters demands, and thus give an abbreviated picture of what goes into a treatment design for the Children Who Hate.

1. A House that smiles, Props which invite, Space which allows

It is amazing how sensitive even otherwise defensive children are to the "atmosphere" which the very location, the architectural design, the space distribution of the house, the arrangement and type of furnishings, the equipment, the style of housekeeping suggest.[4] This alone is a subject on which organized research is badly needed and it would have to be research of an "interdisciplinary" style: architects, interior decorators, sociologists, psychiatrists, psychologists, social group workers, and experienced housemothers should cooperate on it. For we have a difficult time trying to describe what we are very obviously reacting to when we enter a place. Being able to break down into observable units what we now do know about the "mood" contagion that emanates from places and things would be a great boon. In the absence of such help, let us at least try to hint at some of the thoughts we would list if asked which facets of the physical design should be considered and in which way:

---

[4] For a fascinating picture of the work and skill that goes into creating a relaxed and emotionally nutritive atmosphere in a small children's institution see Eva Burmeister, *45 In The Family* (New York: Columbia University Press, 1949).

The avoidance of sociological shock

It is not necessary that the detail of all the elements of the style of life of the natural habitat of the children be imitated—in fact, it certainly would not be desirable to build up another slum just so that some of the children would feel at home. On the other hand, it is essential to avoid too great extremes, which would lead to "sociological shock." For at the same time at which a youngster is supposed to do a good deal of internal reshuffling of his personality, it would be too much to load him with too heavy a "newness panic" on other counts. On top of that, some architectural design really fits only a certain style of life and produces anxiety or the desire toward cynical opposition in anybody not leading a compatible life. To illustrate what we mean:

If tough youngsters, for instance, would have to do their daily living in the sedate austerity of a "library atmosphere," we mean the type a well-to-do connoisseur of rare books might have left as a legacy, we would have quite a time to "outlive" the clinical wrongness of that milieu. For the sedateness of the atmosphere suggested would have either of two effects: either it would make them feel like "whispering" all the time and thus not able to be noisy and relaxed without guilt when they should, or the sublimation challenge of sedateness would work as an irritant, stirring them up into special features of rebellious triumph over the architectural attempt at tyranny and control. Both effects would hamper the therapist way beyond what would be reasonable and could be coped with at all.

Action-invitation versus action-Verbot

There is something in a way furniture is designed and arranged, and in the way toys or books are kept, that immediately betrays the owner's desire for either having them happily used or proudly protected, revered, and preserved from too consumptive interference. Workers in institutions will remember how often the primary task of institutional personnel may become that of protecting equipment against children, or how often spatial arrangements are so unfunctional that they have to wage a constant battle against even otherwise permissible mobility, because it would endanger the prize gift of a watchful donor or board.

Leeway for extraneous use

It is interesting to watch how sharply youngsters size up a home or youth center not only in terms of equipment itself, but in terms of the potential leeway of fringe behavior which might be implied. By this we mean the question whether equipment which is offered for the use it was designed for can also be used, occasionally, for a certain margin of gratifications which become important at the time but were definitely not "built into" the equipment by its original creator. Sofas, for instance, are obviously meant to sit on. Yet, for lively children, a total Verbot of ever jumping on them even during the pursuit of an exciting game would seem like a cruel limitation of their mobility. This does not mean that they expect to be. "allowed" to do anything they want to with that couch. It does mean, however, that they expect to be able to trespass somewhat the fringe of "legitimate use" under certain circumstances without having to expect too severe punishment or having to produce too severe guilt feelings. Some homes may be very "permissive" as far as the absence of special punitive rules may be concerned. Yet, the way the house parents look whenever a slight deviation of the original use of the furniture is tried makes one feel like a criminal so that one might as well forget about ever trying it. It is the whole attitude of over-solicitousness with which furniture is often regarded which betrays such implications immediately to the watchful child. For this very reason it is much better to have much "old stuff" around, especially in the places in which rougher behavior is to be expected, or modern furniture which has been really built with the awareness of the type of use and marginal use it will have to stand from children. This cuts down on unnecessary worry on the part of the adult, avoids embarrassment on the part of the shy child, takes away the spice of triumphant rebellion from the otherwise harmless liveliness of the toughie.

The psychology of space arrangement and sublimation dosage

The moods and activity needs between which children move can be somewhat anticipated. Unless the designer and furnisher of the home makes use of this knowledge, he may throw unnecessary blocks in the path of the staff, who will then spend more of their time in "outliving" the wrongness of the place and its design than they can devote to the treatment ingredients they could otherwise add.

Knowing the frequency with which aggressive children may have to switch from quiet to overactive games, it is essential to have a place available in which wild running, shouting, gesturing, throwing of balls, roughhousing can be allowed with no problem at all. If such a place is available, the adult who has to interfere in a scene of wild ball-throwing which may spontaneously develop in the living room can easily do so by simple "geographical redistribution." His interference can be done with the implication: "I love to have you have this kind of fun; there is nothing wrong with it, really. Only, let's go to the place which is designed just for that purpose, that's all." Without such facility any such activity would have to be totally blocked and it is easy to see what this would do to the adult's role: from a friendly redistributor of geography, he becomes a gratification-forbidding blocker of mobility. What a difference that can make!

The very arrangement of space, too, can be of utmost strategic importance.

Very often, what started out as a group may have to be divided into subgroups, and sometimes a larger activity pattern "breaks into pieces," in a friendly kind of way. Of the five children, for instance, starting out playing blackjack, three may tire and want to start a ball game. The other two may want to continue with cards. The situation is not strained enough so that total reprogramming must become necessary or that an additional adult needs to be involved. If spatial arrangement allows, the adult may spend the time with the ball throwers in the larger play room, while the two card players continue in their living room, which is adjacent with the doors open. Even though the adult is physically only with the ball players, he is still, in that case, psychologically not entirely out of the life sphere of the others. In fact, verbal remarks may even be exchanged between the rooms, and he can easily enough float from one to the other whenever that seems wise. This same scene would look very different if the only usable rougher ball play space is in the cellar, five flights down as we have once seen, while the quiet game rooms are at the top of the building. In that case, such a situation always becomes an "either/or," and an adult who would float between these two places would not be a natural "marginal figure" in both, but would be a "checking-up-on-mischief" supervisor in either. Clinically this may make all the difference between ego support and chaotic confusion.

Destruction leeway and margin for waste

In a real treatment home destruction and waste are not to be chalked up to "the unavoidable weakness of human nature and the imperfection of any supervisor's eyesight." They may become essential ingredients of the treatment process itself. It is therefore important that the amount and type of materials available and the budget for them are directly proportionate to the specific clinical task, not to the average customs of budget committees or material-producing firms. Bruno Bettelheim for instance advised us that, under certain conditions, heavy and comfortable chairs are much more economical than lighter ones, in spite of their higher purchase price, because the latter continually offer themselves as throwing objects even in mild tantrums, while the former don't. In order to get youngsters who fear or hate arts and crafts material to develop the taste for creative self-expression, it may be quite important to forget, for a while, about all limitations of economy of material. They could never even approach the creative use of a piece of material if we loaded their ego at the same time with demands of calculated cooperative economy. Yet the trick can often be done if we temporarily sacrifice the latter so that the former can blossom out. The same is true, of course, for items like food, much of which may have to be uneconomically prepared, so as to symbolize sociological taste patterns out of those children's past, and much of which may have to be calculated to be wasted, in the symbolic use of defiance against the love-offering adult. It took many smashed-up and thrown-around cakes and pies and superhuman restraint on the side of our brave and wonderful cooks until the love that was baked into a birthday cake could finally really get across to its consumer. When it did, though, it was worth the sacrifice in flour and sweat that went into its less fortunate predecessors.

The economy of seduction-avoidance

In work with ego-disturbed children, however, it is important to stress the danger of going too far in a triumphant policy of permissiveness. The kind of children we talk about have low temptation resistance and few controls, and even those are easily swept away in moments of excitement, or overstimulation, into which they drift with dangerous ease. For their ego to keep some level of reasonable control, therefore, it is also important that open overstimulation or overseductiveness of surroundings and props is carefully avoided. Policies about access to rooms and equipment with which they have no business must be clear and firm even though the occasional trespasser may be handled with all the wisdom of clinical thought. Adults must definitely know what kinds of things and situations expose those youngsters to uncontrollable temptation and should not expose them to more of it than their ego can be expected to cope with at that time. The popular yarn about the little "thief" who is so impressed with the "confidence" his counselor showed him by leaving his wallet lying around that he stops stealing is a fine theme for sentimental magazine stories but is utter nonsense from the point of view of clinical strategy. It is our task to support what ego strength has remained, not to undermine it by exposing it to entirely unmanageable strain. Much unnecessary confusion can often be avoided if such policy is built into the very layout of the space design itself. If children have to run through another group's dormitory in order to get to common washing facilities, we are asking for trouble that involves no clinical gain. If their life space is crowded with props which shouldn't be touched, if the total range of temptational gadgets in the rooms of the adults is constantly open to unhampered exploration, we are confusing, not improving, our total treatment strategy. Just what should and what should not be accessible is a decision to be made on strictly clinical grounds.

The mental hygiene of housekeeping

Children do not see only the house when they enter it. The whole style of housekeeping, the basic policies expressed in the way a house is run, are also having an effect on them even at the first visit. It is sometimes possible by walking into somebody's home to have some hunch of the degree to which a lived-in quality seems to be preferred by the owner to the protection of the value of the possessions themselves, or the other way around. Youngsters, too, react to the style of housekeeping, not only as part of a realistic regime, but as part of a psychological gesture of the relationship of adults to them. It is obvious that managerial efficiency has to yield in favor of a careful clinical assessment of the psychological implications for the children to be treated. One illustration may be chosen here out of dozens:

The questions of policies about keeping—and keeping track of—the children's clothes many times had high priority in the clinical part of our staff discussions and the policies had to be "made to measure" and changed several times. At one phase, for instance, we were impressed with the great value that came from having the children make the selection of shirts and clothes their first "interview contact" with the housemother every morning. We were very happy, at that time, to sacrifice any ambitions about "increasing participation through self-reliance" in favor of this chance. It was also important, in this phase, that the housemother as well as the counselors not be crowded into the role of "routine nagger." They would, therefore, ignore the fact that socks, shoes, shirts were often left all over the place when the children entered into an activity with zest. On the other hand, we had reason to be impressed with the "seductive" power which a messy living room has if that's the first place the children enter in the morning. During that phase, we carefully gathered all their things after they were in bed, put them in places where they could easily find them without having to start the day off in a squabble over what belongs to whom, and kept what "clothes contacts" we had with the children at a positive optimum. In another phase of our treatment such policy would have been outdated, or would have established a temptation for the children to exploit it for unnecessary overdependence or blissful neglect.

This, by the way, also constitutes an important item in staff selection and staff training. Neither the overcompulsive protector of order and cleanliness nor the happy-go-lucky person who just enjoys a mess is successful. Adults who work in a treatment home need the ability to sacrifice what personal style of housekeeping they happen to be most enamored with to the clinical strategy needed at a certain time. The people who often have to bring the greatest personal and professional sacrifices to the principle of clinical hygiene are the janitor and the cook. They, like everybody else, must be ready to vary what they may have learned to consider "good" practice in accordance with the clinical pace.

2. Routines which relax

The attitudes of people to the concept of "routine" might easily constitute a most fascinating piece of research in its own right. They could be summarized under the following headings:

Most people show an attitude toward routine which one might call "the naïve approach." By this we mean that they either "believe in routine," considering it an important part of learning or an essential tool to make children accept the limitations of reality, or they show an attitude which seems to convey that routines are something which they would rather not have if they could avoid it. Some people go so far as to react to the mere word "routine" as though something akin to goose-stepping storm troops of a fascistic autocracy were involved. This naïve approach is, of course, totally inadequate.

The "professional" approach to routine would take it for granted that we are aware of the complexity of the phenomenon. From this angle, routines are neither good nor bad and one's personal taste for elements of routine is not supposed to be a yardstick for their value for a specific group. Instead, objective criteria must be found on the basis of which we can make decisions as to where in the life of a group of children routines are needed and what kind of routines would be most advisable. The criteria on the basis of which people consider certain elements of routine advisable can be divided into the following two levels:

(a) The *"managerial efficiency"* criteria. Administrators in all types of life situations, not only of children's institutions, will easily tell you that the mere fact of the coverage of the need of a large number of people requires for efficient handling a certain amount of routinization. In a way, for instance, there is no doubt that a hotel which would allow all its guests to come for their meals any time they so chose would require a larger amount of personnel, a greater expenditure of money, and an expanded amount of time for the feeding problem as compared to one in which mealtimes are restricted to certain hours. In the same way it is also obvious that a fighting unit or the crew of a ship which may have to be ready for clear-cut action at short notice will certainly find the practice of routinized shortcuts for getting ready for these tasks a valuable asset. On this basis, many routines are introduced into the life of institutions which are justified by the argument of managerial smoothness.

(b) Relatively recently, another concept has pushed itself into the evaluation of routines. We might call it the *"mental hygiene aspect"* of routines or the "human engineering factor." For it is easy to see that administrative efficiency may sometimes be bought at the expense of the actual goal which an institution may have in mind. It may be more expedient to handle the feeding of hungry children in a reformatory in a certain routinized way. The people in charge of the children, however, might notice that the long waiting in line for the food, the pressures needed to keep them in line, the frustration piled up during the process, would create innumerable discipline problems, breakdown of group morale, increased hostility of children toward each other, etc. Then such a routine would be not an asset but actually a detriment to the institutional goal. It was originally the impact of psychology, mental hygiene, psychiatry, and especially of progressive education which raised the issue of the "mental hygiene implications" of routines. It is to be admitted that the original representatives of this point of view often added to their professional plea a high degree of triumphant opposition to routinization as such on a philosophical basis which we might consider naïve. However, no matter how the process started historically, it seems to us that an increasing number of institutions responsible for the development of children as well as the group morale of adults have come to view routines, not only from the point of view of the unavoidable numerical expediency problem and the advantage of managerial efficiency, but also under the scrutiny of their effect on the lives of people, individually, as well as upon the morale of their groups.

In a treatment home, it is obvious that the original sequence in which such criteria receive consideration has to be reversed. It seems clear to us that the criterion of the mental hygiene impact of routines will deserve priority over all others and that the conflict between administrative efficiency and the clinical advisability of routine elements in the life of children has to be abandoned for good. In more specific terms, the following seem to be the prerequisites of mentally healthy planning of routine elements in a treatment home:

The insertion of "routines" for their ego-supportive value

At Pioneer House, with five children only, it was obvious that many life situations which in larger and less well-staffed groups might require a higher degree of routinization could practically be handled on an individual basis. In spite of this, however, we soon learned that a certain amount of routinization under certain conditions, even where it was not needed for reasons of expediency or administrative smoothness, may actually have the value of increasing the total security with which the child goes through the experience in question. We found, for instance, that the mere existence or evolvement of a time schedule for certain life tasks, the mere repetitiveness of the same or similar situations to be gone through in the morning, in the evening, at bedtime, the mere development of a clear expectation pattern of just what the sequence of evening treat, story telling, lights out, etc., would be, would in themselves, after the first resistance was overcome, have a relaxing, quieting, and soothing effect on the personality of our children and actually, therefore, become an ego-strengthening factor. Thus, even though a nearly endless variety of individualization was open to us because of the smallness of our group, the adequate number of our personnel, and so forth, we soon learned to exploit the *mental hygiene value of routine expectations* around this area of the children's lives for their clinical benefit.

The mental hygiene design of the specific content of expediency routines

Even in areas, however, where routinization as such is unavoidable because of the nature of the life situation or the limited time available for a task involving multiple personnel, the question of what specific form the routine will take is of importance. In the planning of the specific details of such routines, a treatment home will have to demand that managerial expediency give way to the mental hygiene criteria in all points. To use an illustration from our Pioneer House experience:

It is obvious that the awakening of the children and getting them washed, clothed, fed, and started off for school would involve a certain amount of routinization and that the time available for this task is not infinite. It is also obvious that, from an administrative expediency point of view, a very simple regime might be expected to solve the problem. For instance, if the children were awakened by a sharply ringing alarm clock at a certain time, surrounded by enough pressure-loaded staff to get them going, provided with wash room and clothing efficiently prepared, furnished with a good timing of kitchen services in terms of the youngsters' completedness of dressing, the most "efficient" routine could be experimentally arrived at. It is equally obvious, however, that, in a home with any ambition for treatment in its plan, the question of what really happens to the children in the process of this routine is paramount. Taking any one of the frequently recommended and used routines for this process, for instance, we might have saved time, staff, and personnel but we would have started the children off to school with such an amount of mutual hostility, of anxiety or aggressive pressure, of inner group conflict or of destroyed morale in terms of the subsequent school job that the next person who received them from us could not possibly have done anything worth while with them. To plan for an appropriate routine for the morning hour, therefore, it became important to consider the type of procedure which would cope with the emotional problem of the situation most adequately. During one phase of our treatment, Miss Mary Lee Nicholson, our Group Work Consultant, had made a careful analysis of our problem, and helped us to devise the following process, which at the time proved to be the most salutary way out all around:

The counselor would turn up about ten minutes before waking was even necessary, putter around in the playroom and in the children's bedroom, sort out clothes and perform all sorts of tasks, as might a mother in a home who is up before the children are ready for breakfast. Those children who would not gradually wake up in the process would do so when the counselor turned on the radio with a soft volume. The children who awakened would be approached in a friendly way by the adult and they would be reassured that it was *not* time to get up yet, they could still keep their eyes closed and stay in bed for a while, the counselor would come back and tell them when it really was time. At the time when the getting up became essential, some of the youngsters were ready for the process without as much hostility as they usually show in their transition from their sleep and dream world to reality. The other counselors would turn up in the meantime and it would be possible for them to handle as much of each youngster's hangover-resistance as was not covered by the previous process individually and gradually. In a similar way frustration reactions to specific clothing to be worn on that day could be handled gradually rather than in a hurry. Ample time was left for consultation with the housemother, for argument as well as for compromise.

To cut a long description of the process short: while totally inefficient from the point of view of administrative smoothness and economy of operation, from the point of view of creating a psychological set for the day and of coping with frustration-anxiety and transition-aggression, a routine design of this type worked very well.

A clinical reaction to the phenomenon of routine as such

In many institutional settings it is not so much the routine itself and its planning which cause friction but it is the overexcited way in which either the children or the adults react to the item of routine. Group psychological studies make it clear that those two problems are really items of entirely separate nature. The organization of the group in an institutional setting, for instance, might be relatively routine-loaded in content but at the same time a very individualistic, tolerant, and thoughtful attitude might be developed toward those youngsters who are not able to live up to the routines which have been set up. In the reverse situation, it is conceivable that a group may get along with a minimum of routines but that those routines which are once established create such an amount of friction between child and adult or that the demands are met with such adamant uncompromisingness or punitiveness by the institution that the few routines become a more frictional source of conflict than the heavier routine in the institution mentioned before. In a treatment home, this means that, even in areas in which routine has to be designed for clinical or realistic purposes, the question of the reaction of adults to items of their routine is still open to separate flexibility. Thus, for instance, it was obvious to us that the transition from home to the station wagon, the behavior in the station wagon, the transition from the station wagon to the school would have to be routinized more heavily than many other aspects of our life because of the danger involved. At the same time it was also obvious that a treatment home could not afford the simple threat of expulsion or of a type of punishment the effect of which is known to be clinically destructive in order to support or bolster the routine previously designed. In short, even where there is a "set routine," the handling of deviations from it *must not become a routine in itself, but must retain all flexibility of clinical individualization.* The most important job which a treatment home has to face, especially in its earlier stages, is the gradual interpretation of routines as part of the life-facilitating design rather than as a potential challenge to the children for goodness or badness, which may in turn call out reward, punishment, acceptedness or rejection on the part of the personnel. Since many children come to us already with set reactions to routine as such, and since their reaction to routine developed previously often is closely connected with the disturbance that they bring with them, this item in itself sometimes receives priority over many other clinical tasks.

3. A Program which satisfies

It seems that in most of those cases where institutions plan the transition from a traditional children's home to "a treatment home" their main ambition is focused around the creation of sufficient psychiatric consultation and adequate and increased case work staff and the selection of personnel who are nonpunitive and acceptant of the children to be treated. All these items are, of course, conditions of a treatment atmosphere. Often, however, the planning of program and its detail is entirely neglected in such clinical plans. The underlying idea seems to be that, if youngsters are shown love and affection and given enough interview help, the rest of their life is primarily a framework within which individual treatment will take place, and that, as long as the children are more or less busy and kept out of too severe destructiveness most of the time, everything is all right.

This approach is based on an unfortunate misunderstanding of the basic role of the program and of the psychiatric nature of the impact of activity on the total economy of children's impulse-control balance.

For a detailed discussion of the role of programming for ego support see our next chapter.

At this point we would like to suggest the following list of primary criteria for the type of flavor which programming in a treatment home must assume:

Children often appraise the amount of affection or rejection which they receive from adults primarily through activity channels. Besides, the unavoidable frequency of interference by adults or of situations which to the children are frustrating cuts down on the amount of direct love signals which the adults can give. The most friendly and affectionate adult is perceived by them in many moments of the day as a hostile, negative interferer and even as an enemy. A treatment home, therefore, especially in the beginning, has to rely heavily on indirect channels of communication of acceptedness and affection from adults. One of the safest channels of that sort is the amount of gratification the children receive during a day and the willingness and enjoyment on the side of the adult with whom they are allowed to receive it. In fact, children may engage in the happiest recreational enterprises but, if they think that the adults frown upon them, they then interpret these enterprises not as a symbol of love from adults, but as a triumphant prize won against their vigilance. It is, therefore, important that the institution as a whole and every person in it are openly and explicitly acceptant of children having "fun." This means that even where fun-bringing activities have to be interfered with, it is the "reality limitations" attitude that has to be conveyed. Hostility toward fun itself must not be displayed by the adult.

The question of what should constitute fun in terms of the desires of the adults who survive with the children or the clinicians who hope to improve their sublimation level eventually and the question of what is really fun for the children at the time at which we start are important ones to consider. Educational institutions are tempted to try very quickly to smuggle higher levels of recreational activity into the children's diet. A treatment home cannot afford to go at too fast a rate in this direction. It is essential that the type of life experiences which is involved in recreational activities and other satisfactions of the children is designed close enough to the natural fun level so that activities are free from strain in terms of sublimation tension, frustration tolerance, etc., as far as the children are concerned. The design of recreational activities for our Pioneers, therefore, had to take careful account of the children's natural sociological taste pattern, avoiding too middle-class-limited activities for quite a long time, and at the same time had to be highly flexible so that momentary need coverage which is always experienced as gratifying by children could be planned for whenever needed.

Thus, it is basic that the priority criteria for the setting up of recreational activities are those of fun-satisfaction on the children's natural habitat gratification level. This principle, of course, must be kept on a sliding scale. With increased ego improvement and frustration tolerance, as well as increased adult-identification, the specific content of what can be considered gratifying for them can gradually move upwards on the sublimation scale. At all times, however, the feeling of the children in the home has to be that the adults are strongly interested in their "having fun." Satisfaction and gratification are not a bribe or reward thrown at them for the production of good or for the avoidance of bad behavior but are a basic part of their accepted diet which they can expect as securely guaranteed even in times which involve trouble. This implies that treatment homes have to use primarily clinical criteria for the establishment of their program activities, that discomfort and risks involved in low level fun activities have to be countered by sufficient staff, provision, material, equipment, that adult behavior toward the children must keep careful track of potential confusion in the children's minds as to the adult's own reaction to their having fun, and that all forms of educational bribe and blackmail, rewards and punishment techniques must be carefully separated from the problem of programming. It is hard to show the extreme difference in design of the activity content of a treatment home as compared to the traditional concept of even progressive and highly child-acceptant recreational levels. We shall have an opportunity to follow this item in more detail in one of the following chapters.[5] At this point, we want to imply, however, that the degree of fun acceptance and strategy is one of the most basic characteristics of a treatment home and that the children's perception of the treatment home as a fun-acceptant institution is one of the primary conditions for developing an atmosphere in which they trust the assurances of adults that they are wanted, accepted, and liked.

4. Adults who protect

We, too, started out with the assumption that a child-acceptant and affectionate atmosphere is one of the most important primary conditions in a treatment home. We soon had to learn, however, that children, over and above wanting love, affection, and friendliness, demand an additional role from the adults who have charge of their lives. This role is that of the adult as a "protector." The children we were dealing with seem to need for their inner balance protection which is primarily in the following areas:

Fear of other children

It is unavoidable that the exposure of different disturbed children to each other involves and produces much interaction. Much of this does not happen in the line of our treatment goals. It is also important that the children have a natural leeway to learn to size up their reaction to each other and the limits to which any one youngster will tolerate interference from any other and just what he will do about it. It is also taken for granted that quite a wide leeway for the "direct solution" of conflicts through fighting, hitting, etc., will be allowed, as it is to be expected in the natural neighborhood style of the children's original habitat. On the other hand, it is obvious that the production of some clearly pathological behavior like extreme temper tantrums or the extreme destruction in which some youngsters will indulge when irritated beyond their breaking point

[5] Cf. Ch. II, "Programming for Ego Support."

may create an actual problem of fear or helplessness in children. It was found important that our children learn that, while leaving them to their own devices to a high degree, at certain points the adult can be safely expected to interfere, stopping aggression which becomes intolerable or teasing which goes beyond the point of endurance. Adults who would not show clear-cut enough patterns of "limit interference" would make the children afraid and insecure and this insecurity about their potential protective role would be deducted from the quantity of affection with which they otherwise would credit such an adult.

Fear of own loss of control

Even children with severe ego disturbances have some points somewhere in which their ego is strong enough to realize the necessity for control but is incapacitated in terms of actual impulse blockage. It is in those areas that the youngsters expect the adult to take over. They may struggle vehemently against such adult interference at the time, but, in order to be happy in a home, they expect a certain guarantee of protection from their own impulses. It is not enough, therefore, that a youngster with extreme rages of destructiveness or aggression knows that the adults with whom he lives like him and will not be too punitive if a symptom carries him too far. He also needs the inner guarantee that, at certain extreme points where he would go beyond what he himself could really tolerate, the adult will use protective interference as a reliable device. It was interesting to watch how, whenever we failed to recognize this item, the youngsters would not only get wilder and more irritable but would afterwards react negatively to the adult who missed his function of protective interference and therefore left them to the fear of their own impulsivity without help.

Fear of outside interference

Many of the youngsters carry with them anxieties, realistic or delusional, about their previous lives or their contemporary outside lives and the consequences upon their life at the home. The fear of parents turning up unexpectedly, punishing, reproaching or taking the youngster away, the fear of the police taking vengeance for some yet undiscovered misdeed, the fear of some dangerous person from their previous lives suddenly appearing on the scene of the treatment situation constitute for many children an item deducting from the security they can find in the home. It is important that the children are given ample direct and indirect assurances of the protection which the home will offer against these interferences at all times. However, there are realistic limitations to the power of the home. They have to be made clear so that they are separated from delusional anxieties along that line. This statement is in direct opposition to a general theory of total openness and accessibility of the institution to all outside people as well as of total openness of the institution to the children implying that they can leave any time they want to. For some types of disturbances, in fact, Dr. Bruno Bettelheim has shown convincingly that a community-separated and closed institution is a primary condition to assure children protection against those anxieties mentioned here. For other youngsters, a combination of open door policy with clear-cut limits and lines of protection from outside interference as well as from the chance to get themselves into conflict with the outside world establishes a fascinating strategic problem.

Fear of extreme situations

The impact of group psychological intoxication often leads ego-disturbed children to degrees and stages of destructiveness and recklessness which trespass even what each individual would have contemplated by himself.[6] The awareness that the adult would interfere if the whole group got into a stage beyond control is another one of the essential conditions which create a security minimum in a treatment home. Thus, while temporarily fought and resented, protective interference by group leaders in moments of mob outburst constitutes an essential basic security device without which affection and love are not adequately communicated.

It is easy to see how this "protective role" of adults renders highly questionable some of the sentimentally generalized theories of total permissiveness. It is our conviction, and this conviction has been solidified during all of our experiences, that children either do not perceive total permissiveness as an affection symbol or that, as far as they do, an affection symbol of that sort constitutes only half the basis which they need for security in a treatment home. The combination of gratification offering through symptom tolerance and noninterference, on the one hand, and the establishment of a clearly protective role in the areas mentioned before, on the other,

[6] See *Children Who Hate*, p. 89.

constitutes one of the most important treatment strategies in a home. We shall try to clarify this vital issue later on.[7]

5. Symptom tolerance guaranteed, old satisfaction channels respected

One of the sharpest dividing lines between institutions with a primarily educational goal and treatment homes can be drawn around the concept of symptom tolerance. Ordinarily, institutions convey to the child the expectance of as much positive behavior as they can produce and load undesirable behavior with a variety of punishments or avoid its production altogether by restrictive programming or heavy impulse limitations. It is obvious that this cannot be the basic strategy of a treatment home. A treatment home is interested, not in avoiding and squashing the problem behavior resulting from the disturbances of the children, but in giving it a chance to come out in the open so that it can be manipulated and used for treatment purposes. This means that we must convey to the children from the very outset the awareness that the difficulties which are part of their natural problem can be expressed and lived out without too severe consequences or rejection from the adult. On the other hand, it is equally important to avoid the impression of "total permissiveness" in the children's mind. For, if they thought we not only tolerated but really enjoyed or did not mind their disturbed behavior, what motivation in terms of gradual treatment changes would there be left? In a nutshell, the treatment home must convey to the youngsters from the very start a climate which could be summarized in the following words: We like you, we take you the way you are, but of course in the long range we'd like you to change. Just how to convey this atmosphere seems to be one of the most serious strategic problems. We shall describe techniques used for this purpose in the following chapters. At this point, it may be sufficient to suggest the following basic conditions for the treatment atmosphere:

[7] Cf. Ch. III, "Techniques for the Antiseptic Manipulation of Surface Behavior."

Design for a wide leeway of symptom expression
without problems attached to it

This means that basic rules, regulations, the availability of equipment, the total programming, and sufficiency of adult personnel will make it possible for the child to produce a good deal of behavior which is natural to his disturbance, even though it is conflicting, risky, and undesirable. He must be able to produce it under conditions under which it can remain harmless or can be handled adequately without recourse to extreme interference. This means then that a wide leeway of confused behavior is built into the expectation of institutional life.

Antiseptic handling of problem incidents

Wherever interference is needed for realistic or clinical reasons, it has to be done in such a way that the basic policy of the interfering adult and the institution in which he operates has a chance to sink in eventually. This means that the manipulation of the interference in undesirable problem behavior which is still germane to the basic difficulties because of which the child was sent to the home has to be handled in such a way that a child knows what the limits are, that his behavior is not really acceptable, but that, at the same time, he as a person is not being rejected for showing it and remains safe from extreme consequences of what he does.

Limit interpretation

We must keep the children from confusing toleration of their symptoms with an actual indifference to or even permissive enjoyment of their problem behavior by the adults, and care must be taken to operate this principle on a sliding scale. This means that what at one time is considered an unavoidable problem symptom, as, for instance, temper tantrums, at another level of treatment in which this type of behavior is not a necessary symptom of the youngster's basic disturbance anymore would be considered in a different way. The development of realistic and flexible concepts of what does and does not constitute "unavoidable symptoms" and of where expectations in terms of levels of aspiration for improved behavior set in establishes one of the most complex treatment problems we can think of. Notwithstanding the strategic problem and the many conflicting issues which evolve out of such a policy, it is obvious to us that the basic atmosphere of "symptom tolerance" is probably the most essential primary condition for anything like a treatment atmosphere to come into existence.

6. Rich flow of tax-free love and gratification grants

Nothing seems more natural to the educational adult than to use the need of youngsters for his affection, as well as for experiences which are happy and a lot of fun, as bargaining tools in his educational task. Thus, it is normal in all homes, schools, and institutions that, once children show a certain amount of desire for adult affection and for certain types of enjoyments and activities, heavy strings are tied to those grants of affection or gratification. In short, the affection of the adult is assured as long as the youngster shows effort along the line of educational improvement and is withdrawn for misbehavior. The "privilege" of happy program experiences is available under the condition of good performance and is reduced in varying degrees for misconduct. We have no quarrel with such a policy as part of the process of acculturation, socialization, and education. In fact, some of it remains a basic principle, at least in the later phases, of treatment policy. However, the degree to which such policy can be afforded is different in a home with clinical aspirations. In order for ego-disturbed children even to begin to function adequately, it is essential that they get a heavy dose of affection, as well as gratifying life experiences. They need these doses as the basis on which treatment can even be considered, not as the removable reward for good behavior. That means that in order for them to develop a treatment rapport at all, a high amount of basic affection from the adult, as well as a high amount of really happy, gratifying program experiences, has to be guaranteed as an *unbudgable quantity*. The children must get plenty of love and affection whether they deserve it or not; they must be assured the basic quota of happy recreational experiences whether they seem to "have it coming" or not. In short, love and affection, as well as the granting of gratifying life situations, cannot be made the bargaining tools of educational or even therapeutic motivation, but must be kept tax-free as minimum parts of the youngsters' diet, irrespective of the problems of deservedness.

It seems to be this principle which runs most counter to the notions of lay people and educators and which is hard to maintain even for clinically oriented adults. It is also obvious that with increased improvement a higher degree of conditionedness of affectionate gratification and security, on the one hand, and affection symbols by the adult, on the other, can be introduced into the style of institutional life. However, the use of affection and gratification grants as an educational tool constitutes the end rather than the beginning phase in a treatment home.

It is to be granted, though, that for the children who hate this offering of such heavy love guarantees and such large gratification quantities does constitute an initial problem. We have described the confused stage of "Treatment Shock," which consumed about three months of our first work with our Pioneers.[8] Yet, even at that price, the conveyance of this basic policy, in spite of the strategic complications it involves and the temporary setbacks made unavoidable by it, seems to us one of the most essential conditions for achieving anything resembling a treatment plan in a residential home.

7. Leeway for regression and escape

The very nature of the disturbances of the youngsters we are talking about suggests two problems which we will have to expect: No matter how well designed the institutional diet may be, how adequately constructed the program and handling, how well planned the amount of gratification grants or the degrees and levels for protective interference, many of the children won't be able to take it all at certain times. In short, even in matters as simple as that of timing, the exposure to an organized game for which four of the youngsters may be just about ready may be too much for the fifth. Or, the participation in a friendly group-atmosphere-loaded event of story reading, highly desirable for most of the group, may at this point stir up too much anxiety around the reception of affection in one of the youngsters so that the whole situation becomes unbearable for him.

A treatment home has to anticipate this problem as best it can and create as part of its total strategy an emergency measure: "Ample leeway for escape."

At a certain time in our development, it was felt advisable that the housemother should not participate in the actual program but should stay in her room engaged in sewing, reading, or some other activity

8. See *Children Who Hate,* pp. 211-238.

which could be interrupted by the children without too much concern. At times at which we tried to expose our children to program activities of a somewhat higher structure, a youngster for whom the structure became too disturbing would have the possibility of moving from group exposure to the private relationship to one person, his housemother, that is, from a more structured activity to simply loafing around the person he liked at any time he so chose. In the same way, the participation and nonparticipation of a youngster in a more challenging program situation like a game or a visit to a factory would frequently have to be decided upon this basis and ample flexibility for variation and escape from too frightening experiences would have to be built into the total plan. Needless to say, this policy requires a great amount of program flexibility as well as a large available staff. This is one of the reasons why residential treatment is so expensive.

It is also well known that children with the type of disturbances we are talking about will, in the course of their treatment, go through severe phases of regression. By this we do not only mean the well-known return of the old disturbance after a temporary phase of improvement which even clinically untrained educators have learned to respect, but we mean a more severe regression to earlier depths of child needs and behavior, which may even have to be solicited as part of the treatment plan. Children, for instance, who have covered their early disappointments about lack of affection from adults with a hard shell of tough behavior and by open rejection of adult affection will, after the first exposure to the treatment plan has softened them up, suddenly go through a period where they may have to go back to a very infantile level of greedy consumption of adult affection. Such regressions constitute a severe problem in the actual handling of the children but are an unavoidable and essential phase of the treatment process. In a residential home it must be possible to build phases of nearly total regression to earlier childhood developments and infantile need demands into the total style and to still be able to manipulate the more realistic level of operation of a total group at the same time. The practical and strategic problems which such a policy involves in a multiple situation arc obvious and will be described in detail elsewhere.[9] It remains the task of a treatment home, however, to be equipped to handle them in a variety of ways. As far as the children go, the awareness of a chance for regression in treatment-essential areas without loss of prestige or danger of rejection and ridicule

[9] See especially Ch. III.

must be conveyed from the very outset in clear terms. If an institution were to supplant this policy in favor of one which implied the rejection or punishment of regressive behavior, it would lose its therapeutic chance.

8. Freedom from traumatic handling

An experience may be traumatic for an organism on two counts. Either it hits too close to home in terms of experiences which have happened to that organism before and have produced a disturbance in it, or it is so wrongly constructed by its very nature that the organism afflicted by it could not be expected to stand up under its impact. In short, you can produce a traumatic effect either by mild pressure on an already inflamed corn or by dropping a fifty-pound weight on a healthy toe. Whether an experience will have a traumatic effect or not, and which experience will, depends, therefore, to a high degree on (a) the previous traumatizations which have taken place in the earlier history of the children and their specific nature, and (b) the structure of the life situations to which they are exposed and their impact on the specific developmental stage of the child. It is well known that all children are exposed to many wrong situations and to much wrong handling which can hardly be avoided, partly because of the emergencies of daily life and partly because of the unavoidable imperfections of even kind and well-meaning adults who meet them as parents and educators. It is also well known that children have some considerable resilience to a certain amount of traumatization and most of them can take a reasonable dosage of wrong life situations or wrong handling in their stride with little more than temporary reactions to it.

When a child is so sick that exposure to a total residential treatment situation seems indicated, it is obvious that we have to redesign very carefully our thinking of what might or might not constitute a traumatic life situation or traumatic handling. It is also clear that a treatment home must, in its very design, avoid to the greatest extent possible exposure to situations which are liable to be of a traumatic nature for the children it works with. This means, thinking of disturbed children of the type we are describing here, that a variety of institutional policies will have to be designed in terms of this traumatization problem rather than in terms of conventional customs or other considerations. For instance, the questions of when the child should visit his home and of how long he should stay, of at what time visitors at the treatment home should be admitted, of the specific way in which such customary festivals as Christmas or Halloween are handled, of policies toward professional visitors from the outside, etc., may have to be revised time and again in terms of the specific treatment phase in which the children find themselves. Policies which may have become customary in many good institutions and which may be perfectly adequate for them may constitute severe traumatization in the one or other phase of the life in a specific treatment home. Nothing is more dangerous than the taking over of customarily routinized practice without reconsidering it in terms of the traumatization problem in the life of specific disturbed children.

It is also good to remember that total protection from "traumatic" life situations can hardly be achieved. An institution will be happy if it can avoid any type of exposure to traumatization situations in its own programming, handling, and design. Even then, the traditional customs around Halloween or Christmas, for instance, will often expose the youngsters to orgies of emotional problems which at that specific time may run counter to anything that would be clinically wise and yet because of cultural demand will have to be gone through and handled. Also, even the most protective policies of visitation, etc., will leave unavoidable mishaps in their wake and occasional exposure to temporary traumatization will not be avoided. Those, however, will constitute unavoidable life accidents against which the design of the institution protects itself to the highest degree and which, if they happen, will force the institution to abandon other objectives entirely and turn its full force on the detraumatization of the incidents involved.

The most important item, however, which sharply marks a treatment home as different from any other form of institutional care is that of total avoidance of traumatic handling by all institutional personnel. It is customary in the tradition of institutional policies to hope for the best and take it for granted that many people in institutions will be badly trained or that some of their skills will have to be bought at the expense of a bad temper or of extreme emotional needs for specific satisfactions which the personnel get out of working with the children involved. It is also customary to consider of primary importance the handling of the children on the specialist level by the psychiatrist, case worker, etc., and to accept the use of untrained and only partly qualified, basically friendly but professionally naive, laymen as a reasonable risk to take. It is clear that in institutions designed for clinical objectives and catering to children who are severely disturbed such a policy must be rejected completely. Conceding to it would be comparable to the situation in which a hospital would take care to hire the most expert surgeon to perform an operation but would leave the postoperational care to untrained lay people who have a great deal of love for their patients, are proud of the self-sacrifice involved in their service for them, but have a total unawareness of or even disdain or hostility for the most primitive requirements of antisepsis. We might even say that in a treatment home the importance of total hygiene in every moment in the child's life assumes a priority position. This means that it may not be avoidable that a youngster runs into a community problem around which an irate neighbor makes a dramatic scene which is obviously of a traumatizing nature, or that he succeeds in fooling a stranger into giving in to his cute attempts at begging, which may feed his pathology. It is absolutely paramount, however, that no traumatic handling is being risked *from the personnel who constitute the representative of the institution to the child*. Thus, while the mean temper tantrum of an irate neighbor may constitute an item which has to be handled and can be handled with a combination of realistic and clinical concern, the same type of irate temper tantrum shown toward the child by anybody identified with the treatment home in itself would establish an unpardonable traumatization which must be excluded by all means.

The implications of this principle of the freedom from traumatic handling impose on any home which has the ambition to be a residential treatment institution the following two basic categorical demands:

(1) Absolute avoidance of unhygienic handling by institutional staff. Under no circumstances can a person in an institution afford techniques of handling children which by their very nature establish a traumatic risk. Thus, any form of physical punishment whatsoever is totally excluded, the use of threat or promise in order to handle the momentary comfort of the adult is out, the absolute avoidance of exposure of the children to threat or fear, on the one hand, or overcompetitive challenge, on the other, must be enforced. Life situations which would involve the adults in getting rid of the children for their own comfort or fun, or which would involve the

tactless talking with each other about children's problems in front of them, or would imply embarrassment, ridicule, exposure to anxiety, or the strong display of personal affect unrelated to the situation in question must be excluded entirely. Needless to add, open contradictions among the adults handling the youngsters, conflicting policies, the exploitation of one youngster's feelings over and above others, or an unprofessional reaction to his conflict with an adult colleague must be equally avoided. In short, the whole gamut of handling by adults which is even slightly hygienically suspect must be absent from any phase of life in a treatment home. All staff including managerial personnel, cook, janitor, etc., are subject to this policy. A cook who plays favorites or rejects some children whose needs are not as gratifying to her pride as others could wreck in one mealtime what the total treatment design has tried to achieve in weeks.

(2) Over and above this guarantee of freedom from traumatic handling, it is important to remain sensitive to the previous traumatization history of a child. In this way, for instance, the rate at which a youngster's demand for adult affection should be met must be decided entirely on the basis of the youngster's previous life trauma and on the clinical criteria established at the time of the specific treatment phase, and must remain independent of the adult's actual need for or aversion to the affection-gratifications of the special child. The question whether a housemother, for instance, will give in to the demand for bandaging a delusional body damage or whether she will ward off firmly but kindly such demands must be exclusively answered in terms of the youngster's previous problem and our present clinical strategy and must remain independent of the issues of her time, her readiness, her fatigue, or her general principles about such matters. In the question of clothing, of Christmas presents, of what type of party should be planned for, in short, in every phase of institutional life we must consider the previous traumatization and the impact of the present situation as a primary criterion.

Thus, a treatment home will have to try to avoid the exposure to traumatic life situations by its very design and to handle such traumatic life situations as remain unavoidable because of the interference of outside personnel, community situations, cultural customs, etc., very carefully and with specific thought. It must be designed with a guarantee of the absence of traumatic handling of any child by the institutional personnel. This means that it is impossible to staff any treatment home with well-meaning lay people who like children or have only special skills or special administrative or other capacities. The actual minimum requirement beyond that for all personnel employed in the treatment institution is either careful training in the past or present exposure to participation in a training and clinical planning process which involves every one of the institutional personnel. Even the professionally untrained part of the personnel must have a share in the excitement and enthusiasm which are involved in the planning of clinical criteria for the selection of policies and for the handling of children. The so frequent lump acceptance of a great deal of wrong handling by adults because of the lack of training of the personnel must be excluded in the setting up of institutional design, personnel choice, and budgetary principles.

This is one of the reasons, by the way, why it probably will be paramount for the next few decades that specific treatment homes be kept small. Even among trained people it is hard to find adults who can remain clinical and hygienic in their handling toward too wide a range of disturbance types. Thus, an institution coping with the problems of extremely withdrawn and shy children may attract personnel who will do a beautiful job with this type of child but who may not be able to take the behavior of openly rebellious, value-rejective delinquents from a tough background. It is possible that the very limitations and ranges of intake which an institution should cater to at any one time may have to be realistically designed in terms of the personnel available and the type of atmosphere needed for the treatment of the specific disturbance type. Sometimes it may be possible to carry varying sets of disturbance types in smaller subgroups and still involve them in a well-balanced total institutional design. Where the personality characteristics needed to do the one or the other job are too conflicting, however, it would be wiser to set up separate institutions with a consistent design of staff selection as well as treatment policy in each one of them.

9. Ample flexibility and emergency help

Every phase of life in a treatment home must be made to measure to fit the existing clinical needs. One must recognize a variety of essential demands upon the total design of a treatment home.

This variety is an essential factor which must be injected into the whole atmosphere of living together with the children. This means that, where there will be a mixture of some life areas which are more routinized and some which are left to the decision of the moment, the children living in a treatment home must gain the impression that the handling of what really counts comes first and everything else comes second. They must have the impression that their feeling of upset will be given the attention which it needs even though this includes discomfort, problems, or difficulties in the life of the institution or the adult. They must, at the same time, get the impression that their attempts to use routine or opposition to routine for their personal pathological gains will be effectively counteracted. In short, it is the coverage of the youngsters' needs and the battle with their pathological techniques which will have primary weight in the planning of institutional designs. Leaving the discussion of the detail of some of this for a later chapter, we would like to list the following items as minimum requisites for clinical work in a residential setting.

Group units must be kept small, grouping must remain flexible

Partly because of the nature of the disturbance of these children who find larger set-ups too confusing, overstimulating or anxiety-producing, the treatment home for ego-disturbed children must have the possibility of keeping the basic units very small, and re-grouping must be entirely dependent on the problem of clinical consideration and free from other pressures.

Intake and exclusion policies clinically defined

It is impossible to keep the atmosphere of a treatment home intact if outside pressures like Board or community feelings have the chance to destroy a consistent atmosphere whenever they feel like it. The staff of a treatment home must be able to decide the intake or exclusion of a child on entirely clinical and group psychological criteria with no other strings attached. This will involve a good deal of community interpretation, since referring agencies, as well as parents, have quite different views on who should or should not be taken. The protection of professionally clean intake and exclusion policies is a prerequisite without which no treatment home could keep its clinical integrity intact.

Leeway for immediate program change

Whatever the expected program of an institution may be, changes which become necessary for clinical reasons must be possible at any time under all circumstances. This means that an institution attempting clinical work must be equipped with enough personnel to split groups in half when needed, to switch from indoor to outdoor activities, to change from a planned trip outside to a stay-at-home activity, to upset kitchen routine at practically any time, to develop substitute facilities, and must be amply implemented in terms of tools, equipment, art materials beyond the risk of the creation of traumatic incidents.

Sufficiently adequate personnel for all types of emergency help

The criteria on the basis of which we decide whether one person is sufficient to be in charge of the program of even a group as small as one with five members must be none but clinical. In some cases, one person may be sufficient or even advisable; in other cases, one leader may be adequate for the supervision of the children but, because their emotional needs may require multiple adult relationships, two or three people may be demanded on the program scene. The decision as to whether the group should be led by an outside person, like a recreational expert, cannot be made as a budgetary excuse for saving on the time of institutional staff. More often than not it will be necessary that the natural group leader of the group be present as a participant in the same activity even though from a supervisory angle this may look to custodial institutions like a waste of personnel.

Hierarchical role distribution on a planned design

The function which different people have in an institution is frequently designed by a pre-set hierarchy. Thus, the leader of the group may consider certain tasks his main domain and would regard the appearance of the institutional head as either a special show of interest or as an annoying interference. On the other hand, the head of an institution frequently reserves certain disciplinary rights and decisions to himself and policies in general are distributed in terms of pre-set arrangements. A treatment home, too, has to have carefully defined hierarchical distributions but this definition itself has to be made entirely on the basis of clinical needs. Thus, for instance, the head of an institution may have at one phase to assume the role of the negative limiter, drawing upon himself the aggression and hatred of the children and thus decontaminating the actual scene of recreational activity with their natural group leader. At other times, it may become more important that the natural group leader assume the role of interferer and use the representative of the total institutional climate for anxiety-assuaging support. The decision about which functional role would be played how and when must be a constant concern of planning and replanning among all parties involved and the development of a consistent role expectation in the children, even though with changing content, becomes an important task.

Ample supply of materials and props

The most difficult interpretation a clinical institution has to make to its Board is that of the clinical importance of supplies and the clinical interpretation of "waste." Yet, the presence or absence of sufficient materials to replace lost or destroyed objects may mean the success or failure of a vital program situation or may make all the difference between ego support or traumatization. The definition of how much money shall be used for what purposes may need redesigning in different phases of the treatment process. Questions of pocket money, cigarettes, candy, amount and form of accessibility of them, of policies about presents and extra treats, of the financing of gifts which are needed as a symbolic reassurance of an adult leader leaving for or coming back from a vacation, all these must be totally subject to the clinical needs in terms of the total treatment plan.

Whether the design of an institution claiming to do treatment is consistent with the claim can sometimes be seen by just running through its structure on any one of the above-mentioned points. Failure of those items to live up to clinical expectations may mean a failure to even have a chance to reach the total goal involved.

10. Cultivation of group emotional securities

Some of the security out of which children receive so much ego-supportive value does not come directly from the behavior of the adult. The fact of multiple clientele which so far seems such a complicating element in our clinical policy also offers a variety of technical advantages, because it involves the possibility of creating group psychological types of emotional dependencies. It is true that with ego-disturbed children the fact that they are physically living in a group situation does not immediately imply the development of treatment-favorable group psychological factors. In fact, one of the most disappointing angles of "therapy through the group" is the difficulty of establishing an emotional meaning of the group first in order to use it for therapeutic ends. However, it is also easy to observe that from the very beginning a certain amount of group psychological ties begin to emerge which can be increasingly used as security symbols and as conveyors of a total affection atmosphere even at times where the individual relationships of people to each other are conflict-loaded.

The most important areas in which a treatment home will exploit the possibility of group emotional securities by cultivating them are these:

The production of group-emotionally loaded situations

It is interesting to watch a variety of life situations which seem to produce conflict or to give ample opportunity for its discharge while others seem automatically to assuage existing frustrations and aggressions and suggest something like a "cozy group atmosphere." Even in the early days it was noticeable that occasionally and, admittedly, for only very short duration, our youngsters, whirling in their pajamas around the story-reading adult or sitting by the fireplace and listening to a radio program, actually seemed to be more of one "mind" than at other times. There were moments in which the very structure of the group situation would keep the individual confusions submerged so that the children actually lived a little bit above their means because of the support which they gained out of the very nature of the group situation in which they were engaged. It then became possible to cultivate such situations with care. It is obvious that we have to be clinically cautious not to impose group emotional elements to a degree to which they are threatening rather than ego-supportive, but it is possible to catch on to the natural trends of the children toward group emotional sensitivity and to exploit the cultivation of such situations in the daily program. Thus, the increase of situations which are group-emotionally tinged, as well as the participation of adults as part of the group in such situations or in certain types of games, is supportive of an attitude of "we, the group," with the adults included. This is the exact opposite of what the excitement involved in the daily disturbance of the children's personal pathology would otherwise suggest. The exploitation and production of a reasonable amount of such situations means the cultivation of security sources over and above other techniques available in individual treatment.

The support of subgroup ties even in anti-adult mischief

Some of the group-emotional ties which the children enter into definitely arise as defense against the world of adults and of institutional policies rather than as a desirable product of sublimation. Thus, for instance, the closeness of several youngsters with each other temporarily may only mean a joint insurance company against adult interference and may actually constitute a severe discipline problem for the supervising personnel. In treatment homes it becomes extremely important to notice the group psychological value of such adult-hostile subgroupings and to keep them protected and intact even where the actual event or enterprise around which the group emotions were developed has to be interfered with.[10] The policy of cultivating even defensive and anti-adult group-emotional possibilities is an important clinical device which individual treatment cannot employ. They will foster the later development of adult-positive group-emotional life situations.

Emotional tie-up with group symbols

The home in which youngsters live eventually becomes more than just a place to live in. It assumes something like a symbolic meaning in their life. It may be symbolic of many things, negative as well as positive, in terms of our treatment goal. Occasionally, the institution becomes the hostile represser of personal desires. Or it may become the avenger of undiscovered misdeeds, the triumphantly fought enemy, or the ridiculed power of outside authority. Whatever symbolic meanings the institution temporarily

10 See pp. 134-135 for an illustration.

assumes in the children's minds, it is possible through consistent policy by the treating adults to create, exploit, and expand a positive use of the institution as symbol in the youngsters' lives. Thus, at certain phases in the youngsters' treatment "we, the Pioneers" became an actual image of quite considerable power even at a time when the youngsters had not developed individual ego ideals worth talking about. For we found that guilt feelings about different types of misbehavior like stealing from an outsider might actually be producible if the institution was involved even though an individual value argument at that time would not have much of a chance. It is possible for a variety of techniques to suggest, simplify, and support the development of the function of their home, their group, as a symbolic unit toward which independent emotional relationships can be developed which can become valuable in the treatment process. Treatment in, and through, a residential home will heavily rely on the production and exploitation of group emotional securities of this type. It is one of the techniques which make the difference between a place where children live to receive individual treatment and a residential treatment home.

Summary

In this description of techniques for the creation of a "treatment climate," we have attempted to show that the very nature of the physical equipment, the very design of rules and regulations, the basic policies governing the behavior of adults as well as of the children, and the very strategy employed in the selection of life situations to which the children are exposed and in the decision as to how they will be handled, that all this basic design is an essential element in the treatment of the children over and above the individual handling from case to case. We are convinced that the therapeutic impact of the total treatment climate hits the children on two levels. The first one is obvious; it is an indirect one. It is the basis of the clinical design which defines the selection of life experiences as well as the behavior of the adults and through these indirectly conveys to the children affection and security, acceptance as well as limitation, reality demands and therapeutic goals. We are convinced that the existence of a clear-cut clinical design pervading all phases of institutional life is an essential prerequisite for the "total" effect in institutional treatment, and that such a total design has enormous advantages over and beyond excellent psychiatric services built into or onto an institution as a separate entity. We are, however, equally convinced that the impact of the total treatment climate also happens on a much more direct level. By this we seriously mean that the children "sense" some elements of such a design and react to them even independently of the experiences and of the handling which they receive from the adults in individual instances. At this moment, we are totally at a loss even to describe, to say nothing of explaining, this immediate preconceptual and preverbal reaction of children to the impact of a total design in their lives. However, the sensitivity which children often show to the implicit challenges of a program structure, the design of a room, the availability or inaccessibility of toys, and the degree to which they sometimes seem to be sensitive to underlying policies have been impressive phenomena to watch for all of us. We are also convinced that at times of piled-up conflict and of increased need for interference, and during phases of hostile misinterpretation of adult behavior, it was this total impact of the treatment climate which worked as a helpful counteragent, assisting us in the dissolution of the negative interpretation of individual incidents and in the difficult task of reality discrimination. However, knowing that it would be a hopeless task at this stage of the game to make such a claim stick, at a time when no specific research on an organized basis on these elements has been possible at all, we shall be satisfied if our readers will accept the implication of this chapter on the first level indicated. Of that level there can be no doubt, for it is the total design in its impact on the people who handle the children and whose behavior it modifies which certainly constitutes a demonstrable therapeutic agent. It is also plain that, wherever there are deficiencies in the total design, even the best efforts of the individual therapists and educational handlers of the children will be seriously counteracted and endangered. It is this part of the impact of the total treatment design which we hope will become clearer in the more specific discussion of special techniques used by us in this endeavor and which the following chapters will concentrate upon.

II

PROGRAMMING FOR EGO SUPPORT

What Is a Good Program?

IN the loosest meaning of the term, people use "program" to refer to almost anything children may be doing at a given time, or they use the word synonymously with "play." At the moment in which this is being written, we are watching, through our window, a group of neighborhood youngsters chasing up and down the remains of a house next door which is in the process of being dismantled. There isn't any adult with them and what they do doesn't look as though somebody had given them a blueprint of their recreational schedule between 5-7 P.M. However, they aren't just running around, either. There seems to be some "cops and robbers" pattern to their activity, and a certain semblance to status hierarchy and leadership distribution seems to suggest itself even in the narrow slice of their activity which we can watch from our vantage point. As Group Workers, we would be tempted to exclaim with pleasure: "Look! How wonderfully these youngsters are programming for themselves!"

More strictly speaking, the educator, and especially the recreation leader and group worker, would like to reserve the term "programming" for activities which require a certain amount of definite planning, on the part of the children themselves, of the adults, or of both. In programming, a large number of important decisions have to be made. Especially where the adult considers himself mainly responsible for the planning of a program, such decisions will encompass a much wider range of issues than the little word "program" might make us expect. Sometimes we may think of tool and prop selection primarily. The question, for instance, of just what toys the playroom for the five-year-olds in an orthopedic clinic should contain certainly would be an illustration of the point. At other times, we may be more worried about the problem of building recreational activities into the lives of children in such a way that they do not conflict with such other necessities of existence as, for instance, sleeping, mealtimes, school work, and so forth. On still other occasions the sequence and timing of activities have priority in our minds: should that story hour follow or precede their bedtime snack? Is it wise to schedule this gripe session right after an athletic game in which hot competition issues are at stake? How long can they play "capture the flag" before battle enthusiasm decays into battle fatigue? In still other instances, we would be more concerned with the content or the sublimation level of what they do. We might, for example, find that the activity called "Woodwork from 3-5" consists, in one camp, of a production line of quite perfectionalistically conceived baseball bats, put out under heavy competitive strain. The place where this activity is going on might easily remind us of a classroom more than of a leisure time setting. In another camp, the same shingle on their arts and crafts cabin door might signify a most informal, relaxed expressional orgy of whittling with wood, and the atmosphere in the room might be more along the line of "let's all have fun and don't bother as to what it looks like." Sometimes the concern of the program planner goes toward the question of just which people should be woven together into one and the same activity pattern and in what numbers and with which role-distribution. Occasionally, even such a superficial-seeming issue as the question of sharing limited facilities among a larger number of people or groups may take precedence on our agenda. Not infrequently, the very question of participation in the process of program planning itself may be the main issue of concern. Then, problems like member-participation in policy making and the democratic process of group decision-making will be of relevance. Altogether, the job of the program planner would resemble more that of the dietician than that of the cook—he feels, on some level, responsible for not only all decisions that go into one special meal, but the total intake and style of nourishment that belong to the concept of a well-balanced diet over a given stretch of time.

The main issue, of course, is the question of just what is really a "good" program for children. The average adult, who does not approach this question as an expert but as a parent, board member, or taxpayer, usually has quite firm and clear convictions on this point. His opinions are derived from childhood experiences of his own, from personal taste and comfort speculations, from views as to what money should or shouldn't be spent on, and especially from his own identifications with the customs and mores of the group he travels with. If pressed, he would probably admit that he considers "good" for the children what he himself enjoyed as a child, or learned to enjoy, and what the cultural system within which he lives would regard as being of "value." In most of the larger communities in contemporary America, for instance, there seems little doubt that "competitive athletics," football, baseball, and so forth, are considered "good for kids" in themselves.

If we turn to the people who are experts, not in program planning but in the cultivation of the specific skill which certain types of activities demand, we find an equally clear-cut value conviction, only sliced in a somewhat different direction. It seems without doubt that most "experts" in certain skill fields consider quantities of what they themselves happen to be interested in as the safest prescription for good programming. Everybody seems to recommend as being "good for children" the very commodity he happens to present on the market of recreational services. Thus, the athletic director of a playground program is convinced that youngsters should have plenty of that. The art instructor is sure that more cultivation of art and art appreciation would be a safeguard against the delinquency problem. The cherisher of good music recommends classical programs for all school children as the greatest blessing for the nation's youth. And every summer, thousands of American children in hundreds of camps shiver in the cold morning air before their prebreakfast dip, even though so far no known research has discovered any connection between goose pimples and character formation.

It is clear, of course, that the very question of what program is good for children is a nonsensical one to begin with. For things are not just "good" or "bad" for people; they are liable to have a quite specific effect which again will be tied to very concrete conditions. Neither salami nor sulpha is good or bad for everybody; it all depends. But there is no excuse for not raising the question of just what it will depend on, for that can be answered quite precisely. And the most important problem is, of course, just what tricks is a specific program supposed to perform? If a program is supposed to be "good," we had better ask right away: *good for what purpose?* As far as this question is concerned, we have, fortunately, a number of quite strongly defended theories to point to. For Educators, Recreation Leaders, Group Workers, Psychologists, and Psychiatrists have given this issue considerable thought. Unfortunately, there is still a paucity of really organized research in this field and many people who plan or supervise or encourage and discourage programs for children are not necessarily trained philosophers of program planning, child psychologists, or practical program experts. Consequently, in many places where children live, a consistent program policy may not be visible, nor may people be quite aware, philosophically, what they are trying to do. However, from what they say and from what is being done in children's institutions, schools, playgrounds, settlements, neighborhoods, homes, the following eight purported "goals" for the use of program can easily be distilled: [1]

Current Approaches to Programming

Program as a counteragent against destruction and sex

Many parents and educators hope that children engaged in activities which they enjoy will forget some of the basic urges of human nature. They are also convinced that children without "constructive program outlets" are liable to be found engaged in exploits of destruction or in the precocious enjoyment of sex. While this theory is rarely propounded as bluntly as this in print, it can clearly be heard in board and staff discussions, or over the luncheon table, and it can more clearly be seen as implicitly involved in many of the suggestions made for the type of program that should be developed for the youth of a community. Especially recreation programs suggested in connection with the Juvenile Delinquency

[1] In Rudolph M. Wittenberg, *So You Want To Help People* (New York: Association Press, 1947), the reader will find a helpful discussion of the use of programming and the group process in general in a variety of kinds of community programs and settings. This same theme is developed in S. R. Slavson, *Recreation and the Total P￦ sonality* (New York: Association Press, 1948).

issue quite often bear the stamp of this philosophy and it is often openly referred to when a reformatory tries to "apologize" for its emphasis on recreation, or to defend itself against the accusation of "coddling" its inhabitants. In fact, one of the purposes for which even the reluctant taxpayer is half way ready to shell out some money is exactly this use of program as a safeguard against youthful destruction and sex.

Program as a disciplinary device

Some institutions, among them, again, especially reformatories and detention homes, have another way of justifying the increasing amount of attention which they give to recreational programs. The fact that they have to "justify" this is in itself a symptom revealing more about the hostility of adults toward their youth than the "Century of the Child" would like to admit. Implicitly or openly stated, the extensive emphasis on "program" is often based on the assumption that activities which children like can be taken away from them when they don't deserve them. In short, program in those cases is inserted into the lives of children as a bribe, and at the same time as a potential tool for punishment or threat. In our own experience we found that especially institutions which have, happily or reluctantly, cut down on the cruelty and restrictiveness of their previous punishment system point with great pride and enthusiasm to their ample use of "withdrawal of privileges." In all those cases it becomes painfully clear that, no matter what educational or clinical objectives a prospectus may claim, in reality program has become a disciplinary device.

Program as a concession to human rights

Some educators will convince you that they have no ulterior motive when they demand an increased amount of recreational programming for the children of their community. They will insist that the pursuit of happiness is one of the basic rights of an individual and that a democratic society, therefore, must make it one of its goals to insert constructive forms of happiness into the lives of its children. They will emphasize that children should be exposed to many such activities just "for the fun of it." It is especially the "progressive" educator who considers the right of children for happy program experiences as something that should be guar-

anteed, because enjoyment of life and happiness constitute values
as such.

Programming as a tool in the educative process

One of the most well-known educational theories about recreational programming holds that, while enjoyable and pleasant in
itself, recreation can also be used as a disguise or vehicle for educational goals, and that a good deal of learning can take place under
its cover. On this basis, the educator would concede the values of
informal recreational activities and play, provided they give the
child a chance to learn, to practice skills which in themselves can
become an important resource in his later life. Or he would approve
of forms of play which bring the youngster in contact with activities
or people which may widen his horizon, without involving the
strain of a more formalized or routinized learning process. Hence,
the cultivation of music and of travel, the value of useful discussion groups connected with play programs, and even the value of
organized play or of intellectual or physical games of skill have
been openly and strongly advertised as educationally approved. In
all those cases, though, recreational programming is really suggested
because it lends itself indirectly as a better tool for learning, offers
a better way to improve, or helps children mature.

Program in the service of socialization

By this we mean the attempt to use activities which are fun for
children as a device to pull them out of individual isolation, bring
them in contact with other people, and help them accept personal
frustrations in favor of adjustment to larger groups or bigger goals.[2]
In this connection the value of team spirit has frequently been
alluded to as one chance to socialize children or to make them
group-conscious. The value of adding the pleasure of a friendly
group atmosphere to situations which otherwise might involve individual frustration has been mentioned before. Thus, the youngster
who may have to learn to domesticate his urge to "hog" the ball all
the time may be expected to be ready to accept a more group-
related role and the temporary frustration of his play impulses, in
view of the reward of triumph of a team victory. Another socializing

[2] See Grace Coyle, *Group Work With American Youth* (New York: Harper
& Bros., 1948) for a more extensive treatment of the philosophy on which this
type of programming is based.

function of program activities has been claimed to be the learning of "functioning in a democracy" through experiences of participative planning. Practically all so-called "social skills" needed in any society can be translated into game activities which combine the value of acculturation and socialization with the experience of happiness and fun in the process.

Programming as a crutch for the emotionally handicapped

Sometimes programming assumes a function similar to artificial feeding. Some children are not able to receive the diet, to incorporate the vitamins of certain life experiences through the traditional channels by which other youngsters can take them. In that case, short cuts are sought or program is considered a substitute for other channels of vitamin supply. For instance, some children are "emotionally" too handicapped to accept intellectual stimulation through regular learning situations in school. They couldn't take the exposure to waiting, manipulative frustration, routine, etc., which school implies. Group workers are convinced that some of them can gain through ingeniously constructed play channels what others can absorb through formalized instruction in the usual curriculum. Other children, again, are so full of aggression and individual restlessness that their participation in community-offered settlement or playground programs becomes unfeasible. Yet, the group psychological value of a club or camp experience is as necessary a part of their developmental diet as it is of that of any other child. The task of programming, then, becomes, not to cure these children of their basic pathology, but to supply them *even while they are still disturbed or incapacitated* with the same ingredients which others can easily find for themselves from the various offerings in their neighborhoods. For the visibly physically handicapped child this function of programming has long been well known. For his emotionally disturbed contemporaries, it took longer to see and develop parallel styles of "special group work with the disturbed child."

Program as a counteragent against wrong life situations

It is a fact that children often have to be exposed to life situations which do not contain the ingredients which a normal life diet would demand, or which are downright loaded with the impact of poisonous effects. Children may have to be kept locked up in limited and unfit quarters for a variety of reasons until the court has been successful in taking steps toward a more adequate re-arrangement of their life space. Or it may be unavoidable to expose children to life in hospital wards, an experience which is obviously fraught with the danger of a severe pauperization of their normal life diet. In those instances, program has been discovered as a po-tential counteragent against the damaging effect which such life situations would have to involve. Thus, for instance, activity pro-grams developed in hospital wards of bedridden children may coun-teract the boredom and individual isolation which children would otherwise experience, and may give emotional support to their or-ganism, enabling it to "stand" the difficult, wrong, or artificial situa-tion into which it is thrown. Again, some of the psychiatrically more sophisticated workers in detention homes have demanded that chil-dren who are exposed to long-range storage and waiting for un-avoidable reasons through the breaking up of family life, and even children who have to be locked up because they are aggressive and have done destructive things in their communities, should not be exposed to the danger of boredom and anxiety which such inactive storage or lockup would imply. They need, as much as any normal child, or even more so, an adequate "program" to structure their psychological life space, to supply them with the vitamins of inter-personal relationships, of engagement in a meaningful activity, of expressional discharge of surplus tension, and so forth. Before the question of actual "therapy" is even raised, such children need their "program" as a protection from the disastrous effect a "wrong life situation" would otherwise have on them.

Programming as a diagnostic and cathartic device

Ever since psychiatrists and psychoanalysts got interested in working directly with children, they have faced, of course, the ne-cessity of using play activities at least as a means of communication. Many of the decisions which a modern child therapist has to make are identical with what group workers would call "programming," even though this term doesn't happen to be customary in clinical and psychiatric circles. There are issues of just which toys should or should not be purchased for a modern clinic's playroom, there are questions of the sequence in which children should or should not be exposed to certain toys or game activities, there are problems of full exposure to the toy shelves or exposure to only a few preselected materials at a time, there are problems of seductiveness, of overstimulation of certain toys and games as compared to the lack of expressional value of others. In short, whether he knows it or not, the psychiatrist or clinician of today is also a program planner. The purpose for which we would think of such activities in clinical practice, though, over and above their use as vehicle for rapport, would be clearly focused around two issues. The *diagnostic* value of many play activities has by now been so fully accepted that we hardly need to try to justify it here. We might want to encourage, though, more organized research than we have available to date on the question of just which activity brings out what in children of certain ages, disturbance types, sociological backgrounds, etc. The other purpose of play in child therapy quite clearly is that of *catharsis*. Many therapists even today consider this as its main function. They hope to obtain from the expressional gratification involved in certain play activities a direct cure via the very fantasy or impulse push which is being discharged. The psychoanalytic school of thought has long tried to debunk this assumption as a naïve illusion. The child analyst today would grant occasional strategic value to the expressional relief through certain play activities, but would insist that the real therapeutic process is much more complex than that and that discharge alone does not guarantee treatment at all.[3] It is amazing, by the way, in spite of this, that even the therapist who rejects the simple catharsis assumption may sometimes regress to the older assumption of "catharsis as the main value for programming" as soon as he does not talk about his own work with the child but views programs where the child plays with somebody else. This may become painfully clear when he is asked to participate in the program design of an institution for children, where the very theory discarded for his own use seems to be often considered good enough for those who meet the child "only" as educators or play leaders. At Pioneer House, for instance, we lived through several embarrassed silences when an occasional psychiatric visitor would ask us in amazement why we didn't focus our recreational activities around a punching ball, "so that these children can work out their aggression." Such statements, by the

[3] This point of view is expressed quite clearly in Anna Freud, *Psychoanalytical Treatment of Children* (London: Imago Publishing Company, 1946), which stresses the interpretative and other manipulative behavior of the therapist necessary to effect cure, beyond mere cathartic release.

way, would usually be followed by the question whether our group therapy would take place in the morning or the afternoon hours.[4] . . .

Programming as a full-fledged therapeutic tool

The eight types of "goals" for which "programming" seems to be used do not claim to be mutually exclusive, nor is it our intention here to weigh their merits and defects more in detail. For, more important than the question of just which "goal" programming sets itself is the spirit in which any one given program goal is pursued. And in this respect the last few decades have really brought with them a contribution to the field of recreational and group work programming without which the mere idea of a therapeutic use of programming would have remained indeed unthinkable. What we refer to here may summarily be described under the title of: *The Mental Hygiene Approach to Programming.* This can easily be depicted in its crude outlines as follows:

No matter which "goal" we have in mind in our program planning, whether a given program is any good or not depends primarily on the question of *whether it achieves its goal without doing damage to the individual or the group involved in other respects.* Let us use just a few crude examples as an introduction to the problem. Even a "good" program in terms of efficient competitive athletics may sometimes be ill-designed for some of the members of a team. With too heavy insistence on athletic triumph on high levels in the foreground, individual participants may be thrown into the doldrums of inferiority feelings or of anxiety about rejection by their own group for not meeting the standards. Groups which are not adequately prepared for a specific level of competition may be thrown into stages of triumphant snobbishness, real hostility to the opponent instead of fair team spirit, or apathetic withdrawal out of discouragement after defeat. The demand of the "Mental Hygiene Approach" to programming would, therefore, not be to substitute different goals for the original ones, or to substitute mental hygiene speculations for program goals, but to scrutinize *what is being done to people* under the title "programming" from the viewpoint of *mental hygiene effect.* In this way, for instance, sometimes

[4] See Erik H. Erikson, *Childhood and Society* (New York: W. W. Norton, Inc., 1950), Chapter 6, "Toys and Reason," for a fascinating exposition on diagnostic as well as therapeutic aspects of play.

the goal of using the phase of a program for the "socialization" of the youngsters involved might be retained, but different specific games might be selected, or the way in which children are handled while engrossed in those games might have to change. The modern trend in mental-hygiene-conscious group work is to retain the value of originally designed program goals but to blend criteria for good programming from that angle with the mental-hygiene-produced awareness of its effect on people. This development of a "mental hygiene approach to programming" has first led to a debunking of the original naïve concept of what constitutes a good program as such. We have learned to consider the importance of making the program fit the needs and readinesses of the children rather than expose children to activities which are traditionally considered "good" for them without mental hygiene scrutiny. In this way, the mental hygiene point of view in programming has already, even on the straight group work scene, developed much more "psychiatric sophistication" in the field of program planning, even where no direct therapeutic tasks are involved.[5]

The step from this "mental hygiene approach" to any and all program planning to the *special use of programming for therapeutic ends* is not far. Relieved from participating in the usually naïve and somewhat salvational program enthusiasm of the layman, the psychiatrist has raised hopeful eyes to the potential which more sophisticated program planning might contain for his task. Not too familiar with and never exposed, in his own training, to any organized thought on such issues, he has nevertheless expressed much confidence in the value of "recreation and group programs" as an adjunct to the treatment in psychiatric institutions. On the basis of such developments, a clearly expressed interest by the therapeutic field in the contribution recreational and group work programming may have to make is well evident by now.

The issue we want to focus on in this book, however, is still one step beyond this. For reasons which will emerge soon, we are convinced that a "supportive" use of programming, to further the success the individual therapist can have with his client in his interview room, is not enough. For the type of children we are talking about in these studies, we boldly claim that the function of pro-

---

[5] See Gertrude Wilson and Gladys Ryland, *Social Group Work Practice* (New York: Houghton Mifflin Company, 1949), which presents a wealth of technical detail and rich recordings on programming for normal youngsters.

gramming must move directly into the core of the treatment process itself. The practice and theory of the use of programming as a therapeutic tool would be a theme worthy of a book of its own.[6] In the following pages we shall have to confine ourselves to describing only a thin segment out of the total programming field, namely, its use for one specific task within the therapeutic process, that of Ego Support. Needless to say, the fact that we limit ourselves to this small segment of the total issue in no way reflects lack of appreciation of the importance of other phases and of the uses of programming for other tasks in therapy. Nor does it indicate that we underestimate the great importance and challenge which use of programming even as support for individual therapy deserves. We only want to restrict the total scope of our discussion of programming for reasons of conceptual economy dictated by the nature of this present book. We hasten to add another apology before we begin—even the description of the use of programming for ego support challenges us toward more theorizing and the formation of more new concepts than we can possibly load this practitioner-geared book with. We resign, therefore, any claims to a logical sequence and to a grand conceptual architecture, and list under headings and in a sequence which might make sense to the practitioner what we have to say. The discussion and clarification of theories, assumptions, auxiliary concepts, and so forth which are buried beneath the descriptive layer of this presentation will have to be saved for a future chance.

1. Impulse drainage

It is characteristic of disturbed egos that they cannot manage any amount of piling up of impulsive energy. Where the normal ego would still retain enough judgment or power of control even when desires or needs have been stimulated to a high degree, the disturbed ego is not able to cope with such situations, and reckless and disorganized discharge of whatever impulses have been piled up is the result. If this is so, then it becomes important to help sick egos to cope with such impulse pile-up. It may even become important to spare them too frequent exposure to unendurable impulse pressure altogether. Thus, even "weaker" egos can be helped to maintain a more successful control of a child if a preventive drainage of

[6] In Gisela Konopka, *Therapeutic Group Work With Children* (Minneapolis: University of Minnesota Press, 1949), the reader will find valuable materials on the use of program with disturbed children.

part of the impulses is made possible. This is where program planning comes in handy. For instance, the exposure to long stretches of manipulative frustration at school, coupled with feelings of anxiety and irritation which had to be subdued temporarily, often confronted our Pioneers before the school day was over with a tremendous piling up of aggressive impulsivity which they could barely keep in check. If, at this time, we had exposed them to a program activity which again would have made similar demands, a disorganized blow-up of their aggressive energies with all of the subsequent problems around it would have been unavoidable. Instead of that, we tried to help the ego to manipulate the situation by creating program structures which would provide a chance within program control patterns for the discharge of the very impulse which the ego alone could not have manipulated. Thus, for instance, a number of exciting seeking and running games or tumbling activities in the protective framework of our own home would drain off some of the impulse accumulation which would have invariably led to disaster if the youngsters had been exposed at that moment to a passive program like watching a football game. It was our feeling that the sum total of control over impulses in a child would be increased if appropriate impulse drainage could be inserted into program planning when surplus impulse pile-ups were obvious. Thus, the program structure became an aid in offering channels for harmless discharge of impulse pile-up where the ego alone could not have kept enough judgment to seek such channels or enough control over the impulses had no such channels been available. Of course, a program activity that is primarily designed for impulse drainage would be structured very differently from one whose primary purpose is educational learning, practice of social skills, or what not. A treatment home may have to have a wide range of program activities, sacrificing all other goals, which are primarily designed to give ego support through impulse drainage of a very specific type.

At dinner tonight Mike was impossibly obscene, using various items of food as sexual symbols (sauerkraut for pubic hair; wieners for the inevitable penis), and had to be removed from the table, after repeated warnings, to eat in the other room with a counselor. His removal came too late, however, for the others, since by this time he had contaged the group with so much erotic fantasy and acting out that it was nip and tuck through the rest of the meal. Andy went into his obscene clowning and took the Verbot just in time to avoid being bounced. Bill giggled and provided all the audience appeal that Andy needed and supplied items of his own when the show lagged. Danny caught the infection via his own anal obscene route and converted the sexuality of the others into anal equivalents. Larry, except for a few raucous guffaws, seemed to withdraw into his own autistic world under the barrage of primitive stimuli from the others. I didn't remove anyone else because they did not go to the extremes of Mike but showed at least a little response to insistence to tone down, even if this did have to be repeated about every two minutes. The evening counselors gulped through the last part of the meal in order to prepare program material in the upstairs playroom. They had scheduled finger paints and had them strategically placed around the room; they also had some athletic equipment on tap if this didn't seem to do. As soon as the children hit the playroom they gravitated toward the finger paints and Danny began to daub huge masses of it on the paper. The others began fingering around a little more delicately and then Danny, with a belly chuckle, said, "Hey, look guys—look at me." He had daubed his whole arm a rich orange. This contaged the others immediately. Mike followed by peeling off his shirt and painting his chest; Andy got the idea of painting up as Indians, and the whole group swung into this beautiful piece of sublimation of many of the body-related impulses running rampant through the evening meal just a short time ago. They spent the good part of the evening whooping around through the upstairs in a variety of loosely woven and rapidly shifting Indian fantasies; they also wrestled and stalked each other and subgrouped around various themes. Bedtime was benign with everyone in good spirits. (Entry: 5/25/47, David Wineman)

Although many localized impulse patterns can be observed in this sequence of behavior, basically they can be grouped into two themes:
  (1) body-related fantasy needs
  (2) group orgiastic enjoyment needs arising from mutual contagion signals.
Basically, the materials prepared for the evening program have many more potentials for constructive goal attainment than here exploited. Aware of the immediate needs outlined above, however, the group leaders wisely confined themselves to the simple impulse drainage aspects involved. By the way, it should be obvious that inert materials in and of themselves could not have done the whole trick. It was the attitude which the group leaders took which made

a somewhat wild but still enjoyable group experience out of what otherwise could have ended in disgruntled mayhem.

The group had been playing ball this afternoon at the gym and were all hepped up. There was a great amount of dirty language, especially toward me. I had to bounce Danny because he threw a knife at Andy and he went upstairs, refusing to eat when I offered him his plate in the living room . . . After dinner the group was still wild, especially Mike, and full of sex gestures, swear words, insults, and fight. There was some card playing which had little chance to succeed in their mood. The evening counselors moved in with their program: tin plates and parts to glue on so that they could be used for musical rattles. This was a great success, leading, of course, to tremendous noise. At one point the phonograph was playing, the group were pretending they were a tin pan orchestra, and the radio, on full blast, had the Lone Ranger trying to out-drone us. Later Emily (housemother) succeeded in starting an amateur show suggested by Andy's presentation of tricks with a coin. This took up the rest of the evening, the kids putting on a costume show and doing a clothes change several times. (Entry: 2/21/47, Fritz Redl)

It is important, by the way, to keep in mind the difference between what we are trying to do in these instances and the usual idea of treatment through simple "catharsis" or "abreaction" of impulses and emotions. In their behavioral results, both may seem quite similar. The purpose for which all this happens, however, is of a very different nature, indeed. When setting up an activity structure so as to enable our youngsters to get rid of "piled-up" impulsivity, we have no illusion at all that such expressional discharge will change anything in the quantity and nature of the impulses which these children have and produce. In fact, many of the impulses discharged under those conditions are in themselves quite "normal," and no intent at therapy for them is implied. Others, which turn up as part of their fantasies, may indeed be sick and pathological altogether. Yet, we know that nothing will be changed, as far as these fantasy needs and impulses are concerned, by merely draining them off. That part of therapy is a story in its own right and belongs to a much later and quite different phase of our treatment effort. The use of programming as a means of impulse drainage simply has the purpose of helping the *ego* of the children in its formidable task, not of changing the content of their desires and needs. It helps the ego in two ways: one, by simply reducing the amount of impulsivity that needs to be kept in check at any one given time.

For a "weak" ego this is a considerable gain. The other is by offering outside support and structures and patterns for impulse discharge on a feasible sublimation level, where the ego alone would not have been able to invent or produce such channels of expression at all. For egos as disturbed in their function as those of our children are, this sometimes makes all the difference between reasonably controlled wildness and total destruction or panic-producing breakdown of behavioral controls.

2. Frustration avoidance and frustration budgeting

Among the defects of disturbed egos are the inability to manipulate frustrations for any length of time and their low level of frustration tolerance altogether. Thus, any activity, even though basically desirable and potentially pleasurable, may become inacessible to a child because the barriers of frustration intolerance constitute an insurmountable handicap. Therefore, program planning may sometimes have the primary purpose of inserting into the youngster's life activity structures or enjoyment patterns which are planned in such a way that frustration is avoided or at least budgeted in terms of the low level of ego control of which the youngsters are capable at the time. For instance, during one phase of their development our children were ready to engage in some level of mildly competitive games of skill. These might include dropping clothespins through a bottle neck, trying to hit targets in dart games, hopping in relay on one foot, etc. In fact, partial elements of such game structures had already been successfully indulged in and had assumed the proportions of a potential satisfaction image in the youngsters' minds. Yet, if such games were organized in such a way that a youngster would have to wait his turn, that the amount of activities available at the time would be limited, that he would have to compete for accessibility to the activity with the other youngsters, that pins that were lost in the shuffle could not be replaced fast enough, the low frustration tolerance of the youngster's ego would have made continuation of this game impossible. The purpose of program planning in this instance, then, would be to arrange the satisfaction potential in such a way that frustration is avoided or is budgeted only to tolerable amounts. For instance, by having several such activities going on simultaneously, each youngster could be engaged in one of them instead of having to wait as an impatient onlooker until someone else was finished.

By having sufficient supplies ready, they could avoid the frustration of having to look for a lost clothespin by supplying another one and leaving the looking for later. By having enough adults around to support the youngsters in going through this process, waiting lines could be avoided or the frustration for some of them having the game held up by the temper tantrum of one child could be excluded entirely. It is our impression that the ego of the children is supported, in these instances, by carefully sorting out frustration potentials which could be avoided through wise planning. By removing them from the activity pattern so that the diseased ego doesn't "stumble" over them through its low ability to cope with frustration hurdles, we open up to the organism channels of expression and enjoyment which would otherwise remain blocked to it for quite a while to come.

During the early part of treatment we observe that Larry has infantile temper outbursts in frustrating and competitive situations. In checkers, he has to win and in order to do so insists on playing "baby checkers," which virtually means that the adult gives him all the moves so that he can win the game. After a few experiences where his pattern has been observed, we make the following arrangements with him: We will play one game of baby checkers and the next game of checkers regular style, selling this on the basis that he has to do this to learn how to play the game correctly and this is what we know he would like to do eventually, etc. This is acceptable to Larry and he can bear the frustration imposed by regular rules for periods of time if this is interrupted by the gratification of some of his infantile needs. At the same time the reality-educational element is preserved and represented to him and, in this style of more or less staggering his frustration, we pull him gradually toward a more reality-loaded approach to games.

At a certain time it seemed desirable for our youngsters to have some experience in making something they could use which would require only one short session of work. Aware of the potential frustration problem involved in such tasks, our counselors went to great lengths to reduce to a minimum the complexity of functions involved in the program.

Today the afternoon program was making shoe sox. Vera (co-counselor) and I cut out the patterns for soles and stitched together the sox before the group came home from school with Dave (Executive Director). Thus, all the children had to do, with our help, was to sew the soles (already cut out) to the sox (already stitched)—a single operation. (Entry: 2/19/47, Pearl Bruce)

Even so, the thin margin with which the shattered egos of our children operated was painfully evident and the staff had to be continuously alert in order to rescue the experience (at least for most of the children) from the particles of frustration still inherent in even the simplified job. Let us continue with the above entry:

Even with this much elaborate preparation to reduce frustration, the boys barely got through the activity. Mike was the only one who stuck to the original stitch pattern shown him. Danny abandoned the original stitch, made his too close together, noticed it, blamed us for it, saying that we wouldn't help him, though he had resisted help when offered. Larry made huge stitches to beat the others. He had extreme difficulty in pulling the needle through the sole and requested help at practically every stitch. When I tried to show him a very simple way of grasping the needle to pull it through, he refused to listen. Then Mike and Andy got mixed up, each taking by mistake wrong side soles for one foot which meant they had taken each other's soles. This produced a short blow-up in Andy. He threw down his slipper, snatched it back up a couple of minutes later, was very irritable, would accept no help, and began deliberately making large, careless stitches. When his needle got stuck, I offered advice, urging him not to pull it so violently. He threw down the sock, stalked out of the room, screaming that no one would let him make his slipper the way he wanted to. Yet, all the time he was angry at the way he was making it! (Entry, 2/19/47, Pearl Bruce)

3. Concessions to sociological taste patterns

One of the difficulties of youngsters with poor ego equipment is their incapability of appraising fun potentials in anything which they have not been frequently exposed to before. Also the threat of a new situation with its very newness or strangeness is enough for their egos to give up when more normal or more organized children would use exploratory experimentation before they made up their mind.[7] The impact of this on program planning is obvious. Program planning has to start with activity patterns which are familiar to the sociological framework from which the youngsters come and are not loaded with an undue amount of new elements or strange gratifications.

[7] For a more detailed discussion of the reaction to new situations of children with the type of ego disturbances we are focusing upon, see *Children Who Hate*, p. 98, "Newness Panic."

By way of illustration, at a certain phase of our development we felt that the youngsters would be ready to throw some of their naive narcissistic enjoyment of body movements or gestural clowning into a more structured pattern of pantomimes or short stunt dramatic performances. At the same time, such an activity or game which is perfectly customary in middle-class circles would have involved a tremendous element of estrangement for the youngster, and embarrassment about engaging in it would have produced giggles, confusion, or outright rejection. We were successful, however, when we hit on the idea of tying up this kind of activity structure with a type of game which was very familiar to the youngsters and which they often had played in their natural habitat. We preambled our dramatic stunt by a treasure hunt and we gave the treasure hunt a style very similar to that of the activity youngsters would indulge in in their usual alley exploration and neighborhood roaming. Thus, we hid a variety of clues all over the house, in the alley, in the yard, in the coal pile. Looking for those clues involved alley roaming and the inspection of neighborhood ash cans. As a culminating clue, we inserted one for the pantomimic production of the title of a song, which again was familiar to the youngsters from their previous style of life, and it was through this device that the resistance, the anxiety produced by the newness of the activity, was minimized through the increasing of familiarity with the old.

Before we arrived at this stage, we had to make even wider concessions to the original natural habitat customs of those youngsters because any introduction of even partial newness would have confronted their ego wtih new suspicion and anxiety blocks. Thus, some of our early games actually consisted in participating with adults in alley roaming and activities of a similar kind. It was also easy to notice, however, that the increasing frequency of the experience of taking some elements of newness finally led to a point where greater deviations from original familiar structure could be risked since there was more probability that they could be coped with by their egos at that time.

Sometimes, newness or strangeness panic would attach not so much to an activity itself, as to the accompanying behavior which they were or were not allowed to unfold, or the "social climate" which a certain life situation seemed to breathe. Thus, we could risk exposing them to some "new" and quite frightening situations, such as a visit to friends of ours whose style of life definitely was "strange" to our youngsters, provided we could be sure that those friends would not object to the youngsters acting in their "natural" way. Exposing them to the strange situation and at the same time having to insist on the production of middle-class politeness or vocabulary tonedown would have led to total ego breakdown in a short time. Sometimes, the problem of taking the sting of "strangeness" out of a life situation or of a demand we were trying to make forced us to imitate their own behavioral style up to a certain point for the sheer purpose of communicating meaning to them which otherwise would not have sunk in.

Yesterday, the director of one of our cooperative agencies had come for a visit to Pioneer House. We could afford that because she knew what we were doing and we did not have to tremble with embarrassment at whatever might happen. The drama of that evening is a story in itself. Today, however, I had reasons to think I should lay down the law about some of their swearing. I told them we weren't fussy about it, as they knew, but they had really done more of it recently than had been necessary, especially in front of the visitor last night. I told them that in such situations I would have to insist on somewhat more control of their language when guests were here. I explained to them that this was not an attempt to lead them into hypocrisy, since this particular visitor was our friend and would understand. But, I wanted them to know that the reason for this request was some need for a certain amount of courtesy toward visitors. The only illustration I could find that would—and did—make the point had to be taken out of the orbit of their own sociological taste pattern. I finally got them to see the light when I told them that I knew they were sometimes kidding each other by farting at each other in fun. "But you don't fart a visitor in the face"—this finally got the idea across. (Entry: 12/14/47, Fritz Redl)

Sometimes it isn't so much a matter of tying up new activities with old taste patterns as of making concessions to their customary neighborhood style in the behavior accompanying activities they indulge in, as the following card playing incident may illustrate:

Most of the time when we played cards, they were in good humor and showed what seemed to be a lot of parental style behavior: On lucky plays, there was raucous thumping of the table with shouts of "Son of a bitch, that was a bastard, wasn't it?" etc. As a matter of fact, Joe would express the same mixture of blasphemy and delight when he would just lose by a close one. It is clear that in these sequences swearing does not denote insult, hostility, or the like, but really is a cultural pattern for vehement or emphatic expression of positive feeling, sheer good spirits or pleasure, etc. Thus, our policy toward terms like "bastard," "bitch," etc., would have to vary in accordance with our differential diagnosis of emotional context from time to time. For example, when the Director just beat him by a close shot, Joe most good naturedly called across the table, "Jeez, that bastard Fritz did it again." Now this is entirely different than when he says to the Director, as he did one night, "I'm taking this pop upstairs, you bastard," after the Director had forbidden it to the whole group on the grounds that it would interfere with the bedtime routine.

The same consideration of the strategic importance of our concessions to their sociological taste patterns would also have to govern much of our policy as to just which customary activities children should or should not be allowed to engage in. It is easy to see that a treatment home, if not well understood on this score, may come in for considerable criticism by those who dislike certain movie, television, or comic book *contents* and are not at all aware of the clinical relevance of the "sociological familiarity issue." The Saturday movie, for instance, is almost a taken for granted "must" in the child-rearing culture of certain neighborhoods in our country. The same holds for the "permission" to read, possess, and swap "comic books." The idea that an adult who otherwise makes pretenses of a friendly attitude to children would suddenly come out with a sharp tabu against such pleasures would be unimaginable to children like ours. Thus, while we tried to retain some marginal control on availability, budgeting, timing, and dosage of such enjoyments, and on selection, we knew we had to allow a wide leeway to this item of "sociological taste pattern" and swallow some of our personal aesthetic disgust or even clinical concern.

Two factors were interesting to observe, by the way, if we may be permitted to throw in here a remark that really belongs somewhere else: One is that the experience of Saturday movie going as a totally taken for granted part of their culture made it possible for our children to stay within the framework of normal movie behavior without any presence of staff. Even from the very beginning, when unsupervised activities at home or on trips even for a short period of time would have been quite unthinkable, we could keep up the practice which we maintained all through the Pioneer House duration of driving them to the movie, dropping them there left all to themselves, and picking them up afterwards. Their behavior there was no wilder than that of other lively but not so pathological children, and they were usually punctual and quite cooperative on the problem of post movie pick-up. The other item of interest is their

selection of and reaction to different types of movie programs. This
theme is clinically interesting much beyond the attention we can
give it at this point, but it might be worth while to remember that
our youngsters had an obvious preference for Western movies. The
wild aggression portrayed there seemed to help them channel their
own by way of vicarious identification, and anxieties stirred up by
such movies seemed to be amply counterweighted by the opportunities to hang on to security-giving symbols and scenes like guns,
victorious escape on horseback, muscular strength of the "good" figures in the movie, and so forth. In contrast to this, we noticed, several times, severe stirring up of anxiety without a chance to cope
with it when we had exposed our children to the artistically more
valuable productions of the fairy tale type of movies, as, for instance, Walt Disney's *Snow White*. It seemed that the portrayal of
such obviously psychotic anxieties as the child being attacked by
trees and weird figures while panic-stricken in the woods left them
all at sea, and that such movies did not offer nearly as many
"built-in" anxiety-assuaging devices as the Western ones do. In
contrast to the rather customary layman's objection to Western
movies and similar types, we also might want to add that we did
not notice that these movies increased or mobilized undue aggression or delinquent desires in our children. And, remembering the
ease with which our youngsters would usually follow temptational
chances along that line, that is saying a very great deal. It seemed,
rather, that the very stereotype of these movies was ego-supportive
—they knew from the very outset that the hero would be quicker at
the draw and would emerge triumphant, that the villain would get
his due, and, no matter how delinquency-prone they happened to
be in their own lives at the time, they all obediently identified with
the hero and despised the villain. It also must be remembered that
our children, no matter how sexually crude and sophisticated they
seemed to act, were definitely in the preadolescent phase of their
development. They were, therefore, relieved that in all those West-
erns the libidinal angle is definitely played down. The role of the
girl is limited to the purpose of portraying her as the desirable prize
in an aggressive masculinity contest, and whatever love scenes are
inserted are sketched in with only enough color to help the youngster's self-image as a future he-man and regular guy. The fact that
the length of time during which the outcome of any one doubtful

fight or danger remains unsure is not too great also seems to be well in line with the short frustration range of our type of child.

4. Individual antisepsis

Sometimes a program may be "good" on a variety of counts, but it so happens that a particular child is allergic to some of the ingredients it contains. In that case, it would still be counterindicated. This is especially the case with youngsters who were previously traumatized in the very area in which the secondary involvements of an activity structure may lie. If that is the case, a particular youngster shies away from any and all engagement in such activity and loses this avenue as an ego resource in times of conflict, boredom, or emotional need.

For instance, a youngster may be perceptive of the satisfaction potential involved in finger painting, especially as an expression for some of his fantasy needs. At the same time, it so happens that he may have been traumatized in terms of previous reactions of adults to his productions. Thus, the fear of doing better or worse than a sibling, or anxiety about adult reactions to his fantasy content, may block him from using this avenue for expressional discharge. If that is the case, all the counselor in a treatment home has to do is to be careful to avoid putting any emphasis on the end product, avoiding rivalry situations or competition when engaging in this activity, and otherwise dunk the whole finger painting activity into the antiseptic fluid of his clinical concern, and then a youngster who otherwise couldn't touch such activity may have it opened up for him without conflict or anxiety display. Another youngster may have needs for some mild, competitive gamble with destiny of the type which games like checkers sometimes represent. Some of the fun of trying one's luck and skill would be a satisfactory outlet for a number of the youngster's needs in a variety of situations. Unfortunately, in the case of the particular child we may be thinking of, previous traumatization around playing such games may have been so great that it becomes impossible to engage in them with another child. The fear of losing, or the anxiety about the child's own feelings of hostile triumph should he win, may become so strong that the whole game is rejected entirely and this particular child is left resourceless where other children happily get over a stretch of activity emptiness with this easy resource available to them. In such cases it is often possible to start such an activity between this child and the adult alone, wisely manipulating gain as well as loss and keeping it from getting entangled with the old traumatic traps. Or, it is possible to be sure a rapport-loaded adult is always near and at hand, should the child make his first steps into trying such a game with another child. Or, it may be wise to avoid such activities, or at least their competitive counterparts, for quite a while to come. In other cases, again, we may run into a child who could use a certain muscular skill activity very well for a variety of reasons. It so happens, however, that in his case the level of overstimulation which he can manage is still rather low. If this is the case, he may still be helped to participate in some muscular skill activity, provided enough trained staff is around to give him personal support the moment he reaches his breaking point, or it may be wise to protect him from exposure to such activity until the time he is ready for it, in which case no such program for the group must be planned in a way which would make nonparticipation in such activity too face-losing.

In short, we mean by this somewhat artificial and strained term "individual antisepsis" an attitude toward program planning which carefully considers all marginal or even subterraneous effects which participation in an activity might involve for a particular child, no matter how high in the general cultural evaluation scale such an activity may be rated, or how desirable it may be for other reasons. We think of it especially as a guiding principle modifying and sometimes countermanding decisions made on general program ideas of the educational or recreational type. Needless to say, this principle is basic to any real "treatment" intent in a residential home. It is this very principle of antiseptic programming, by the way, which constitutes one of the most serious stumbling blocks in the improvement of children's institutions and in the development of real treatment homes. For to most people it seems to sound like heresy if we insist that an activity which is culturally and traditionally considered to be "good" for children may, at times, be bad for a specific child on clinical grounds, or that often a much more primitive, a simpler and rather valueless exploit should be preferred to one of more obviously "desirable" high level content, at least for the time being. The existence of such a principle invariably reduces the eagerness of volunteers and of untrained personnel, and often enough wipes out the enthusiasm of those who want their donations to be translated into activity forms of which they themselves could be proud.

Just what constitutes "antiseptic programming" for a particular child will, of course, differ widely. This raises the additional problem of program choice where a whole group of children is concerned and underlines the overwhelming importance of group composition, mentioned elsewhere in our studies.[8] For the staff of a treatment home, the most difficult training task seems to lie in the need to combine with the usual resourcefulness and enthusiasm of a good group worker or recreation leader the very restraint of the subsurface-wise clinician without losing out in either capacity. Much research is needed before we can offer the field at large the data it needs to make this principle usable for a wider and larger group of practitioners. Just a few illustrations will be listed here, for almost any illustration relating to all other program techniques unavoidably is, by the very nature of our work, also an illustration for this principle of individual antisepsis.

Larry is a horrible singer—atonal, stammering, etc. Every time he tries to sing in the station wagon on trips, which he wants badly to do, the others jeer him into bruised silence. Because singing is such a favorite and enjoyable group activity on these trips and sometimes after dinner at home, too, we want very much that Larry have a chance to join in. Finally, one of our counselor staff devises a piece of strategy to work Larry in. On one trip the counselor focuses their attention on some favorite camp songs where the emphasis and interest involvement of the group are not oriented towards singing. Rather the interest is in the inventiveness of new variations in verse which each child makes up as he goes along. The song has a refrain: "On the dummy line, on the dummy line," etc. After this refrain, each person makes up a verse, then the whole group sings the refrain, then another verse, etc. At this, Larry shows good inventiveness and makes up cute verses when his turn comes. So, he gets in on the "sing."

Andy, especially during the early part of treatment, showed a delusional attitude toward fate or destiny. When he lost in any game of chance, he always construed this as a special victimization of him by luck and he would have extreme rage reactions in which he would displace responsibility from pure chance onto his opponent or a counselor, frequently fling down the cards or whatever game tool was involved, accuse the others of cheating, etc. On one such occasion after an unlucky run at

[8] See Ch. III, "Techniques for the Antiseptic Manipulation of Surface Behavior," pp. 199-202.

Blackjack, he stomped out of the room with his usual accusations, then returned about ten minutes later, hovered around the players, detached and sullen, fearful of trying his hand again. The Executive Director, who had observed the whole sequence, chattered with him for a few minutes on some neutral subject and then got him interested in some dominoes that were lying about. Instead of playing dominoes with him, however, he showed him how, if you stand up the dominoes close to each other, then knock down the first one in a row, it will fall on the second, this on the third, etc., producing a chain reaction until all the dominoes have fallen. Andy was delighted with this chance for total manipulative mastery after his (to him) overwhelming experience with unmanageable destiny at cards before. So, he fascinatedly arranged the dominoes in many different designs—first a straight line, then a circle, then an arc, etc., tasting deep of his power to make them *all* fall just by touching the first one. This so restored his spirits that he wound up the evening by joining a final round of cards with great gusto.

5. *Group psychological hygiene*

We have made much of the fact that most of our activities happen in "groups," and of the advantage which group psychology in general offers the therapist, and we certainly do not mean to belittle it. It would be a bad mistake, however, to forget that this obvious technical blessing of "group therapy" is not a blessing without a price. The very fact that most residential life is really group life also backfires at times, or, at least, introduces a few variables into the picture with which we had better learn to deal. The factor which we have in mind under the term "group psychological hygiene" can easily be defined. It is developed in analogy to the principle of individual antisepsis just dealt with, only stretching it so that it applies to the group as an organism. In a word, some activities or phases of the program may be perfectly all right for most children, or desirable in themselves. At a certain stage of its development, however, a specific group may not at all be able to digest what a normal group's stomach would visibly thrive on. Exposed to such an otherwise desirable program phase, it would show acute signs of disorganization. The implications of this are enormous —it really means that we have to add to the already mentioned cautions in terms of individual antisepsis also those of group psychological hygiene in every step of our work.

The following illustration is typical of the speculations our staff were confronted with in all phases of their program planning. Sometimes we felt that the youngsters were ready for a somewhat more complex game structure—in terms of actual frustration tolerance and activity level involved. That meant, for instance, that they could "really" have played some kind of team game which would involve choosing two sides, then running and catching opponents from the other team—variations on well-known types of not very complex games. Such a game, at a certain time, we felt would have the advantage of diffuse discharge of excited mobility in running, and the opportunity for mild levels of aggression involved in catching and holding on to an opponent for a short time (with a clear-cut group tabu excluding the chance for wild fighting as a result). It would also offer the ingredient of some mild competitive challenge through the idea of one team or the other "winning in the end," without having this competitive element too heavily loaded, or the final outcome too far away, so as to create achievement anxieties or tension about the end result. In addition to that, we could be sure that our youngsters, by that time, were improved enough to be able to take some defeat, so that the frustration of having been caught in such a game would not any longer produce the severe form of temper tantrum it would have ended in a few weeks before, and they even could take, by now, the tension of waiting for the starting of a game by a given signal without showing all the variants of their frustration intolerance and their confusion about time. In short, we had here a situation where a specific game seemed to fit perfectly the purpose we had in mind and seemed to meet all the qualifications on the basis of "individual antisepsis."

There was only one thing wrong at the time about which we talk: the game involved the problem of choosing sides. At a certain moment in the development of a group, this very ingredient of the game alone may be enough to counterindicate it, or at least to require serious modifications and careful manipulation by the adult. In the case in question, for example, this very issue of choosing sides would have thrown the group we are thinking of into complete confusion. Whoever would have chosen sides would immediately have produced a line-up of the children in terms of already established subgroups, the game would then have turned into a continuation and climaxing of, rather than a counteragent against, this subgroup hostility, and whatever would have happened during the game would have added to an already dangerous group psychological cache of dynamite. In short, while perfectly all right on most other counts, this game had to be omitted for the time being for reasons of "group psychological hygiene." Sometimes it is not omission, but manipulation and modification which are required. For instance, in another case it might still be possible to play the game provided the adult in charge of the group happens to be equally popular with all parts of the group, provided he chooses the sides and does so fast and enthusiastically enough so that the group doesn't notice the fact that their basic battle alignment has been broken, and provided that the game is terminated before they find out and begin to realign.

In other cases, the staff may take a chance, play the game, and then hope to be able to "handle" emergent conflicts so skillfully through humorous exploitation that the very fuel which the game seemed to provide for the original subgroup tension is turned into an asset and brings the subgroups together more than they were before.

Be this as it may, just which of these alternatives will be available cannot be predicted. All that we have in mind here is that this factor of "group psychological hygiene" becomes in itself an issue that has to be reckoned with, and one that may turn a poor "program risk" into an asset, or raise havoc with what originally looks like a sound "activity choice." Needless to add, these group psychological considerations assume top priority in program planning, when the group leaves its familiar habitat (trips to factory, museum, other towns), when it mingles with other groups ("Can we as yet afford to pick up their own suggestion to play a competitive match with the kids from the other school?"), or when other groups *in toto* or by representation are invited to invade our native premises ("Who will have to represent Pioneer House at its worst if we invite a teacher or kids from their school to spend an evening with us, and who will be scapegoated in the process?" or, "Can we take the chance of having the kids invite all the girls of their gym class for a party?").

By the way, the illustration used here to develop the thought only happened to involve the item of "subgroup hostility" as the main point. The list of criteria around which such speculations of group psychological hygiene will have to develop is nearly endless. Among them is, of course, the question of "group resistance to fatigue," "danger of group psychological intoxication," "competitive challenge readiness," and many others.

This afternoon the group was on a hysterical bender unparalleled in our seventeen days' experience with them to date. This is absolutely correlated to the Christmas excitement, which is like a violent poison on top of their total day's function pattern, for tonight is the Pioneer House Christmas party. Blow-ups, all sizes and shapes, occurred by the dozen. Dave (Executive Director) and I took them on a tobogganing trip to Rouge Park to get them out of the House. On the way out we passed, here and there, department store Santas out for their lunch or a cup of coffee, and each time they saw one they exploded in a shower of obscenities—"Yeah, goddam double bald-headed bastard Santa Claus—Shit —I'll kill the bastard—Just let me get my hands on him." This from Joe. Danny seconded this with, "the dirty butcher," and the others added their several cents' worth. Obviously, of all the hoodwinked children, ours, least of all, can tolerate the myth of jolly old Santa who rubs their deprivation patterns in the wrong places. This tipped me off to the real possibilities of group riot should I come to the party tonight in a Santa costume complete with beard, belly, and all, as the staff had planned— so right then and there I scotched the scheme.
Epilogue: I wore only a Santa hat tonight and even that was almost too much. Their excitement-loaded aggression was unbelievable. Imagine if I had really dressed up! (Entry: 12/16/46, Fritz Redl)

Most activities involving our Housemother were extremely loaded with special risks. This was due to violent sibling rivalry tensions which exploded around her with much greater volatility than around other female staff, because of the obvious impact of her mother role. Any situation in which she was the central figure in the group activity had, therefore, to be handled with hair trigger sensitivity on her part. On one occasion, for example, she started to read a story to the group while they were munching their "treat" upon return from school. She was sitting on the couch and the group was ranged on either side of her when suddenly bickering broke out about who had the right "to sit right next to Emmy"—Larry, who was on her right, was viciously slapped by Danny, who in turn began to draw fire from Mike, Andy, and Bill. Group riot looked imminent when Emmy suddenly broke in with "Hey, wait a minute—I've got an idea. I'll read campfire style." "Campfire style— what's that?" Danny asked as they temporarily stopped their milling and mauling of each other. "Oh, I'll be in the center and you'll make a circle around me—that'll make me the campfire and each of you will be the same distance away." This worked out to divert them from their feuding for that afternoon's story anyway.

During the later stages of treatment, Andy would frequently ask the Director, when the latter returned from a trip out of town, why he did not take the Pioneer Group on a trip some place during one of the school holidays or on summer vacation. This was discussed from the program point of view during many staff meetings. For example, they could be taken to nearby Ann Arbor, Michigan, or even to Chicago. After all they were only five—it wasn't as though we had a large institution of seventy-five or one hundred boys. From the point of view of physical management it was entirely feasible. And yet in each and every staff meeting, when the plan was broken down into pros and cons, we always came out with the same dismal conclusion: None of the kids, with the exception of Andy, could handle it. Mike, for example, even when we occasionally exposed him to thirty minutes in a restaurant, could never tolerate the frustrations involved in waiting for the waitress to finish with other customers ahead of us so she could take our order. As for waiting for the order once it was given—that was next to impossible. Mike would wind up by snarling insults at the waitress whom he held personally responsible for his frustration. Danny had similar troubles, and, in his way, each of the others was totally unready for the complex demands of a two or three day trip out of town, even though as a group they had made impressive gains over their earlier patterns. Andy alone could have handled it perfectly. In fact, a variety of reasons seemed to suggest that such a special experience of an exclusive trip out of town with the Director would be clinically a great advantage as far as Andy was concerned. Yet we could not even dream of taking him alone, ready though he was. For this would never be understood or forgiven by the others. They would not be able to grasp the real issue—that Andy could cope with the situation and they could not —but would see it as a betrayal and rank piece of favoritism.

This principle of "Group Psychological Hygiene" must not be interpreted as suggesting that any individualization of handling of different children would be disastrous for the morale of a group. Far from it. There are a vast number of life issues in any given group which allow for considerable variety of handling without any group psychological disturbance at all. At the same time, for instance, at which we had to decide against the special trip for Andy, and when the housemother had to perform such mental gymnastics to handle sibling rivalry when she was in a focal position of direct group leadership, as in the "reading scene" above, we could easily afford a rather wide leeway for individual experiences of the children with the housemother. For instance, while some of the youngsters would be happily engaged in some program activity, it was often perfectly possible for one of them to wander off into her room and have a story read to him by her without any stirring-up of group tension and sibling rivalry.

6. *Organization and sublimation dosage*

It is, of course, the purpose of all ego repair to make it possible for the children to accept exposure to higher demands of organization of their individual impulsivity and to lure them into the ability to gain pleasure from more sublimated outlets of their impulses than they originally were ready for. With children who are not only ego-disturbed but extremely primitive in terms of their level of impulsive outlets, this becomes an especially challenging task. For we know that simply exposing them to or offering them more highly organized or more sublimated channels of emotional expression or enjoyment does not do the trick. On the contrary, whenever we make mistakes of that sort, the total breakdown of their individual ego or of their existing group pattern is the immediate punishment we reap. On the other hand, it is obvious that disturbed children do not have the capacity for looking for or finding a taste for activities of higher organizational demands or higher degrees of sublimation levels all by themselves.[9] The policy in program planning, therefore, has to go in both directions. First, it is important to avoid exposure to organizational structures which are beyond the youngster's readiness and to sublimation levels which must be too frustrating to his actual expressional needs. Second, it becomes essential to discover chances of gradual "increase in challenge" and to give them ample support in the process.

When we talk about "organizational structure," we have in mind the amount of "rules, restrictions, conditions, complexities, group-accepted tabus" and so forth which a game may imply or the amount of "preparatory arrangements, limitations necessitated through the involvements of tools, props, spatial considerations, and laws for the protection of other people's rights and properties" which are somehow necessitated by it. Avoiding a more adequate discussion of this theme here, we might point at the rather customary distinction recreation leaders, teachers, and group workers make between terms like "games of higher organization" (baseball, and all highly or ganized team games) and "games of lower organization" (like Keep-away: a ball game involving the challenge to keep the ball circu-

9 See *Children Who Hate*, "Sublimation Deafness," p. 92.

lating and prevent one of the players from capturing it, or, even more primitive, a simple game of being "it" and trying to avoid being caught). By "sublimation level," we refer to the Freudian implication of that term, the details of which could not possibly be repeated here.[10] May it suffice to say that we have in mind the difference between more "primitive" channels of impulse gratification and more "cultivated" ones. An illustration to the point: the difference between two children engaged in a wild scratching, biting, kicking attack on each other after challenging each other's courage and a game of chess, which also contains the similar element of matching of powers, plus an attempt to triumph over one's opponent, but subjects this end to a much more elaborate process of conditions, and offers much more "cultivated" gratifications than a direct fist fight.[11]

The "level of organization" to which we could subject our youngsters at different times, as well as the "primitivity of gratification" we had to yield to, or the "sublimation demands" we could make under favorable circumstances, would vary greatly. The real problem the practitioner faces in connection with this item is simple to state: We usually consider higher organization levels, as well as less primitive and more sublimated gratification channels, more desirable and educationally "valuable." The trouble is, are they still fun? And while we can lure some children some of the time into concessions on this point, one of our tasks is not only to get them to concede to us their participation in activities which demand higher organization and higher sublimation levels, but to get to the point where they can even enjoy them. The educator usually hopes to move them to "higher levels" on both counts. The clinician wants to be sure he knows just how much organization and sublimation they can really take without their ego being loaded with an unbearable weight of frustration or anxiety. The clinician, then, would make two demands on program planning: one, that it be "realistic," so that it will expose youngsters to activity levels which they can

[10] A large number of papers on sublimation have accrued during the past three decades from the contributions of psychoanalytic therapists, too numerous to mention individually. A condensation of many of these is reflected in Otto Fenichel, *The Psychoanalytic Theory of Libido* (New York: W. W. Norton & Company, Inc., 1945).

[11] See Karl Menninger, "Chess," Part VI of "Recreation and Morale," *Menninger Clinic Bulletin*, Vol. 6, No. 3, 1942, p. 83, for a very fascinating analysis of the psychodynamics of chess.

enjoy without having to expose their ego to a breakdown, and, two, that it be "challenging" in the long run, which implies making provisions that the ego gets enough support, so that it occasionally can cope with higher organization and sublimation demands than it otherwise could. In the beginning of treatment, of course, what we called here "clinical realism" was the primary task for us. How far we often had to compromise in order to make activities at all possible may be shown by an illustration—and may the disciples of the royal game of golf forgive our souls:

Took over as counselor tonight in absence of Bob Case who is attending a conference. After dinner took the group out to Palmer Park for golf. Golf à la Pioneer House is stripped of all of the niceties of that aristocratic game. We had bought up about ten old clubs—mostly driving clubs—from the Salvation Army and gave one to each kid for his very own. There is no attempt to make a score. We simply drive and drive and drive. Tonight the kids covered vast stretches of the Palmer Park course. Whenever they hit the ball they squealed triumphantly. They found old pins and battered discarded balls and stuffed the latter into their pockets or simply smacked them gaily into the distance, as their whim of the moment might dictate. Mike and Andy tried some more systematic driving on the real driving range and became a little frustrated, as it began to get too dark to see what they were doing. They were in a fine mood, with all of the space and freedom for large motor release, and when the time came to come back to the wagon, they came readily at my signal—two honks—across a quarter mile of golf course. We had treats and drove home quite relaxed. (Entry: 5/2/48, David Wineman)

It is well known, by the way, that the more complex activities and games often are composed of parts which, by themselves, may be somewhat too complex for individual children to endure. Sometimes, however, it is possible to insert these parts of more complex activities into their lives and make them acceptable to them by themselves, or in gradual accumulation—thus paving the way for exposing the ego later to a much more complex challenge. Our tumbling activities, which played a great role in the Pioneer's life, are an illustration to the point:

Tonight Joel used his forte—tumbling and acrobatics with the group. He set up the upstairs playroom like a miniature gym, piling tables and chairs ingeniously together and using old mattresses for mats. The kids who had been tearing around like wild hyenas before and right after dinner were tickled and even calmed down enough, especially Joe and Andy, to help him set the stuff up. They seemed to accept immediately the need for each child to wait his turn and shared Joel beautifully in this respect. Although each was itching to show off for me and especially Fritz (Director), who both functioned as audience, they waited patiently for their turns. Joe, who has a natural grace and litheness, was the star performer and the most daring of the group, also the quickest to learn more complicated leaps. Larry was on the other end of the scale and Sam is only fair. Still, in some miraculous way, this didn't seem to bother them and they all spent a good hour and fifteen minutes in this activity. Actually, with the exception of Joe, the standard act was simply to tumble off the high perch with a simple somersault onto the mats. They are so thrilled at the power and total narcissistic enchantment of the movements themselves that they don't seem to care how complex or simple they are—so long as they start up high, sail through the air somehow, and land on the mats. (Entry: 1/13/47, David Wineman)

In this sequence of events it seems quite clear that the children's ability to take a higher organizational challenge—waiting in line for turns, helping to set up and, later, clean up the room, sharing the leader—is related to the very low sublimation challenge of the activity itself. Anybody can fall through the air onto a soft mat and, in transit, gratify any number of narcissistic, body-power fantasies.

The "complexity" of an organizational pattern need not come out only in game situations. And it need not limit itself to the actual organization of playing the game, but may refer to the complexity of the social interrelationship a game or situation requires. Both are exemplified in the problem we had with gifts. This is, of course, an issue that reaches far beyond this item here. Picking up only what relates to the point in question and leaving the emotional involvements with gift and giver out for the time being, we can say that we had to be very careful for a long time to create situations which helped the children cope with their confusion around receiving gifts. This means that, since a lot of potential sibling rivalry, as well as greed, anxiety, individual involvement, and ambivalence, was invariably stirred up when we brought the children a present after being away, let us say, on a lecture trip for several days, it became especially important to create the most ego-supportive conditions for giving them those gifts. For a long time, it would have been impossible to bring them one thing which they all could share. This would have led to total mayhem. The best we could hope for was that they might survive a situation in which each one of them was given things of the identical type, color, weight, size. If this were not done, we were faced with a riot. The demand to "organize" their group relationship into using one toy in group play would have been overwhelming, until very late in the treatment period. It was quite a departure, and clinically quite a risk, when we dared to deviate from this practice for the first time:

Tonight on my return from a lecture trip out West, I presented the group for the first time in their career with a single gift for the whole bunch—a real lasso. Also, I gave each one an individual gift: a conch horn. Previously on all of my returns home—and there have been at least one and a half dozen such incidents since the opening of the home —I would always use the following formula: one big gift of the same kind for everybody, like a knife or a flashlight—king-size—and one different gift of smaller economic stature, like a pocket comb or pencil. They were really thrilled with the lasso. There was no bickering and they didn't even have to make a schedule to use it. It simply made the rounds as it would in a normal group. Each kid tried to do something fancy with it and then Danny contaged them with the murderous fantasy of stringing up Mr. Wineman (Executive Director), whom they knocked off his chair in a good-natured (?) way in acting out the fantasy. Upsetting his chair gratified enough of their impulse and they swooped out into the backyard with the lasso, with which they fooled around for about thirty minutes before swinging into the planned program, which was a ride down to the River with treat out. (Entry: 4/4/48, Fritz Redl)

7. Insertion of depersonalized controls

Some of the aspects of programming for the "children who hate" seemed nearly hopeless to us for quite a while. There are, especially, three factors which seem to pile up on each other in order to form an almost unsurmountable block. For, by their very definition, our hyperaggressive and extremely destructive children are in need of a good deal of program activity which involves the happy discharge of surplus aggression, diversion of destructiveness into excited large-muscle activity, and so forth, along the line of already illustrated points. At the same time, however, these children suffer, not only from a surplus of piled-up hatred and aggression, but also from a severe disturbance of the very control machinery which is supposed to cope with it. This means, then, that, if we expose them to program opportunities which involve activity and aggression, they can rarely take them without much interference from the adult to "keep things going" and to "avoid the worst." This is, however, where the worst aspect of the problem hits us directly in the face: for remember, these are also the "children who hate." This means that adult interference, rather than being considered a welcome help, is rejected or reacted to with fury and counterattack, and even the helpful attempt at umpiring to make a game possible is usually interpreted simply as the hostile meddling of an enemy from above.

It was while in this predicament that we felt the discovery of the wide range of "depersonalized controls" as a special relief. This is what we mean: In almost any neighborhood, there are certain activities, behavioral customs, and games, the "rules" for which, though unwritten, are well known and automatically accepted "by everybody." Even our very disturbed youngsters commanded a halt to their total rule rejection when it came to such well-ingrained "neighborhood codes." In fact, sometimes it seemed to us that those were the only areas where something akin to a conscience or a feeling of decency seemed to be left. Not that they wouldn't break these self-imposed rules, too. But hardly without feeling somewhat bad about it—and whoever wanted to support such native behavior code items had an easier time of it than in other behavioral ranges. In short, while their judgment of what is reasonable or not, dangerous or daring, decent or mean is highly impaired, as long as we deal with rules which are clustered around certain group-code-loaded game situations, we can count on a much higher degree of "readiness for the acceptance of controls." This means that behavior which is tied up with playing such games fairly finds more of an echo in the youngster's control system than any area of only adult-defined conditions of life. Thus, for instance, even with our type of children, a game of "hide and seek" has certain unspoken but very clearly drawn licenses and tabus built into it. Even where individual youngsters might cheat, they would still expect group criticism were they found out, and would accept it as such, and they know that they have to expect group ostracism if they go still further than that. Being summoned to play the game fairly and according to rules is considered, even by them, as a "reasonable request," even though it might come as a reminder from an adult whom they regard, at that time, as an enemy.

What a wonderful aid in our desperate predicament! If we could only find enough such activity structures with their natural group codes encrusted around them, then we really could "step out for a while" and let the built-in behavior codes of the game in question do the controlling. Or, at worst, the adult could step into the role of marginal reminder of group-code-demanded rules rather than have to act as the hostile limiter of illegal fun from the outside. What a strategic gain! The discovery of such opportunities sent us, of course, scrambling for game structures of this type. We wished there were organized research on this. As it is, we had to worm our way through trial and error and through frantic efforts of "game analysis" in terms of "native group code relevance." Our findings are still deplorably thin compared with what we think can be found in the uranium mines of psycho-sociological research, were we only given the chance to exploit them.

Most "games," by the way, seem to have special "impulse-encouraging" promises in them, but also have, as a "built-in" device, automatic limitations and heavily code-loaded tabus to guarantee unconflicted fun as far as possible. There comes to mind a game frequently played by children which runs somewhat like this:

The group divides into two equal teams each standing behind a chalk line. The idea of the game is to yank the person immediately in front of you over to your side. At the signal, the pairs of opponents begin to struggle. If an opponent is pulled over, you have to stop yanking on him because you have already captured him and then he is obliged to fight on your side. The two main rules of the game are that you can't step over the line in order to get somebody and that you have to stop yanking on him once you get him, and, if either of these two rules is broken, then a foul is declared.

Such a game obviously offers a variety of gratifications, partly along mildly aggressive lines, but it also has its "built-in" control switch in terms of group-code-loaded limitations to guarantee some protection from too uninhibited abuse. Let us assume that we can find many patterns like this. The strategic advantage for us is obvious: some of the time the youngsters can be engaged in somewhat complex and impulse-gratifying activities "under their own steam," so that adult interference with all its ambivalent implications is avoided. This provides a "breathing spell" in the life with children whose need to battle the adult, either on real or on delusional grounds, is so great. Besides, where conflict is unavoidable, where the game structure is too weak to limit the exuberance of our youngsters, or where the pathology of an individual child is too heavy to be domesticated even by the self-imposed group code, the adult may have to interfere—but then he is in a much more advantageous role. For, helping a group to "play a game fairly," if well handled, is a chore that makes you the "servant of the group code," a sort of self-appointed "traffic aid," which is quite a different role from the usual one of "hostile society code enforcer" to which the children usually doom us no matter what the real issue is.

It is also fascinating to watch not only how well-known and neighborhood-tradition-loaded games can assume this function, but how sometimes a group of youngsters will make up their own games spontaneously, and for the time being give the behavioral code making that game possible as much power over their lives as a normal child would give to the societal demands of lawfulness and decency.

In the meantime, Mike, Andy, and Larry were playing cards and Bill was playing the policeman who stood around with three comic books rolled up in his hand and struck anybody who cheated over the head with this weapon. This continued for half an hour or more and even when Bill set the cheating penalty at ten blows on the head there was no resentment from any member of the group. In fact, they were getting considerable fun out of it and would tell Bill when someone else was seen to cheat. Actually, they were cheating as a sort of joke and getting a hilarious, though not riotous, bang out of the whole thing. In the process of the game, Bill played no favorites, though Andy probably got many more blows than the others—all in all I should guess about fifty to seventy-five whacks across the head with the roll of comic books. Surprisingly, nobody got mad. Eventually the game died out and they grouped themselves around Emily, who had been sitting watching for a while, and had her read comics to them for half an hour or so. (Entry: 11/2/27, Bob Case)

Sometimes we could observe a gradual "behavioral group code" in the making, and combined with it the amazingly accepting attitude of the children to adult behavior which is supportive of group game code. Acting that way around a routine issue, the children's reaction to the adult's interference would be different, indeed.

We went upstairs and found Mike sitting on the saw horse, trying to lasso the andirons. I immediately structured this into a game and soon Bill and Andy joined him in a marvellous game of Rodeo, with me as an announcer reporting what was happening over the radio, and in this way intensifying the fantasy of a lot of recognition for each of the kids. Each was allowed three tosses, first taking the names of various cowboys, then of various Indians. At first they roped broncos, then more dangerous game like cobras and tigers. There was some obscenity invited in the choice of names and Bill made sexual advances to the "horse" in order to clown for the others. When I told him to stop it, the others did not only not rebel but they, themselves, limited Bill—Mike insisting that it was a rule that if anybody was dirty he would have to leave the game. This calmed Bill sufficiently for the game to proceed with few interruptions. (Entry: 11/26/47, Paul Deutschberger)

Occasionally, a combination of the direct power of "depersonalized controls" and the marginal interference of the adult, but one well in line with the basic game code demands, created control patterns which made a much more complex activity period possible than the children were, individually, really ready for:

The kids had been playing "Monopoly" before supper and continued it after supper until nearly 8:15 p.m. Danny dropped out about 7:50 to listen to a radio program, play with a new jigsaw puzzle, and read comics. Larry dropped out about 8:00 because he said he was getting too confused. They simplified it at several points and overlooked various rules, but it still involved numerous transactions, purchases, loans, rent, sales, etc., which they handled surprisingly well. I was called in very occasionally to settle differences about arithmetic or playing directions, but they settled most of the problems and conflicts themselves. Andy obviously dominated the game. He handled the banking in addition to his part and made many decisions and interpretations of directions and rules. Some of these were challenged by one or another of the group and, though he sometimes overrode them, he not infrequently admitted to an error. There were numerous conflicts, usually involving quite a bit of shouting and some anger, but the surprising thing is that they were all resolved sufficiently so that the game continued, and the two drop-outs left, not in anger, but because they tired of the game. Danny, of course, overreacted to what he took to be wrong moves on the part of the others, as usual condemning them furiously as "goddam liars," etc., but only once did I have to interfere with him and that was when, in a moment of particular exasperation with Bill, who wasn't backing down in an argument with him, he leaned across the game and slapped Bill's jaw. I took him out of the game and told him that such action was inexcusable and that he could not continue in the game if he couldn't handle himself any better than that. Then I softened and said that, if he'd refrain from any further outbreaks and if Bill was agreeable, he could return. Bill said he could return under those conditions and the game continued. Three or four times during the game Bill got up and walked away in anger, sometimes in tears, because of alleged cheating or continued irritating interference by Mike. Each time Mike repented and told Bill he'd stop if Bill would return, and Bill returned, except for the last time when Mike and Andy were about ready to quit too. So the game folded up, and, with a little urging from me, the four of us picked up all the pieces of the game and packed them away, and Bill's irritation was apparently dissipated. (Entry: 1/15/48, Bob Case)

We found the insertion of such stretches of self-run activity patterns without involvement of adult domination issues a tremendous relief in the total budget of adult-child relationships. Since at those times the children's egos could function without severe conflict, the exposure to increased frequency of such stretches of unconflicted ego functioning under their own steam could be considered a definite item of ego support. When such games could not be found, it was important to develop them, insert them, or to create a structure similar to originally known neighborhood games into which the neighborhood codes about what is decent or indecent, fair or unfair in a game could easily be built in. Once we had developed more traditional patterns of such game structures, a process which in itself requires some of the techniques listed later, we could actually use the exposure to depersonalized control patterns as a conflict-relieving and, therefore, ego-supporting device. Sometimes the development of such group-accepted, automatic behavioral codes was possible through a variety of techniques and through geographical separation. Our youngsters, for instance, would invariably consider the interference by an adult in the dangerous use of a knife or a dart as just that much evidence that the adult was hostile, mean, and didn't like children, no matter how wisely and realistically the adult handled the situation. This inability of their egos to "get the point" seemed to be so extreme, however, primarily when such instances happened in their play room, in the bedroom, or on a trip. The same youngsters seen at about the same early treatment phase, showed much more automatic understanding and reasonable respect for realistic limitations when interference had to take place in the use of tools downstairs in their workshop. In fact, the careful structuring of organizational limitations around the use of tools, the consistent interpretation of reality implications, the arrangement of tools around clearly drawn places on the walls, and the cultivation of a certain code of pride of the "efficient toolsman" soon became independent items to which the youngsters would respond irrespective of the adult present. The fact that the same youngster's ego would not develop similar judgment or realism in other life areas at the same time, handled similarly by the same personnel, shows how these patterns of "depersonalized control," because of their entrance into the group code, had assumed a power over our children which less well-structured life situations could not claim. Technically, this suggests the interesting possibility of increasing realism and acceptance of limitations, tabus, and demands for control around clearly defined and group-code-loaded structures at least in parts of a youngster's life space, even before total ego improvement sets in.

8. Protective timing

Whether a disturbed ego can manage its tasks seems not to depend only on the intensity and piling-up of the impulses to be controlled. It seems to have an amazing and somewhat mysterious relationship to the duration of its problem. Thus, all practitioners in recreation, group leadership, and teaching develop some kind of hunch of just when a game has lasted so long that it has "worn out" or when it has become so overstimulating that from now on a loss of control would be expected. This peculiar law of adequate timing is a factor in the activities of normal children and adults, as well as of disturbed ones, but with the latter group it assumes nearly fatal proportions. If this is so, then it is obvious that one of the most important aids to a disturbed ego would consist in avoiding wrong timing so as not to confront it with unmanageable tasks. This means, for instance, that the exposure to a happily and mildly competitive game for a few minutes may stir up a great amount of excitement which may very well be stopped at the right time, in which case it may contribute to an image of satisfaction which can be well used later as a new program resource. If allowed to continue beyond a certain point, frustration will result or difficulties of the ego in manipulating anxiety or aggression produced in the game may become so great that the activity at first enjoyed may lead to a total breakdown of individual or group morale and the whole thing may end up in hopeless destruction or in disgust, bickering aggression, and mutual irritation. To gauge the optimum of time exposure for different types of activities, as well as the sequence of such exposures, becomes one of the most important parts of program planning. This element of timing plays an important role in all phases of children's lives. We know from life with normal children that sometimes, for instance, the exposure to exclusion from an activity as punishment for misbehavior may have a reasonable effect if kept up long enough to make its point, but not so long as to expose the youngster to the aggression and frustration of boredom and of envious observation of others enjoying the activity. When mistakes in timing are made, even with normal children, the effects of such otherwise reasonable temporary punishment may be destructive and disastrous to the greatest degree. This element of timing rests on the correct prediction of the length of potential ego control and the need of interference by the adult before collapse of ego control sets in. Such timing is important, not only in terms of ongoing activity, but also in terms of the balance between present experience and future gratification. Events promised as an appeal to gratification expectations of children in order to bolster their morale or their ego strength but which are yet too far away may have a destructive rather than an ego-supportive effect and the question of just how far away an incident on which planning is done by a group of children can be and what the optimum distance is becomes one of the most fascinating problems to figure out. Needless to say, since ego-disturbed children have a poor sense of self-timing, this often involves an artificial interference by the adult in terms of planned activity sequences or patterns in place of an attempt to let children decide themselves. Most of our youngsters would interrupt activities because of the mildest impact of frustration long before they even got the taste of them, or, on the other hand, they would continue activities which were stimulating to those of their impulses which were related to their pathology far beyond reason and then get into stages which would lead into absolute loss of control.

This element of timing has to be considered on an individual basis but, of course, it also involves group psychological elements. The problem, for instance, of total frustration tolerance of a group in terms of length of time, as well as the problem of the duration before group psychological build-up into overstimulation, is one of the most fascinating puzzles and one on which we wish we had more organized research. Fortunately, it becomes possible for most group leaders to develop a certain anticipatory judgment about the length of time which it takes a group to get going and also about the length of time beyond which an otherwise enjoyable activity will lead into secondary individual or group psychological disaster. Needless to say, that same element of timing is also an important clinical issue to watch in terms of the working of individual temper tantrums, the duration of individual sulks, and particularly of the most opportune moment for the interview handling of problem incidents. This part, however, relates to more specific treatment techniques and will be discussed in connection with them.[12] The development of skills in clinically adequate timing constitutes one of the most important problems of the training and self-training of staff. Most adults have a tendency to let activity patterns drag and, in work with disturbed children, to miss the natural timing rate of their confused egos. This problem is well known in group work and recreation as one involved in all construction of "larger" programs. With disturbed children as much effort in the planning of antiseptic timing may have to go into a three-minute activity as we otherwise would only use on the development of a concert evening, an open house program in a settlement, or a morning celebration in a school assembly.

Occasionally, soft, harmless substances like wallpaper cleaner can be allowed use as throwing tools. Thus, we had "wars" in which the boys would use this material as ammunition. This placed very high priority on sharp diagnostic hunch skills on the part of counselors as to when to divert or limit such an activity before it transformed itself into unsublimated rock throwing for honest-to-goodness member-to-member hostility flareups. On one such occasion, wallpaper cleaner was being used by four boys out of the group quite acceptably. They had divided into two amiable teams—Larry and Andy versus Bill and Mike. Then Danny, who had been peacefully occupied in the house reading comic books and listening to the radio, lumbered into the backyard where the "war" was going on. Since he is a group scapegoat, as soon as they saw him, the two sides combined into a single coalition against him. The activity should have been stopped here, but it wasn't. Result: a full-fledged gang attack soon involving throwing stones, pieces of board, and branches at Danny, who became so helplessly and murderously enraged that he had to be held through thirty minutes of tantrum.

[12] Cf. Ch. IV.

Hide and seek, a game that always lent itself well to after-dinner programming, had to be carefully watched for overstimulative implications for the subsequent bedtime routine. In the cold months it was played upstairs, involving the use of the upstairs playroom and sleeping rooms. Especially if a female counselor was on duty, this game had to be stopped a full thirty minutes before bedtime routine was instituted. If not stopped, the highly exciting search for the female counselor in their own darkened bedroom, or the waiting to be caught by her, produced too much erotic overflow, resulting in sexual acting-out during the reading period while the same counselor would be reading to them in their sleeping room. This reaction could absolutely be controlled if early stopping of the hide and seek took place with a buffering activity like group singing downstairs around the piano between the game and bedtime.

In the following program the breaking down of total activity into small time units was necessary to accommodate poor time adaptations of the various children. Even within each time unit, ample flexibility was retained to meet emergency needs as they arose. In addition, three counselors were on duty as a special protective measure.

Larry and Mike had both been into Vera's (co-counselor) room to see what was going on in preparation for the evening program. When Mary Barker (co-counselor), Vera, and I went into the living room, Larry came with us. Andy and Danny were absorbed in reading and games and didn't respond immediately to Mary's question, "Who's ready for a mock track meet?" The curiosity about the props helped and the kids came up, Mike trying to grab props at every step. I resisted this, holding them away until we got upstairs. He picked each object up, handled it, and then helped set the things out on the table. Andy and Mike had already practiced the obstacle race with hazel nuts before Danny arrived. Mary announced that there would be a trial heat and then each would have two tries.

No. 1. Obstacle Race: Andy did it quickly and nimbly. Mike hit one and swore he wasn't going to play. No one paid any attention to him. Next round Mike beat Andy's record and Andy hit one, a fact that he refused to admit. He sulked for a minute or two. He demanded more heats and everyone else agreed—after four heats we went on to the next, after some persuasion. Danny's performance times varied widely. Larry did it slowly and carefully, each time a little more quickly.

No. 2. Javelin Throw: Object: throwing paper straws for distance. There was some argument based on a tie score between Danny and

Mike. When it was announced, Danny, who had picked up his straw, insisted that it was not put down in the same place and that he had really won. He blew up and started to storm out of the room but instead turned away and said he wouldn't play. Mary, Vera, and I all united in verifying the scoring and, after a minute, I asked if he were going to play. Yes, he was! The element of chance here was good because everyone seemed to gain some points during the several trials.

Nos. 3 & 4. I forget the mock track names for these but the events consisted of measuring the lengths of the kids' arms and feet. Danny, of course, came out ahead in this and he beamed expansively throughout the entire procedure. During the measuring of arms Andy protested that Mary was measuring from a different point on him and it wasn't fair. Mary calmly said, "No, see it's the same place on your shoulder," and measured him again. He said, "Aw," but made no further comment.

No. 5. The 5o Yard Dash: Object: to sew around a piece of cloth six inches square, taking at least twenty stitches. Mike exploded after a minute, before it began, saying he wouldn't do it, "You can't even get your needle in the damn thing!" However, when the signal was given, Mike began and finished first with exactly twenty stitches. The others worked industriously, Larry and Danny forgetting about the competition and going right on to see how many stitches they could take even after Andy had come in second, and Larry third. Mike pulled his stitches tight and made a kind of cap which he presented to me.

No. 6. Discus Throw: Object: to throw paper plates as far as possible. There was some difficulty here because someone hit the wall first and then bounded back and was farther back than the others. However, Mary declared a "wall hit" the highest and everyone was satisfied.

No. 7. Fishing Toothpicks from the Water: Object: to "fish" thirty toothpicks from a basin of water by using your mouth only. Everyone enjoyed this immensely because of the opportunity to splash. Larry got carried away and finally began to spout water furiously.

No. 8. The last event was a turtle race. At the beginning Mike blew up because he thought the turtle everyone said was his was dead or dying. Danny also complained that his was dead. By dunking them in water, movement was produced and it was decided that all could enter the race. The turtles were placed in a small circle within a large circle and at the signal were released. Mike's turtle moved rapidly out and went across the finish line. Larry's did likewise, followed by Andy's. Danny's just stayed but Danny didn't become excited. After everyone's was out it came to life and slowly and deliberately got out. In the next heat Larry's reached the finish line and, instead of crossing it, began to follow it around. Everyone got a lot of fun out of this and even more when Danny showed that the turtle followed when he snapped his finger in front of it. Vera started to say, "Everyone get his turtle into "p.j's," and everyone laughed. This made the suggestion of p.j's a little easier to take. Downstairs, while having "treat," the subject of prizes came up and Vera promised to make ribbons if everyone would tell her the name of his turtle. Mary read a little before they went up to bed. (Entry: 2/15/47, Barbara Smith)

Besides the ingenuity which the staff displayed in handling moments of potential crisis and breakdown, hair-trigger sensitivity in the timing of each one of the subunits of the total activity was of the essence. Had any one of the activities been allowed to continue too long or had it been terminated around a frustrating incident, the program would have ended right then and there with the usual symptoms of group disintegration.

9. Manipulation of hangover effects and transitional confusions

The idea that the effect of the pattern of an activity the children are engaged in is terminated just because the activity itself has been stopped is a naive illusion, indeed. In fact, any pattern of activity whatsoever has quite a severe impact on the economy of impulse and control distribution within the children engaged in the activity and some of this pattern takes some time to fade out or needs to be definitely reset before another activity can take hold. For example, a group of youngsters playing tag are acting under a clear-cut pattern of impulse distribution and limiting controls. For one thing, impulses related to running, catching, and mildly aggressive triumph over an opponent are given free rein, while impulses of following up mild aggression with more severe hostility or more drastic exploitation of triumph in terms of throwing a youngster down or fighting him are definitely tabued and have to be avoided even on the basis of the native game code. At the same time, needs for the more quiet enjoyment of a daydream or fantasy and desires for the elaboration or the nursing of a hurt or indulging in a masochistic daydream are definitely excluded during the activities thus indicated, and needs for personal privacy or playing with a preferred toy are obviously frustrated for the time being. Whenever this activity is stopped and the children are expected to make a transition to another pattern of activity, a severe rearrangement not only of the types of needs which will be satisfied and those which will be frustrated, but also of the conditions under which both events will happen, takes place. A group of children, for instance, arranged around a campfire listening to a story after such a tag game, suffer a severe reversal of the basic structure into which they are expected to fit. Now, the relaxation of personal activity into the passive comfort of resting is given as a possibility, while the stopping of still existing needs for running, catching, and triumphing is demanded. The passive enjoyment of an atmosphere of friendly indulging in a specific fantasy involved in the story to be read has to take priority over other interests which may still be frustrated in either of the activities mentioned here, like the play with preferred toys or with a newly received gift. It is obvious from practical experiences that very often the very transition from one activity pattern to another constitutes quite a problem in children's lives. Very often our programming demands such transition with too much rapidity so that actually some of the behavior shown during the second activity can be considered to be a hangover of patterns of need and impulse demands stirred up in the one going on before. Sometimes the next activity may happily terminate what had become exhausted in the previous one and may now give a chance to have needs satisfied which were frustrated in the activity before. Such is the case when a group of youngsters, after listening to a quiet story, are given a chance to play a game of tag. On the other hand, the rate at which children make such transitions and the problems which are involved in the making of those transitions constitute difficulties in themselves.

With ego-disturbed children the managing and anticipation of what we call hangover effect and transitional confusion becomes a separate task. The adult has to be aware that his first function may not be to plan for the next activity but to plan for the coping with impulses stirred up by the previous ones and with frustrations enforced by the structure going on just before. Thus, for instance, an exciting ball game in a gym class on a rainy day during the last hour in school will send the children into the station wagon in an entirely different frame of mind than if the last hour at school is a spelling drill. It is to be expected that ego-disturbed children will have specific problems with such transitions which more healthy children may take in their own stride and that some of the planning for ego support has to go into the offering of transitional structures

and the planned relation of subsequent program units in terms of
the coping with leftovers from the previous one. Thus, not only the
type of program activity to be selected, but the conditions of transition from one to the other, as well as the sequence in nature of
those activities, become a terrific concern to the clinician.

For children with severe ego disturbances, the aid in the transition from one activity to another and the skillful manipulation of
hangover effects and transitional confusion may be the very task for
which the adult may have to plan as carefully as for the program
itself. While their egos may be in good enough shape to take the
first, as well as the second, activity, they may not be ready to manipulate the transitional problem in their own stride. The implication of this item for the practice of programming is so great and so
fascinating that we regret, at this point, not to be able to give it
more space. For the same issue has become a stumbling point in
the programming for normal children, in such things as the scheduling for school subjects. Needless to say, even in normal children
mistakes in the evaluation of and planning for hangover effect in
the sequence of activity structures and in the manipulation of transitional problems sometimes give rise to the more severe discipline
problems which may have nothing to do with the personalities
involved but may be primarily due to the task of transition itself.
While such planning for the manipulation of hangover effect in
the hygienic sequence of activities and in the support in transition
from one activity pattern to another is important in all program
planning, it assumes a nearly fatal importance in such areas of
daily life routine or programming toward which the children have
a natural resistance or which establish, because of previous traumatization, conflict areas in themselves.

If we know, for instance, what tremendous anxiety, frustration,
and potential aggression are involved in the waking-up process of
disturbed children and their transition from their sleep and dream
world into a phase of rebelled-against reality like a school class
in a subject they feel bad about, we realize that we have a very
difficult task of supportive treatment in trying to cope with and
manipulate the transitional problems.[13] In the same way, if we
know what it means to children to surrender the activities they are
engaged in and the presence on the scene of adult life in favor of
withdrawal into their beds at a certain hour, then we can easily

[13] See Bruno Bettelheim, *op. cit.*

develop policies and ways of handling the transition which will be
designed not to increase but to cope with their feelings and to
make them ready for the next stage. We have already mentioned
some of this under the item of routine, our routines actually being
very similar to what in other situations would be called games
and programming. To use a concrete example, under certain conditions the resistance of our youngsters against going to bed was
not a rebellious objection to adult demands but resulted from a
hesitance to leave the happy game situation or even a friendly
adult-related chat around the fireplace. The problem is then vastly
different from that of a straight aggressive episode, a riot, or a
temper tantrum attack. The main resistance now comes from a
fear of loss of the pleasant atmosphere around the adult and the
engagement in activities which are basically satisfactory. In such
cases, for instance, it was important to supply in the very process of transition some of the elements of both situations, the one
before and the one after. That would mean that the adult would
make a game out of taking the children to bed, would carry them
up pickaback in sequence or even repeatedly, would then stay with
them in the new situations in which they were to relax, would
change the structure of activity from playing into reading, but
would stay related to them and talking to them or even let them
discuss things for quite a while. Yet at other times this would have
been disturbing rather than soothing.

Sometimes the support which the egos need to be given to manipulate a problem of structural transition has to be more detailed
and more specific than that. For instance, occasionally we know
that youngsters are ready to switch from a running game in the
rumpus room to a quiet arts and crafts activity connected with
preparing decorations for Christmas. We also know, however, that
the actual problem of transition will be very great. That means
that the breaking up of the running game will create frustration
aggression around the interfering adult which will easily make
them meet their arts and crafts activity with more destructive impulses than our arts material can stand. Or, the frustration of having to stop a wild active game combined with being taken into a
room in which they must start an activity of inventiveness and
creativeness will mean too much of a task at once. In such a case,
the previous activity and the later arts and crafts activity might
be tied into one pattern. That means that the youngsters will first

pick up or make things to decorate themselves with and then continue running around in the new decorations for a while until the making of more specific decorations is something they are ready for. Or else the equipment and props needed for the next activity will all be pre-set by the adult before the children are interrupted in the first one. In that case, the game in the rumpus room will continue while another adult will actually prepare, not only some of the arts and crafts materials, but also examples of the type of things which could be made out of them, so that the youngsters, when coming into the arts and crafts room, will meet an inviting structure which will help them over the hurdle of imaginative gaps and will take on the job of suggesting the satisfaction value of the next structure so heavily that any disappointment caused by interruption of the first one can easily be coped with. Without such a preparation, with the youngsters meeting the bare arts and crafts room without the suggestive seduction from satisfaction potentials in front of their eyes, such transitional problems will lead into apathy, disgust, or rebellious aggression.

Among other types of hangover effects are those that derive from activity structures creating heavy physiological fatigue, such as overnight hikes, all-day trips, etc. Upon return to the Home, after such a program and with a few hours to pass away before bedtime, the children often tried to work off fatigue tension through different varieties of rather wild motor behavior. This set up a vicious circle, since originally the problem on such an occasion is rooted mainly in fatigue and what they did was to build up more fatigue so that actually they would keep getting wilder and wilder. What seemed to be called for is what we would call a "quiet" but highly structured program which will permit physiological rest while at the same time the children are engaging in some absorbing activity which does not require movement. Under these conditions it was found that a simple routine consisting of hot showers, changing into pajamas (since it was usually an hour or so before bedtime), followed by table games (checkers, cards, bingo, etc.) or picture puzzles or comic books, worked very satisfactorily.

We learned early to expect regular transitional confusions in any "swing over" interval of time, viz., between getting washed and ready for bed and actually getting into bed, or between breakfast in the morning and getting into the station wagon and off to school, or between typical in-the-house activity and being ready to go on an out-of-the-house program like a station wagon trip. Thus it was found extremely valuable to have "on the spot" programming to sandwich into these structureless intervals of time. These are some of the activity patterns which we found especially valuable in these periods:

1. Group singing. The group leader floats over to the piano and picks out a tune which is known to most of the group. Usually they will cluster around and kill some time this way before moving into the coming activity or routine. The whole group may not participate; one youngster may be sitting and reading a comic book or engaging in some other activity. But basically a kind of polarity in this group situation is built up where the adult figure at the piano and a few youngsters grouped around serve as an activity resource at this moment, which otherwise is structureless.

2. Story-telling, or reading of comic books and funnies. These were almost sure-fire bets as far as absorbing transitional tensions are concerned. In these instances, the adult will usually tell the group a story, or, if comics and funnies are involved, will read them to the group.

3. Work on unfinished project. Frequently, youngsters during these in-between moments will pick up some half-finished arts and crafts project which they want to work on. Thus, in our case, casual working on material was a frequent short-range activity in the morning before getting into the station wagon, or, occasionally, going down into the shop to do some sandpapering on a boat or model plane worked very well.

4. The use of table or "quiet" games. Transitional periods are nicely filled out by the use of checkers, cards, or almost any variety of quiet games. Competition tension is usually low because the children realize that the game is being played only until everybody is ready to do something else or until the station wagon is ready to leave for school, etc. Thus, nobody really expects to finish a game that he starts at a time like this but it can serve as an activity anchor.

5. Utilization of the outside or of out-of-doors play equipment. Usually out-of-doors equipment comes in very handy during these transitional moments. For example, a swing rope which the youngster had suspended from the upstairs part of the house so that it hung over the downstairs porch was constantly used by them to solve a variety of the transitional activity problems without very much active supervision from the adults. They could frequently be observed using this rope after their breakfast, before going to the movies on Sunday (between dinner and time to go to the movies), or after dinner during the week before evening programs had started, etc. In the same way, certain kinds of climbing equipment can be used.

It is easy to see from even these few illustrations that the anticipation of transitional problems, the assessment of what impulse satisfaction and impulse frustration are really involved in the previous and the subsequent activity, and the offering of structural helps to the child's ego to make the transition are probably one of the most essential crutches of ego support which children may need in order to get benefit from the activity diet to which they are exposed.

10. Protective and preventive interference

Sometimes ego-disturbed children are ready to enjoy and benefit from a specific activity structure, but are not ready at the same time to cope with the marginal frustrations or the marginal temptations which such an activity structure also implies. In this case, it is important to secure the engagement in the activity structure as such through a variety of interferences of a protective or preventive nature. For instance, a group of youngsters may be quite ready to get satisfaction out of some work with clay. At the same time, it is obvious that clay also contains a seductive stimulation to hyperactive children to be thrown, used as a weapon of aggression, etc. Even if the activity was selected wisely with a realistic appraisal of the youngsters' basic readiness for enjoyment from expressional manipulation of the clay, it still may be important to secure this line of enjoyment against a variety of marginal disturbances from the seductive element included in the material. Thus, some individual youngsters, left to their own devices, would soon yield to the temptation toward the more primitive use of clay as a weapon. All that is necessary in that case is some interference from the supervising adult to keep the activity tied to its basic goals. Sometimes this becomes a group stimulational issue rather than one of individual interference. Thus, for instance, a group of youngsters may be happily engaged in clay activity while one of them, out of the overexcitement or overprimitivity of his momentary mood, may start acting in a much more primitive response to the material at hand. It is to be expected that, in spite of their potential ego control, exposure to such seductive visualization of a more atavistic form of enjoyment will very soon break down the morale of the rest of the group and an orgy of clay throwing will be the result. In those cases, stopping the deteriorating and contagion-loaded exploits as soon as they emerge through a variety of preventive interference techniques may still rescue the value of the challenging program as such. If techniques for such protective and preventive interference can be developed which are reasonably free from a surplus of individual problems, aggression, and conflict with the adult, then it is well indicated to start on the higher level activity for which the youngsters are potentially ready. If the degree of preventive and protective interference necessary to keep the things going becomes too great or demands such heavy forms of interference that the amount of conflict created is too great, then this is to be considered an indication that the planning of the activity was premature. In any case, the point we are trying to make is in some contradiction to traditional concepts of programming for children and groups. With ego-disturbed children it may be important to engage in program activities slightly above their total readiness, provided that it is possible for them to enjoy the basic area of involvement. The barriers of marginal seduction can and must be handled by the interfering adult, or by other techniques. In practice this means, of course, that quite often for the successful enjoyment by even a small group of children of a fascinating and valuable, but otherwise temptation-rich, activity, a larger number of adults have to be present than usual in order to avoid the need for crude interference and to make it possible to *recognize* these youngsters' potential seduction breakdown quickly, to give them friendly and supportive preventive interference before a bigger battle between the seductive impulse and the activity of the total group even arises. Through this technique of preventive and protective interference, it becomes possible for youngsters to be exposed to program situations, materials, or tools which their ego alone could not handle. However, since the ability to find pleasure in such higher level and more complex activities is obviously a clinical goal, this technique of protective and preventive interference can be easily recognized as one of the ways of giving direct ego support. Especially with children with a low facility in the use of verbal interpretation, such preventive and protective interference through skillfully supportive adults in the moment of engagement in an activity is preferable to the interpretive exploitation of disturbances in such an activity in postsituational interviews. In the long run, most techniques, of course, can be combined. Just which techniques can be clinically used in this task of interference in marginal behavior, which others would disturb the total activity of the child or the whole group, will be discussed in the next chapter.[14]

In a card game, especially during the early stages of treatment when the competition tensions of the various children were high, it was necessary

[14] Cf. Ch. III.

to spot and handle all cheating immediately. Otherwise, the game, itself quite gratifying and usable to them because of its high sociological taste pattern appeal, would degenerate into bickering, feuding, rioting, etc. On their own, at this time in treatment, the children simply couldn't handle it with each other at all. Thus, if Mike cheated, Andy, instead of saying, "Hey, Mike, that's against the rules, and if you want to play, cut it out," would go into a real rage in which he would throw something at Mike and leave the room. Or, he might cheat back and, if he won, Mike, forgetting his own cheating, would have a similar blow-up at Andy. Immediate detection and exposure by the adult could keep this from happening, and it was clear here that the protective interference from the adult relieved their already overloaded egos of the job of having to cope reasonably with their own hostility against a cheater, and smoothed over the competitive hysterias.

One over-all protective and preventive interference device is simply to load an activity structure which may have many risks in it but which it is still necessary for the group to have with plenty of staff. Thus, on some programs, instead of using two counselors, three and sometimes four were used. Trips, like those to an amusement park, which had high excitational potentials involving many cases of choice making, handling of money, purchase of food, etc., required almost an adult per child. The same applied to overnight hikes, special events like parties, etc.

No skipper and crew of a warship loaded with dynamite and approaching mined enemy waters could have been more alert to a risky trip than were we with our boys as we faced Halloween Eve. Even for normal children the impulse stir-up of this night often calls for vigilant adult supervision. Thus we had no illusions that anything short of the most intricate program planning could insure safe passage through this mayhem-loaded occasion. Of course our children had their own plans, half hinted at, half uncontrollably advertised in advance. "You know that old bastard who runs that candy store near the corner? Well—!" (chorus of approving cheers from the group). "Hey, how many windows do you guys bet will be left in any car on this block?" After some ventilative discharge had thus occurred, we discussed the evening with the boys and finally worked out a program which, in spite of their lurid expectation patterns of fun on Halloween, was accepted by them with a surprising degree of enthusiasm. We suggested that an overnight camping trip be combined with their Halloween activities. For this purpose we had been promised the use of the University of Michigan camp site, located some twenty miles from the small university town of Ann Arbor. We would drive to the camp first, put on our costumes, and then drive back to Ann Arbor. Here we would stop in on six different friends of the Directors for "begging." We told the boys that these friends, whom they all knew and liked by the way, expected us and had enthusiastically welcomed us when our Director had dropped in on them during the previous week and mentioned that we were going to talk over the plan with the group. "O.K., but how about some house to house begging after that," the boys wanted to know. We assured them that we could do this in Ann Arbor after we had visited our friends. Then we would go back to the camp to spend the night and the next day we could also spend at the camp, which was not being used by anyone else at this time, to do pretty much as we liked. We would return home the evening of the second day. As stated, the combined appeal of a camping trip and regular Halloween fun to boot carried the day. We had really a delightful time, the whole atmosphere of the evening resembling a gay, festive travelling party. Staffing for the trip involved both Directors and the Housemother. Yet, even with the high level of over-all success with which our preventive planning was attended, the continuous need for vigilant protective interference was clearly obvious throughout the evening. For example, Danny, who was dressed as a "lady" with high-heeled slippers and flowing voluminous gowns borrowed from our cook, broke a heel off one of his slippers. Immediately he became quite disturbed and he began to demand angrily that his "goddam slipper better get fixed by youse bastards RIGHT NOW!" Having poorly developed shoemaking skills, we were a little slow and clumsy about it. Danny's frustration tolerance being what it was, he blew up right in the living room of the particular home we were visiting at that moment and such was his physical aggression and obscenity that he had to be "bounced" to the Director's car. Here one of us sat with him for a full twenty minutes, alternately trying to pound the heel in, using the curb as a work bench, preventing Danny from leaving the car because he was still too upset, and also taking some time out to have short range interview moments with him to soothe him, etc. So the evening passed with a very high staff energy output but well worth it in terms of over-all success. The next day at camp was passed in a variety of activities and acted as a toning down of the overflow of Halloween spirits that still remained and would have been difficult to handle had we immediately gone back to Detroit the next morning.

11. The build-up of satisfaction images as resources

One of the difficulties of the disturbed ego, which we have deplored before, is its total helplessness in moments of emergency, crisis, confusion, or at the dropping out of ongoing supportive structures.[15] The healthy child, confronted with a period of waiting or the necessity to stay at home instead of going on a planned trip,

[15] See *Children Who Hate,* p. 110.

is soon able to switch his expected satisfactions to a variety of other resources. He will find some chance for fascinating exploring in some detail of his present environment, or he will remember previous activities which were gratifying in such situations and soon pleasantly fill the otherwise frustrating gap in his life.

Our youngsters were inadequate for either task. Their ability to use previous satisfaction images as resources was poor, their tendency to visualize new gratification potentials in the present situation definitely limited. This means that it would be of great help if the program planner were able to get around this difficulty from both sides at once: if we could find ways of "promotional build-up" or "implementational nail-down" of whatever activity structures do fascinate them now, and if we could create a more "detachable image" of activities enjoyed before for later exploitation. We also would need ways of making the "gratification promise" which the present may hold much more clear to them, of increasing the "seduction potential" of recreational possibilities in a given situation so that it can break through their apathy, disgust, delusional detachedness, or hostility, at the time.

The techniques we used most frequently for either purpose can be listed as follows:

1. Name giving. Wherever possible we would try to give certain names to games and activities or to stress the use of certain terms in connection with them so that later, whenever these terms were used, a recall would be facilitated.

2. Using props which can remain constant. At a certain time the youngsters got interested in some kind of stunt-like performance with a stage originally meant for puppet shows used as a prop. At that time, whenever it seemed indicated, bringing out the stage or pointing at it was sufficient. The production of the stage functioned like the calling of a name; the memory about the pleasant experience they had before would be rallied around their perception and revitalized.

3. Promotional build-up in between. We found that it was worth while to increase the image value of an experience of previous activity by bringing it up in conversation as much as possible in the intermediate periods. For instance, arts and crafts activities which the youngsters enjoyed would be mentioned or brought up in table conversation occasionally even though there was no direct reference to them. New counselors coming into the room would show great

interest in an arts and crafts product which one of the youngsters
had made quite a while ago or in school or in the morning, or
the adult would make it a point to start talking about an enterprise or an activity or game which the youngsters seemed to have
enjoyed. In short, keeping potential images alive in intermittent
periods and keeping their emotional content or some postrecrea-
tional excitement stirred up seemed to help the later usability of
activity images a great deal.

4. Relying on structural support. In the beginning, it seemed
that some previous activity satisfaction images had been created
before our children had come to us because they could be revived
but were not strong enough to be used on a youngster's own impulse. Thus, in moments of sudden program change or during the
difficulties of waiting, boredom, or what not, it would be the task
of the adult either to mention or purposely start off some of the
activities of which he hoped there might be a slight image trace.
He could hope that starting off with such a structure would have
a blood-filling influence on the image itself.

Besides the many illustrations of this indirectly contained in
most of the program descriptions quoted for other reasons, here
are a few special examples.

I set up my bedroll before the kids got up this morning so that they
would be stimulated toward getting moving on the overnight preparations for our trip to the Island Lake Recreation area scheduled to start
after lunch today. They were quite easy to awaken and Mike was, as
usual, the first one through showers. When he spied my bedroll in the
upstairs playroom, he asked, "Hey, what's that?" and I reminded him of
our overnight. He whistled and shouted, "Hey, now," and dashed into
his sleeping room to get his blankets and sheet. The others, attracted by
this flurry of activity, galloped in from the showers and immediately,
with the exception of Danny, pitched in. Half of the bedrolls were done
even before breakfast and this set a good mood for the rest of the morning's preparations. (Entry: 8/13/47, Henry Maier)

Today we scheduled kite-flying at Palmer Park. Before the children
came home from school, I completely rigged each kite for each member, string, tail, and all. Then I placed them in the living room, where
they usually have their afternoon snack. As they burst into the living
room there was scarcely any need to announce the program and, stuf-
fing their mouths full of cookies, hastily gulping down some milk, almost all of the boys seized their kites immediately and dashed for the
door. Bill, the most adult-hostile during this particular period, tried to

start a counterprogram with "Hey, let's us go down to Wayne and smash windows," but even his closest and beloved pal, Andy, could not be diverted as he ran toward the door of the station wagon shouting, "Let's go someplace where there is more room." Seeing his plug for delinquent mischief fall on such deaf ears, Bill then succumbed to the group involvement with the kites and, seizing his, tore out after the others. (Entry: 4/2/47, Barbara Smith)

The boys were working with asbestos this evening. When they gave unmistakable signs of really enjoying themselves, I began to "smuggle in" some conversation about craft projects they might like to do in the future. They were quite responsive and almost all of the group participated in the ensuing talk, working the meanwhile on their asbestos. In view of their haziness about recent experience, I kind of summarized certain activities that I knew that they enjoyed when we had done them, to start the ball rolling. "Oh, yeah," Danny said, "I'd like to do that woodburning again," this after I had reminded him during the "review" that we had a good time the evening we had done that. Larry wanted to do spatter work, Andy to work with plastics, Mike to repeat what we were doing tonight. Some of these ideas were new, not just repetitious of past program. Then Andy said, "Let's vote on them." So positive was their mood that I felt a vote could be safely resorted to and they did in fact vote in every suggestion that had come up with spontaneous and amazingly orderly "ayes," except spatter work. (Entry: 3/11/47, Vera Kare)

12. The cultivation of interest-contagion

With children whose egos have such trouble becoming resourceful and developing intensive and sustained interests at all, we are, of course, happy if we suddenly find they do, and we are constantly looking for means to encourage such opportunities. Two channels for the intensification of the experience of being really "interested" in something stand out among our tools: one is the contagious effect which the interest of one youngster sometimes has on the others, or the development of whole group psychological contagion clusters around an activity. Such opportunities can, of course, not be produced by us, but they can be picked up and supported when chance throws them our way. The only trouble with this is that most of the time such "interest contagion" is most effective exactly along the lines we can not afford, has to be cut off because of the overwhelming states of "group psychological intoxication" or general mayhem into which it leads, or definitely constitutes a reinforcement of their delinquency or pathology rather than anything that can be used along "constructive" lines. It is unavoidable, therefore, that some of the best chances to see them develop ego involvement (interest) are therapeutically of no help. On the other hand, it is often necessary to make only slight adaptations in our policy, so that it becomes possible to rescue some of the interest-contagional chances even out of basically intolerable interest concerns.

This is certainly one of the points concerning which the clinician has the hardest time to keep the educator appeased. In the beginning months, especially, we had to be so grateful for the ego-supportive possibilities of moments of high interest involvement that we would go quite a stretch in closing our eyes to the special content of such interest contagion chains in order to rescue some of their clinical value. That means that we had to take many chances, leave much basically pathological behavior untouched, or even encourage the development of some behavior which we knew would confront us with an enormous problem later, just so as not to squelch interest cultivation when we got a chance. Instead of many examples, a more detailed description of the development of the early "club" may illustrate this point:

Before dinner their "club" kept them busy again. This "club" becomes more and more fascinating.

Sam is undoubtedly inventor and leader of most of what happens. He changes plans and content continually; we really know very little about some of its details as yet. Often he will send the counselor out in a friendly but firm way, saying they have "work" to do. Right now he is running a racket: they pay him money, he doles movie money out to them, etc.

This is what seems apparent about the Club so far:

1. It is a subgroup formation as resistance against incorporation of the adult-value-dominated world.

2. It helps individual members to keep from surrendering to us and to Pioneer House, to fight their own individual affections for individual adults.

3. It has at least fantasy play and probably even actual planning of secret delinquencies in it.

   a. Money, hiding things, swiping things. We know of their play money, of couch covers they hid previously. We do not know whether any of the actual stealing was done as a club enterprise.

   b. Sex jokes, sex play—whether officially club-related or not we are

not so sure. It is often hard to separate what club members would normally do and what is being done as part of the club allegiance.
c. Resistance against adults, especially at bedtime. This content is openly revealed through their insistence on the opposite. Whenever Sam was asked by us what the club was about he pronounced: it is to make us good and follow the rules and not get into trouble.
4. It gives Sam the possibility of playing my and David Wineman's (Executive Director) role. This role play is interesting: he does what we do. He has his "office" (that's how it started). He interviews people there; he exercises power over the members whom he tells what they can and what they can't do (only *his* power works).
Question: Should we let this develop further, or should we have Joel (counselor) start a club or become a club sponsor? The pros and cons are many; we cannot as yet make up our mind about it.
While I am typing this, there is a new club development. Gist: Danny hits Sam on the shoulder, Sam takes him upstairs, kicks him out of the Club, insists he take off his badge. Danny says he paid twenty-five cents for it and couldn't take it off or the suit would be spoiled. Fist-fight, I separate them, have to hold Sam for a while, then he quiets down, remains insistent on having Danny's badge, says he will repay him the twenty-five cents. They temporarily sit down in different corners of the room. Upon a slight command by Sam, Larry walks up with Sam to his room, comes down with another badge to be sewn on. Has he been promoted? He paid "a dime and some cents" for it. (Entry: 12/29/46, Fritz Redl)

By this time the club pattern has shifted many times. Different kids have been kicked in and kicked out. Sam is still the nominal head. One of the very interesting sidelights is how the kids have gathered together all of the old mattresses that were once up in the attic and some blankets and have made a kind of tent club house in the upstairs playroom. Of course, they use it for forbidden activities: to hide stolen loot in and also to sneak into at night when they run out of their beds. There we find them singly or in pairs, cuddled over in the foetal position, feigning sleep and waiting for us to catch them. It is fascinating that they finally land here after they have made us chase them all over the place. Obviously, this is the surrender point where they become passive and resistless—it takes on the symbolism of a group womb. While some of its negative features, e.g., management problems and rule consistency, tempt us to break it up, the fact that it may have important group formational elements of not entirely the delinquent sort, plus the fact that they make some positive program use of it, motivate us to let them keep it and even give them additional materials with which to furnish the tent club house. (Entry: 12/30/46, David Wineman)

Sometimes, the problem is not so much to tolerate pathology and delinquent sidelines in favor of the cultivation of ego-supportive interest involvement, but rather to take a chance on having to handle later disappointments, blow-ups, and frustrations, and to refrain from the urge to "show them limitations of their plans" too early.

This evening the boys were quite excited about our gardening project, the first lap of which we started on after dinner. We marked off the plots and at different points all of the boys entered into the activity, accepting the plots we had marked out for them. Mike, in his plot out in front, did a thorough job of digging up the ground. I told him we'd get shoots to plant and asked him what kind he'd like, and he said, "New Jerseys." This was finally deciphered to mean nasturtiums—he had heard me mention them somewhere along the line. He was an enthusiastic gardener and made great plans for his flowers in the future. By this time, the rest of the group had descended upon us, demanding spade, hoe, rake, etc. Soon the fellows were all digging energetically and the pecuniary Larry began weaving vast fantasies of the riches which the as yet unplanted floral yield would produce on the flower stand market. This caught the imagination of the rest of the group, who began digging like fury to work themselves into the flower vending business. By dark they were going ahead on all eight and it wasn't easy to pry them loose for p.j.'s and treat. Bedtime was saturated with schemes of combines and cartels; a dozen partnerships were made and broken because of disagreements on profit splits, all woven around five plots of ground not even completely spaded up. (Entry: 5/9/47, Emily Kener)

The following morning . . .

When I arrived at about 7:45, I found a veritable beehive of activity in the backyard. The kids were all up at the crack of dawn and had dragged together all of the loose lumber they could find—from the shop and from the garage, which still had a lot of junk around left over from the remodeling of the house. They had even scoured the alleys behind Kroger stores for boxes and they were building—flower stands, of course. When they saw me, they descended upon me for opinions as to various items of construction. They wanted more nails, hammers, etc. Although the grandiosity of their scheme floored me, since they didn't even bother to worry about (a) planting seeds or (b) waiting for them to grow, I pitched into carpentry with them and for three hours, until almost lunch, they worked with an unusual amount of energy and attention span at fashioning their stalls. As last night, there was a constantly shifting web of partnerships, monopolies, etc. This finally began to break down into subgroup hostilities and crossfire between individuals but the mood tone was still good at lunch and nobody had yet figured out that business could not start without some stock on hand. (Entry: 5/10/47, David Wineman)

No doubt the reader may wonder how we ever worked our way around the potential frustration and disorganization which was anticipated because of the children's lack of realism about where they would get the flowers to sell. Actually, once the stands were built and with their morale as high as it was, it was quite easy to utilize their positive spirits to restructure the situation somewhat so that they sold lemonade instead of flowers. Yet, if we had suggested this during the process of building the stands, they might have lost interest in building them and then accused us of not wanting them to have fun. It was far more strategic to let them finish the stands and then, with such tangible "fixtures" for opening a "business" in front of them, work in the suggestion to vend lemonade instead of ungrown flowers.

Popularly known quiz contests were especially fascinating for our group. One night at dinner, for example, Larry, whose fantasies ever ran to accumulation of vast hoards of wealth, talked incessantly about the Pepsi Cola contest then being sponsored. He found out about it in school and it inflamed his pecuniary grandiosities no end. The other kids were not as hepped up as he but his talk got them going and they began to demand that we get forms to fill out, etc. None of them knew anything about it. Larry said that you had to go to anybody who sold Pepsis and he had forms and information about it. This carved out our after-dinner program, which consisted of everybody piling into the station wagon and going to stores to find out about the contest. Eventually, after the first Pepsi dealer was found, the counselors and group traveled around to a variety of establishments which sold the drink to collect bottle tops since the contest involved making up rhymes on the various entry slips about Pepsi and sending in a Pepsi top with each rhyme. This fed into program activities on successive evenings which involved making up rhymes to send in with their Pepsi tops, etc.

Needless to say, we knew what we let ourselves in for, and how, in part, we really supported or left unchallenged the delusional character of some of the fantasies that led up to the excitement about both activities. And we also knew what a mess we would frequently have as the result of the inevitable subgroup conflict, confusion around money matters, scapegoat opportunities around decisions as to who would get what or be in charge of what, or the mere frustration of getting tired, sore, and disappointed in the process. On the other hand, that is one of the cases where the clinician must make a decision in terms of total strategy. What we did get out of both enterprises was an experience of collective enthusiasm and mutual interest contagion which, at that time, was so hard to produce that we felt it worth all the trouble and clinical anxiety we went through ourselves.

The other technique available for the creation of interest involvement comes from the adult more directly. We might refer to it as "adult interest contagion." It is well known that, at least in moments of a happy relationship, adult mood as well as adult behavior has quite a contagion potential in terms of the actions of the children's group. Sometimes, even if there are personal hostilities blocking the relationship between children and adults, a heavily demonstrated fit of enthusiasm on the part of the adult around an activity may actually become so contagious that it may be able to cut down both personal hostility and activity lethargy or fear. Of course, some adults have more of a "natural" skill along those lines than others, and most of our staff had potentials of that sort in different directions. Rather than compete with each other, it is important that the staff become aware of their own chances and limitations in the program of a specific group, and that they supplement their various techniques. One of our counselors, Barbara Smith, for instance, had a nearly magical effect on the children through her unusually contagious love of music and certain types of records. Introduced to these by her, the children would show interest in types of music nobody else could ever have sold them on. Maybe this was the result of her own fun, the thrill with which she put such records on, combined with her quite conscious efforts to use additional techniques mentioned before, as, for instance, careful "cultivation" of the memory of such songs by naming them, humming them, bringing them up while driving to school, during meals, and at many other opportunities, and other devices. It was through her skillful "interest contagion" that our Pioneers were capable of a level of organized behavior around such enterprises which stood out like an island in the rest of their chaotic lives. The subsequent description of their trip to see Burl Ives backstage still seems to us incredible if compared with what these children at that time were like the rest of the day:

We had some difficulty finding the entrance to backstage and had to wait several minutes, but the kids were really quite patient about this frustration. Ives was sitting in his dressing room and welcomed them jovially. They clustered around and told him how they had liked his songs. Then Andy gave him the valentine which he had had Emily inscribe "From Andy to Burl Ives." This was accepted with pleasure by Ives, and Bill and Larry immediately gave him their Roy Rogers and Trigger buttons and Mike gave his perfumed blotter, all of which Ives accepted with nice expressions of gratitude. When Ives started his thanks and didn't know the names, Danny introduced all the others. Ives offered them some grapes from a large bunch he had. Larry started to decline and then said meditatively, "I think I'll have a few," and took three or four. Mike, I think, also took a few but the others all politely declined. Barbara Smith had been delayed and arrived on the scene at this point with the album of Ives records, and they asked Ives to autograph it. He asked what they wanted him to say and they told him to write "To the Pioneers from Burl Ives," and, after he'd written this and the date, they asked also that he write "Hello to Emmy Kener," which he did. At this point other people were crowding in so we took our leave. (Entry: 4/17/48, Bob Casc)

It is especially important to realize that neither of these techniques makes much sense in isolation, that actual programming usually demands a combination of both of them. With such skillful combination it is sometimes possible to hit levels of ego support which would otherwise be hard to expect. One of our counselors, Joel Vernick, had a special genius for the production of adult interest contagion, and, combining it with well-thought-out techniques of "preparatory build-up," "careful prop-stimulation," and others, was able to produce interest involvements of a level far beyond what anyone else at the house could have hoped for. Needless to add, the following illustration is intended to show just that much. It does not suggest that such acrobatics should be switched on too often. Trying to lure the children through tricks or personal charm into ego involvements far beyond what they really can maintain would not be considered a wise therapeutic move. However, an occasional dose of an experience which is real fun while still somewhat above the level the group could otherwise even have conceived of can work as a most welcome ego stimulant.

For the past few days I have been putting out a heavy dose of propaganda concerning the jet cars that we are going to make. I have been telling the kids that they would be fairly hard to build but that they would be able to do it. I also said that we wouldn't be able to build them in one day. At dinner tonight, I told them that I had mine all done and that they could see it tonight. They kept on asking me when I was going to bring it down. As long as I said "Later," they continued asking the same question. So, I decided to set a definite time for the unveiling, and said that they would see it during treat time. The questions then ceased. When it was time for p.j.'s, I told them that, when they were all in p.j.'s, I would bring the car down. I had fixed up a piece of board to act as a stand and on a piece of cardboard I printed in red crayon "The Pioneer (the name of the car). I covered everything up with a colored handkerchief. We were going to have a real unveiling! I asked Bob Case to come down in time to see it. He preceded me and suggested that he have Barbara, who was playing the piano, strike a fanfare for my entrance. After she had done so, she started to play the wedding march. I walked in very slowly with the board held up high. The boys all crowded around and were just "busting a gut" to see what it looked like. Evidently my propaganda had been successful. I then put the board on the floor and in a very formal manner asked for quiet. When they were all quiet, I said, "Ladies and Gentlemen, it gives me great pleasure to present to you THE PIONEER." With this, I lifted the handkerchief. What then followed is just too difficult to put into words. They were simply tickled to death over the thing. However, it didn't look anything like what they had thought it would. Andy said, "Hey, look at that little thing." Danny said that he thought it was longer. However, even while they were saying this, they were grinning from ear to ear. I explained to them that it would really travel. I decided not to let them handle it. However, I then changed my mind and let each of them hold it for a few seconds. I ran it back and forth across the floor several times and they just chuckled all over the place. (Entry: 11/15/47, Joel Vernick)

During dinner, it was decided by Paul (co-counselor) and me to ask the boys if they would like to start on their cars. We told them that they would have to cut out their own patterns. I had made a set to be used as a model. All accepted the idea heartily. After supper, I said that, if they were ready to get to work, they should go down to the workshop and I would be right down with the necessary materials. Mike, Danny, and Andy did most of the work by themselves, with some help from us. Mike revealed more ability to stick with the work than any of the others. He worked without a stop while Andy said that he was finished for the evening long before he had to. Danny had to quit so that he could have his leg taken care of by Emily. Mike worked even after the rest were upstairs. When they had to quit, it was about time for p.j.'s . . . Andy now seems to be able to make mistakes without getting angry at the material and throwing it around. He used to get very violent at the slightest mistake. This evening when he made some mistakes, and I told him that he would have to do it over again, he didn't say anything but just asked where the wood was . . . They are really excited over the cars. Also, I think that this project marks a new era in our crafts program. I don't think that we have ever tried anything that couldn't be finished immediately in one session. Before we started them, I kept telling them that we would not be able to finish them in one evening, that it would take a few sessions to finish them. I had expected some resistance against stopping work before the car was finished. However, I told them that, when they had done enough, they could put the stuff in the envelopes provided and then finish them some other time. (Entry: 11/17/47, Joel Vernick)

13. Widening the experiential range

We made quite a point at the beginning of our chapter on ego support of the great importance of starting where the children "are," of carefully avoiding life situations, tasks, or activity structures which are either too complicated for them to accept or which involve challenges of impulse control or stimulation beyond what their confused ego is able to cope with. In fact, it must have seemed as though most of our attempts at ego support were directed along this protective line. The underlying assumption is that, if an ego is confronted with life situations and tasks which cognitively and emotionally can be mastered and are free of fatal blocks or problems, the person can gain a feeling of mastery which in itself may have a strengthening effect on its future possibilities. It may appear that we have somewhat overemphasized this part of the problem, at least in the earlier illustrations of this chapter. We want to hasten now to stress that it is by far not the only one. In fact, an exclusive use of such ego-protective techniques would limit our therapeutic scope in a rather unfortunate way.

We would like to underline, therefore, the suggestion that ego support can also be attempted along the opposite line of attack, namely, by offering ego-challenging life situations but ones which are not too far away from the scope of ego control and, of course, with ample emergency help added. In fact, it was through some of our worst blunders that we discovered the ego-strengthening effect of a "technique of challenge." It would happen, for instance, that we exposed the youngsters to a bit of programming which obviously, as we soon had to admit, turned out much too difficult and confusing for them, so that we quickly had the mess on our hands which we deserved. In those cases, however, in which we were at least enough on our toes to handle the mess wisely and fast, we were sometimes surprised by an amazing result which we would have had neither the wisdom nor the courage to produce on purpose: the very experience which seemed such a mess but which had been rescued by our interference acrobatics turned out to be one of the things the kids would "remember and talk about," whose mere recollection would definitely have a mood-clearing, morale-boosting, cohesiveness-increasing effect. This means, then, that our real task should not only be to find out what program experiences are ego-safe and can be used to relax the ego, but also to find the "margin of challenge" which an ego can take, *provided it gets enough help in the process*. This latter, of course, remains a condition *sine qua non* in the picture.

It seems to us that some special ego-supportive force can be derived from the successful meeting of a *challenge*, which seems to be even more powerful than the one coming from the successful completion of a *task*.

Such speculations led us to make a planned approach out of what we first considered "more good luck than we had deserved," and so we began to be on the hunt for chances to widen the experiential range. We would do a lot of planning on life situations and program activities which might be somewhat beyond what the children could take, but which, when surrounded by adequate planning and cautions on our side, could be turned into an asset nevertheless. And sometimes, of course, impressed with the program potentials of an opportunity that offered itself and their possible good effect on individual children or on group spirit, we simply took a chance.

One of the needs we felt all along was to get the youngsters exposed to more traditional forms of entertainment and recreation, the type that all communities and cultures offer people on a large scale. We realized that there was no special hurry for this but that, if it did work, it would add another resource to our possibilities of structuring the day—and, especially, the long week-ends and vacation days—more adequately for them. The idea that sports, especially high mobility and aggression-loaded activities like hockey games, would be a natural solution for this need is true only for children with fewer ego disturbances than ours. Even as unquestionably interesting an event for the usual child as the chance to go to a hockey game is fraught with the dangers of ego breakdown:

I tried to sell them the hockey game in the morning at breakfast. I had little success. The kids didn't want any hockey game; they said they wanted to go roller skating. I did not press the point then. In the evening, Henry was the only one who refused to go. He finally went along when we said he didn't have to go in, but would have to go along because the House would be closed up. By that time, the rest of them were somewhat interested in the hockey game. During the game, Larry sat next to me. He had rushed out of the house at the last moment; he had his face all smeared up, his shirt hanging out, his torn pants on, looking like someone out of a Dickens' novel. He didn't grasp most of what was going on, but made up his own fantasies about what the game was about. He first cheered for the Red Wings; then when the New York team scored a point, turned around in favor of New York; then switched back to the Red Wings and talked himself into: "I have always stuck to the Red Wings, etc." He was temporarily just interested in rocking his chair and crawling around; then suddenly he burst out into wild shouting when he heard others do so. He had the looks and behavior of a moron more than ever before. Whenever he is confronted with so many things he doesn't quite understand, he seems to regress into his most infantile self. Sam had held with New York from the beginning, saying it was because Joel was from New York. He became somewhat difficult once or twice—ran around the building somewhat, went smoking in the toilet with Joe—but he was fascinated by the game most of the time. He cheered heavily for one of the players especially. Danny insisted on having popcorn right away. (He had not eaten dinner, I heard.) He munched his popcorn with the intensive look on his face which he gets before a tantrum and when he is strongly concentrated. Henry watched the game; wandered around the place; had to be prevented from crawling all over the place several times, but did not force the issue when I became firm. Joe sat next to Emily. Outside of the times when he ran around the Arena, he watched intently, with a lot of cheering for one special player. Andy watched; wandered around; showed no remarkable reaction otherwise. After the game the boys rushed to see the players. Joe was the only one who stuck with Emily; he seemed afraid of getting lost for a while. They finally all turned up at the parking lot. (Entry: 12/28/46, Fritz Redl)

One of the most important marginal tasks in program development is, of course, to help the youngsters to be able to widen their own group psychological and program scope. For that it is essential that, individually and as a gang, they must finally get to the point

where they can "take it" to mix with other groups, or even to have
something like a party in their own house. Here is an illustration
of how such plans—provided we wait long enough to dare even to
think of them and then do plenty of thinking about them—look in
the tryout:

This afternoon our party, which the boys have been planning during
the whole preceding week, took place. The group behavior during the
pre-party stages today was all that one could ask. They helped clean up
and decorate the living room, etc., and yet were not insistent on taking
over *all* of the preparations which they could not have handled such as
making punch, etc. *In toto,* we had ten guests, about half of whom were
siblings of the Pioneers, the remaining half school and camp friends.
Although there was not really any fluid interaction, which could hardly
have been expected because of age differences and the degree to which
the children were acquainted with each other, there immediately developed a nice, breezy party atmosphere. Bob Case and Joel Vernick (counselors) facilitated mixing through initiating interest in various games
scattered about, such as pick-up sticks and cards, and then Bob led them
in some organized games such as Musical Chairs. The Pioneers were
marvelous. There was total absence of any degree of wildness or obscenity of either the verbal or acted-out variety. Andy, who might have
been expected to act somewhat disturbed because his girl friend had
"stood him up," was able to meet this prestige threat most gracefully,
managing to compensate for his disappointment with only the mildest
of showing off. Larry, whom one would have expected to withdraw to
some degree, was, on the contrary, very much in contact and participated in all phases of the party. Bill scurried about with the girl he had
invited, dashing around the house somewhat, but nothing really objectionable developed and he remained mostly in the center of operations.
After the inside games and refreshments, some backyard athletics were
engaged in, and here again we were quite gratified to observe our usually competition-tense Pioneers swallow their gripes in good party host
fashion whenever issues arose. This was true not only for those disputes between Pioneer and guest but even among themselves. It seemed
as though the positive party atmosphere had the power to support them
through moments which they otherwise might not have been able or
even willing to handle constructively. (Entry: 3/20/48, David Wineman)

Another challenge to the program planner in a residential treatment home is, of course, the constant criticism that youngsters are
being "overprotected" and through that exposed to too much "isolation from the rest of the community" while treatment goes along.

While we were aware of what the real facts were, the impact of this community criticism of our work still may have led us occasionally to decide a little earlier than we might have otherwise to expose the youngsters to "new situations," even to take chances like accepting the offer of a Board member who owned a farm to visit them. We knew what we might run into, were all prepared to do as much hygienic manipulation of emergency situations as would be needed, and in the meantime just trembled in our boots when we thought of the embarrassment we would probably be exposed to. However, we took our fair share of chances of that sort, some of which backfired miserably, some of which turned into an asset in the long run. An illustration of the latter—just on the verge:

This afternoon and part of the evening was spent by our group at the farm of one of the Pioneer House board members. They started out by dashing about, exploring here and there, and then quickly settled in the barn for climbing, jumping, etc. In this they were sporadically joined by our hostess' children, a boy of eleven and an adolescent girl. Just prior to focusing their attention on the barn, many of the boys had to go into the farmhouse to use the bathroom and handled very beautifully our hostess' limitation about not tarrying in any of the rooms which were being repainted, a temptation resistance of a pretty high order for the Pioneers. In the barn, they were, of course, in their element and executed daring feats of acrobatics off the high bales of hay. When their interest in these activities waned, the boys went off on an exploratory hike in the fields, and Mike gathered some flowers which he tendered gallantly to our hostess for table decorations, supper being in the offing. Danny followed suit. We ate picnic style on a long table outside. Dave Wineman, who had accompanied us on the trip, and I waited with baited breath, geared for antiseptic interference in the events that might occur at supper, knowing full well that the real test of their controls would be in the eating situation. Actually the meal was most pleasant, and we were amazed at the way in which the group met this challenge for conventional table behavior without even once cracking. The high point of comic relief came when Mike asked Andy, "Where is the salt?" Here Dave and I shivered in anticipation. What we both feared was that Andy would yield to the temptation to resort to the use of a mysteriously derived and—within Pioneer House—chronically used idiom which popped up whenever one Pioneer asked another where anything was to be found. This idiom is "Up Moe's ass and down Jake's dick." Whenever one of them says "Hey, where is this or that" sure enough whoever is asked replies, "Up Moe's ass and down Jake's dick." Of course, Dave and I had good reasons to believe that Andy would even be more than usually tempted in the situation we were in. But, wonder of wonders, Andy surprised us. Smiling devilishly at Mike, he got up, and, in the most perfect imitation of Arrow Collar manners imaginable, picked up the salt shaker, and, with a most correct little bow, handed it to Mike over his crooked arm, saying only "Moe!—." To which Mike, in equally punctilious fashion, replied also with a correct little jerking bow as he took the salt shaker, "Jake!—." This started a wave of jerks and "Moes" and "Jakes" from the other kids. (Entry: 6/21/47, Pearl Bruce)

14. Challenge toward participative planning and postsituational evaluation

To think that severely ego-disturbed children would be capable of participating to any extent in the planning of activities or later events or to sit down after something has happened and discuss it in an evaluative fashion, to harbor such illusions would be the most unrealistic mistake a clinician could make. By the very nature of their disturbances, pre-planning as well as postsituational thought becomes either much too complex, much too overstimulating, or much too frustration-loaded to be considered. Thus, the early programming with children with serious ego disturbances bears little resemblance to what we otherwise happily suggest as the most healthy diet of democratic and participative educational processes. On the other hand, it is not true that the ability to participate in planning or postsituational discussion of an event falls into our lap only as a reward for having completed an ego repair job. It seems that somewhere along the line, after the first ego disturbances and ego weaknesses which are most fatal have been repaired, the possibility of a marginal and carefully protective use of anticipatory planning participation and postsituational evaluation can have an enormously ego-supportive effect. In the beginning, of course, the adult would have to plan as he would with very little children. He would have to be on the lookout for even mild chances of participation which involve the youngster in some pre-planning hardly noticeable to him, and it is obvious that the securing of the total structure for the activity needed would have to be guaranteed by the adult. In fact, participative planning might involve as little as just having one's idea picked up by the adult or as taking some share in a partial performance during a game, art activity, or the like. Usually, the participative planning might have to be relegated to the implementation of just which color or which saw we might use, rather than the actual ideational creation of a pattern. It cannot be denied, however, that, to the degree to which participation in some of the planning process became possible for our Pioneers, the group assumed a more normal aspect of functioning during the activities which could involve participation and pre-planning, and we could consider successful completion of such moments a real sign of ego strengthening and improvement on the youngsters' way to health.

In a similar way, the exploitation of an event for the purpose of sitting down and talking about it later offered a variety of valuable chances to use program situations for ego support. Success, as well as failure, could be used for such ends and occasionally this post-situational evaluation would be limited simply to an underlining of the clarity of the cognitive structure. Originally, the process involved would be so simple a thing as saying to a youngster, "Gee, this is swell. Just how did you make it?" Or, when an adult would come in when a game would be going on, he might say, "Gee, that seems to be a nice game, just how does it go?" thus forcing the youngster to go over the basic elements again, to describe the activity, or to make some comments or remarks around it. Later, we could risk more complex postsituational evaluation procedures. For instance, if an activity which seemed to have started off happily suddenly led to a breakdown, it became possible sometimes to get the youngsters together, or at least to have one or two separate interviews, and try to go over it all and see just what really happened: "You had such a good time until then. And then what was really going on?" Such an attempt to evaluate the totality or part of a process required, of course, that we already had given the ego enough ability to cope with anxiety, impatience, aggression born out of defeat, etc., even to "stay put" and accept the situation of "talking it over." Once we had them in that shape, however, the process of postsituational discussion of an experience obviously gave us a widened possibility of supporting ego functions which it was hitherto impossible to use spontaneously.

It seems, therefore, that this technique might be used judiciously with some frequency rather than only in emergencies where the clinician feels he has to talk things over because of a variety of problems involved. The degree to which presituational planning, presituational participation, and postsituational evaluation should be mixed with the actual enjoyment and naïve imbeddedness in activities has to be carefully planned. Mistakes in quantity, in dosage, and in timing can turn what otherwise would have become an ego-supportive event into failure and disaster.

Some of these attempts at "participative planning" would be focused on routines, house policies, the settling of disputes, fights about responsibilities and chores, or money issues. In such cases, what really happens is that what originally would fall into the category of routines is used as a program item to make participative planning an experience.

On the way to school, the boys fell to squabbling over who gets to ride in the front seat on the way home. Danny smacked Andy and called him a filthy name, and accused us simultaneously of always letting the "other bastards" ride in the front. He then suggested, "The hell with it —the first guy out will ride in the front." I was unwilling to reward early birds because Danny, for example, with his paranoid memory would always be the one to remember when to dash out and be in front of the wagon first. So I suggested instead a regular roster of turns and agreement on who was first, second, etc. After some haggling, this was accepted and then we bargained out who would be the one to start off today, etc. (Entry: 1/4/47, Vera Kare)

At dinner tonight a feud started around serving dessert. Everybody wanted to bring it in, to be "cookie." Immediately there was a subgroup flare-up: Andy and his beloved slave, Bill, clamored for Andy to be the one. Mike, inspired by the chance to ingratiate himself with Andy and Bill, screamed out in favor of this plan but said that he would be the next after Andy, which pleased Andy but confused Bill because he did want Andy to be first but wanted to be next himself. Danny began to pout menacingly and Larry responded with a loud, "Aw, heck." Danny had begun to go into the "bastards" routine when Joel (counselor) saved the day by suggesting firmly that they could have a schedule of turns and dashed out quickly, returned with paper and pencil, and in a flash had ruled off squares, written in a column of names, etc. The remaining problem was: what order? The crafty Danny suggested alphabetically (he would be first) and then Andy yelled out, "O.K. but how about going from the end?"—then he would be first. Joel, visualizing a stalemate, said that tonight dessert would be served by a staff person but starting tomorrow scheduling would start. Then the alphabet compromise was decided in favor of starting from the alphabet in the rear. Thus Andy would be the first but Danny could now accept this since, at least tonight, Andy wouldn't serve and this was therefore not a complete victory for the other side. (Entry: 8/1/47, David Wineman)

Tonight, before dinner, Bill burst into my office in somewhat an excited mood. "Hey, Dave, you better get ready to pay for my kite that Shep (Pioneer House dog) chewed up, Andy's too!" I said, "Say we better talk about that, but how about waiting until after dinner?" which was agreeable with him. Thus after dinner we had a "business conference" in the living room. During the meal, of course, the attention of most of the group had been drawn to the topic of Shep's destructiveness and interest was very keen. I opened by telling them that I had a plan which might work: Shep was everybody's dog—Pioneer House's and theirs too. Therefore, everyone was responsible to a certain degree for the damage which he caused. There was some immediate attempt to refute this, but this soon died down and I was able to continue. My proposal was quite simple: for every individual damage which Shep did, Pioneer House would assume fifty percent responsibility; the group the other fifty per cent to be split among them five ways. Larry then brought out the following objections:

(1) That you had to pay in without necessarily benefiting yourself.
(2) That it could amount to quite a bit of money, depending on the cost of the damaged article.

The first I handled by pointing out that, if the plan were adopted, he could become a potential beneficiary if any of his things were so destroyed, since all parties would be pledged to participate in the event of any claim.

The second I capitulated to and established a ceiling of fifty cents as top claim, asserting that articles above this cost should be so guarded that they were out of reach of danger.

Larry began to moan over and over again that I didn't "understand" and got quite emotional about it. Danny supported him but made no suggestion of his own; he spent a good deal of the time hidden behind his comic book but following every detail of the discussion nonetheless. Mike by this time had worked up the angle that he too had had some damages incurred through Shep—a kite string which he claimed Shep ate—so he was all for the plan. Andy and Bill kept plugging for it too. Finally the situation grew into a deadlock, with Danny and Larry holding out against insurance and the trio supporting. I, therefore, proposed that we have a split policy: Mike, Bill, and Andy could form a cooperative group of three, and Danny and Larry could have individual insurance, which meant that, in case of damage to their things of up to fifty cents, we would pay half and each of them half (of his own). The trio chorused "O.K.," and then I began to figure how it applied in tonight's claim; at this point Danny and Larry (the latter the leader) suddenly capitulated and joined up too.

The final agreement, therefore, was that Mike, Bill, and Andy would have their claims paid out tonight, I advancing three cents on everyone's allowance to meet the total claim of thirty cents, which meant: fifteen cents from the group, fifteen cents from Pioneer House. (Entry: 2/23/48, David Wineman)

At other times, program issues themselves lend themselves logically to participative planning sessions:

After Dinner, Dave said that he had an announcement to make. He then said that the boys had wanted to put on a party and he was thinking that perhaps they could have it this coming Saturday afternoon. They all let out shouts of joy and immediately started shouting about whom they would bring. Mike said that he wanted to invite his parents. Andy said that he was going to invite Connie. Bill then asked if they could invite girls. Dave said yes, they could invite anybody that they wanted. However, he mentioned that it would be best to limit the number of guests to two per boy. They all started shouting the names of girls and boys whom they were going to invite. They started explaining about what they would do with their girl friends, etc. At this time, Dave then suggested that they list all the games that they would like to play. Kissing games were very much in demand. After they had discussed the party for a while, I suggested that we go out into the living room and finish the discussion since there was more room out there. Larry and Danny sprawled out and were listening to the radio. Bill and Andy were seated in a chair reading funny books, and Mike was squirming around on the floor. Most of the discussion was carried on by the latter three boys. After games were discussed, Dave brought up the food suggestions. The three had very good suggestions—things that would be expected at any party of this sort—and nothing fantastic was suggested. Bill asked if we could take them all out for ice cream sodas after the party. All during the discussion the boys would get in a few words about what they were going to do with their girls.

The party discussion was one of the most fruitful that I have seen with our group. In the beginning, when we used to discuss something, we would be met either with silence, wildness, or joking. However, this discussion revealed the boys at their highest point of organization. They had good suggestions—ones that would be in order at a party of this sort. The sex talk about their girl friends was held to a minimum. There was no arguing about the food, games, etc. Each suggested what he had in mind and Dave put it down or gave reasons why it couldn't be put in the agenda. (Entry: 3/15/48, Joel Vernick)

Summary: In describing our attempts to use "programming" as a treatment device in the process of ego support and ego repair, we have, of course, limited ourselves to the description of a variety of specific avenues along which we can proceed. The actual details of any one of the techniques listed above are still very sketchy and there is hardly an area with a greater need for organized research than this one. On the other hand, the mere fact that programming can play a specific role in the clinical task on its own, not only as a "time-filling" substitute for psychiatric contacts during the rest of the day, seems to us to deserve heavy underlining. We might add, though, that our singling out of the program as one of the factors constitutes an artificial categorization and does not really mean a separation from other avenues of approach. We realize fully that even the best timing, program construction, or what not, would be either futile or even damaging if it were penetrated by the poison of poor adult-child relationships, of a treatment-unfavorable institutional atmosphere, or of actual bad mistakes in the direct handling of child behavior while the program went on. However, we had to single out programming as a technical area in its own right in order to mark it as such. The actual use of programming for ego support remains, of course, a task strongly interwoven with all of the other aspects of technique as well as treatment strategies. In our evaluation of program failure or program success, or in our attempt to figure out just why a certain life situation could be tolerated, where it would lead to a breakdown and where not, we felt a desperate need for much more concrete research. Most of our evaluations of which factor contributed to what in the total picture were really made on a restrained hunch basis—but a hunch basis nonetheless. We know of no organized research that is really based on the concept of a psychiatric evaluation of programming as part of a treatment task in the way in which we are talking about it here. We realize that, not only the expenditure of considerable sums of money and the use of a large number of persons in different types of institutional or noninstitutional situations would be required, but also that specific research tools would have to be devised for the process. Quite a few people would agree with us that this type of research should deserve priority over many others, especially since the fruit it bears would be directly accessible to practitioners in institutional settings of varying types, with different ages of children, and with different degrees of normality or disturbance. It is our hope that this thin and still rather flimsy model of a concept of therapeutic program use may at least be the instigator of enterprises with more ample resources, more specific research design, and a greater chance to finish the job which they start than we were allowed.

III

TECHNIQUES FOR THE ANTISEPTIC MANIPULATION OF SURFACE BEHAVIOR

IN traditional psychiatric practice, the clinician is primarily interested in bringing about long-range changes of deep-seated problems, in dissolving causal chains that lead to some "symptomatic behavior" rather than in dealing with that behavior itself. He is easily impatient with the educator or parent who plagues him with questions like: "But what do I do if Tommy starts hitting his little brother?"

The person who lives with the child, by which we mean the parent, teacher, group worker, recreation leader, and, especially, the worker in children's camps and institutions of all types, seems to follow a tradition of approaching the problem from the other end of the line. Plagued with the nuisance value of disgusting, undesirable, pathological, or actually dangerous behavioral outbursts in his children, loaded with the responsibility of securing everybody else's survival along with a child's symptoms, he tends to become impatient with the fascinating but rather distant detour into long-range therapeutic aims. He is liable to insist on an immediate answer to the question, "But how do I stop him from doing this right now?" rather than listen to the reconstruction of just what made him want to do it to begin with.

During the last decade or so, especially with the intensive development of "Mental Hygiene" as a sort of buffer state between clinical work and direct handling of the problems of daily life, the "theoretical sting" has been taken out of this problem. The more thoughtful representatives of either field of endeavor know now

that there is really no controversial issue in all this. Their seeming
contradiction and the occasional impatience of the two fields with
each other are due to the limitations and peculiarities of the experiential framework of each field rather than to a contradiction
in basic issues. There is ample reason to hope that a further rap-
prochement between clinical work and psychiatry, on the one hand,
and the practice of the educator on the scene of daily life, on the
other, will be brought about.

For the job we have set out to do, this gap between "naïve educational practice" and "clinical sophistication of causal thinking"
constitutes a challenge which simply has to be met. For, the moment the clinician steps into the natural group- and play-life of
disturbed children, either in a club or camp setting, and especially
in a "residential treatment home," he can no longer ignore the
occasional task of "behavioral interference." At the same time he
must subject whatever interference techniques he may have developed to the discipline and scrutiny of "clinical antisepsis " Whether
the two fields are ready for this or not, in our daily job we have to
come to grips with this issue. Knowing that this has far-reaching
theoretical implications beyond what we can deal with here, we
have to go on record as subscribing to the following tenets in everything we say in this chapter from here on:

1. The clinician will have to face the fact that the person who
directly lives with surface behavior and is loaded with the task of
symptom-survival on the scene of the total life of a child has a
problem to face the technical implications of which transcend
what psychiatry is primarily concerned with. It is the problem of
immediate interference in surface behavior, of the "manipulation
of and survival with" symptoms. Thus, no matter what may be
therapeutically desired, many life situations arise in which the
immediate behavior of children needs interference for reality reasons. For instance, no matter why a boy has been led into the display of sadistic urges, the group leader responsible for the survival
of all the children may have to stop effectively his attempt to
gouge out his cabin mate's eyes. Or, no matter why a girl, at a certain moment of her development, is faced with a great need to
escape from the pressure of certain life situations, occasionally it
may become important to raise, not the question of how she can
be cured of her basic disturbances, but how she can, right now,
be lured back into the group, rather than being left in her movie

seat when everybody else obviously has to go home. Again, let us remember the implications of group psychological overstimulation which we mentioned before. In spite of the best care and caution, a group of children may work itself up into a state of excitement which, as we well know and can safely predict, will lead to the unacceptable danger of clinically wrong behavior the next minute. In that case, the problem of the group leader is to stop the behavior of the most overstimulated child in time in order to avoid contagion and disaster, or to solicit or mobilize opposition to this behavior in some of the more reality-related children in order to develop a group-cohesive counterblock. In all the above cases, the issue is not, "Why do the youngsters want to do it?" or "What has led up to their basic disturbances?" The issue is strictly and clearly the stopping of one brand of behavior or the production of another. This problem of the manipulation of surface behavior is a realistic problem in its own right. The clinician has frequently either ignored it, considering it a minor job and not in his own domain, or has even been fooled into the illusion that total noninterference or total indulgence of behavior is a clinically wise policy in itself, an illusion with which we will deal in subsequent discussion. No wonder, then, that the "practitioner of survival" with overt child behavior, while finding all the contributions of psychiatry and clinical work fascinating and worth while, is constantly left with the feeling that one of the main domains of his responsibility is only partly recognized and certainly not directly investigated and contributed to by the clinical and psychiatric fields.

2. At the same time, it is obvious that the parent, teacher, or group leader with a clinical purpose in mind has an additional problem to face. He is not only after effective tools for the stopping or production of surface behavior, but he has a definite interest in seeing to it that whatever tools are effective also be antiseptic. Thus, for instance, the naïve educator or group leader might be happy simply to have a good trick at hand to get the knife away from our little sadist with greatest dispatch, to get that girl to leave her movie seat and join the station wagon crowd without delay, or to eject the first one who starts throwing things in the dining room before he gets a chance to set off a contagion chain. The clinician, or let us say the clinically oriented manipulator of child behavior, too, will be interested in the efficiency quotient of any one of the techniques which can be used for such purposes of behavioral

stoppage or behavior instigation, but he will be equally concerned that whatever technique is being offered is *at least harmless in terms of its side-effect on the basic clinical goal.*

For it would be of little help to his cause if the price he paid for the behavioral influences he brings to bear would be the destruction of the very therapeutic task which he is trying to achieve. He wants to stop the boy gouging out his cabin mate's eyes—but he does not want to stop him in such a way that he loses all the rapport which he has previously established with the child and which he has worked at for weeks, so that he has to start all over again after this scene, nor does he want the child left with newly generated surplus quantities of jealousy or hatred, of which he already has a clinically challenging overdose as part of his problem. The clinically oriented practitioner, too, would want the girl to go home with the others if they live so far from the theater that transportation has had to be arranged, and if there aren't enough staff members available for individual supervision, or if it would be unwise for reasons of group morale to leave her behind. But what good would it do to get her into the station wagon at the expense of her anxious withdrawal for another week from all the activities she had just begun to open up to? Our clinician would certainly have to be alert to the contagion potentials during riotous moods in larger group settings, but he would not want to take the chance that his ejected boy may now become an outcast among his group mates or run around wearing the defensive halo of one who has successfully proved himself a hero in a mob scene.

In short, whoever tries to combine the goal of total clinical treatment with actual survival of and with the children on the scene of daily group life on a twenty-four-hour basis, and carries the responsibility for their physical safety and health to boot, is confronted with this task of "antiseptic manipulation of surface behavior" whether he wants to be or not.

3. As far as we are concerned, there is an additional reason why we desire a more organized approach to the problem of "interference techniques." For, as we have hinted at before, we do not consider "total permissiveness" to be a wise clinical policy. We, therefore, do not consider "hygienic tools of interference" to be needed only so that we don't do too much damage if we have to stop behavior because of the unfortunate limitations of space, equipment, time, or human nature—of our children or ourselves. We

seriously insist on the suggestion that "planned interference" may sometimes be a clinical tool in its own right. In short, not only do we want to interfere "efficiently and without doing side damage somewhere else," in order to avoid physical or psychological damage to the child or to the group, but we think that the right type of interference strategically applied is sometimes the very thing that constitutes an important step in our direct therapeutic task.

We know that this is an untraditional statement to make, as far as psychiatric and clinical beliefs go. We know that it may even expose us to the suspicion of "going old fashioned" on the clinician. We have to take that chance. We shall try, in subsequent chapters, to develop this idea and its implementation as best we can. At this point the important issue is only that we have one more reason in addition to the ones already referred to why the organized study of interference techniques seems to us such an important task.

The need for developing organized research for the establishment of a scientifically valid "instrumentology of interference" in child behavior has fascinated us for many years. The Detroit Group Project and the Detroit Group Project Summer Camp have given us ample opportunity, and especially very real incentive, to observe, gather data, check findings, and, all in all, develop the rudimentary elements of such a science. The total absence of an organized bulk of such materials has always concerned us, especially when our students and workers expected suggestions from us with more specificity than we could learn from books. We think that, on the basis of our experiences, we have much material that is worthy of elaboration. This, however, is not the place to display it all, and even less to argue and discuss its ramifications in detail. We also know that what we have doesn't even scratch the surface, and we can only hope that the future may hold a chance for us to do an organized job on a larger and more thorough scale.[1]

Since the materials we are presenting in this chapter might be misinterpreted and misunderstood, we shall indulge in the luxury of listing just a few preliminary cautions.

What we are presenting here is only a very thin part of our findings.

[1] For an early and abridged consideration of some of the problems which are discussed in this chapter see George V. Sheviakov and Fritz Redl, *Discipline for Today's Children and Youth* (Washington, D.C.: Washington National Educational Association, 1944).

The techniques we list constitute only a very minor part of the answer to the total problem. The question, for instance, of the basis on which we make decisions of whether or not to interfere at all and the question of what type or which combination of interference techniques to use are as little covered here as the problem of just how to predict which technique will have what after-effect—visible or not. We shall hint, where we can, at some of the most vital criteria for "indications and counterindications," but space allows us very little of that.

Thus we know that without all these specifications our listing of techniques leaves many questions unanswered.

Yet we think we ought to undertake the job. What we shall do is simply to "unwrap" some of the tools that can be used by the clinical practitioner in group situations, and, with modification, by the parent and educational practitioner. We unwrap and describe them a little, that is all. The fascination of elaborating on the groundwork for the badly needed "instrumentology of influence techniques" we shall have to leave for a future publication.

By the way, not a single one of the items listed here pretends to be a new invention. Almost anybody who has any dealings with children has at some time used most of them. It is their planned assortment and illumination under the principle of "behavioral hygiene" that is being stressed.

It is with thoughts like these in mind that we now go into the specific discussion of antiseptic techniques.

1. Planned Ignoring

A good deal of child behavior carries its own limited intensity charge within it and peters out by itself as soon as that is exhausted. Sometimes it serves a specific subgoal and is easily abandoned once either this subgoal is reached or the youngster loses interest in it. By planned ignoring, we mean the skill of an adult in sizing up surface behavior for the items mentioned here and in limiting interference only to those behavioral trends which carry too heavy an intensity charge within themselves or which would not stop from their own exhaustion unless directly interfered with. This skill of selection of which behavior to interfere with and which behavior to ignore because ignoring makes it easier for it to stop is one of the most important practical assets of a group leader. It may seem surprising that ignoring something might be considered a technique of stoppage; but we hope that the following illustration will leave no doubt about the planned nature of this approach.

We know that one of our youngsters has to make a large number of clownishly distorted body motions each time before he sits down to lunch. We also know that, after a variety of tensions are discharged that way, this behavior will automatically subside. It would be silly to waste any effort on an interruption of this behavior. For its primary goal seems to be "tension discharge at the visualization of potential need gratifications." Therefore, stoppage of this behavior would increase the youngster's problem rather than decrease it. As long as this behavior is within the range of tolerability, and as long as contagion initiation for others can be halfway kept in check, "ignoring" leads to faster stoppage, at less expense, than interference would. This is, of course, very different from the case where this same youngster begins to work up into a real prepsychotic attack which looks very similar but feels different for the observant onlooker. Then it becomes important to interfere at the most strategic time so that the secondary effect of the youngster's attack can be successfully excluded. Planned ignoring in such cases would be very much counterindicated indeed. The areas of behavior which call for planned ignoring rather than other forms of interfering have to be assessed realistically and such an assessment sometimes has to be tested from day to day. Of course, a high degree of sensitivity of the adult group leader is essential for this task. The technique of planned ignoring is also relevant when the behavior of the youngster has certain secondary gains as one of its motives. For instance, if a youngster tries to provoke the adult into an act of aggression by accompanying his basically reasonable demands with accusations and insults, he is led to stop his behavior more easily by having the negativistic and provocative implications ignored than by having them taken up and made an issue of.

I came down to the Home at 8:00 A.M. The children awoke around nine. There was quite a bit of confusion and shuffling around about clothing and getting dressed, with no end of bickering and whining, most of which the housemother patiently took care of. Finally all the boys but Joe were ready for breakfast, which began in relative peace and quiet. I had observed that Joe was perhaps more deeply disturbed than most of the others this morning and that he had engaged in considerable neurotic quibbling about clothes he had loaned to the others and now was missing, blaming the housemother for his own lack of care for his clothes, etc. So I decided not to make prompt appearance at breakfast an issue and let him dawdle in peace. He finally appeared all groomed and with a white shirt to boot and sat down meekly at breakfast after asking Henry—the main villain in the missing clothes saga— to help him tie his tie, which the latter did quite amiably. (Entry: 12/8/46, Fritz Redl)

At the barber's, today, Mike had to be sent home because of his obscene antics. When I returned with the rest of the group he greeted me with a "Hi, pigfucker," just bristling for trouble. Under the circumstances I felt my best cue was to ignore the attack and so I said nothing but called all the boys around to finish a story I had started in the station wagon. This rather floored Mike. He looked at me with as much of a quizzical expression as that deadpan face of his can acquire and then abruptly dropped his attack . . . Gradually he edged over to the others who were listening to the story. (Entry: 12/1/47, Barbara Smith)

2. Signal Interference

A great deal of wild behavior occurs not because a child has no judgment about the danger implied or no value sensitivity about its unacceptability but because his ego or superego doesn't happen to be vigilant enough at the moment to prevent it or has been waylaid or swept aside by a momentary upsurge of seductional challenge. There is a difference, of course, between the youngster who is engaged in a feud against a neighbor whom he has placed in the category of an enemy and about the destruction of whose property he has from now on not the slightest compunction and the youngster who is fascinated by the temptation of climbing which the neighbor's cherished hedge may temporarily throw into his path. In the first case, it would be silly to expect him to drop his destructive escapade by any but rather direct and heavy means of interference. In the second case, it may be sufficient to signal to the otherwise vigilant ego or superego of the child which from then on takes over and suppresses the seductive impulse which was just about ready to emerge. Thus, a youngster who is suddenly fascinated by the challenge of hurdling the neighbor's hedge will easily respond if the counselor to whom he is well related and who caught the sudden gleam in his eye makes some clear gestures of disapproval, like waving his finger, or saying "Uh uh," or whatever the customary signal is. Of course, a group of youngsters who are ready to burst into a riotous breakdown of overexcitement around the dinner table will not stop throwing food or knives unless they are actually held or strongly interfered with. If, however, the gradual trend in the direction of that mischief is discovered earlier, at a time when the youngsters are still adult-related and when their original group code about behaving a little more reasonably around the dinner table is still basically intact, it may again be enough for the adult to give a clear signal of unacceptability of that behavior in a friendly way. This signalling of the unacceptability of the behavior will block the rising disorganization. We could furnish hundreds of examples of this sort. In fact, these forms of interference are well known to practitioners in large groups who could never survive unless they made ample use of such fill-in recourse to signal interference anyway. Unfortunately, this interference is rarely considered deserving of the dignity of being called a "technique" and, therefore, when people plan interference techniques, they always seem to have to take immediate recourse to threats, punishments, rewards, etc., rather than realize that the concept of technique implies a variety of interference forms, depending on the preliminary stages in which interference becomes necessary. What really occurs in those cases is clear: the youngster's own judgmental system or value system, or in other terms his ego and superego, would basically be rejective of the type of behavior to which he feels tempted. Only, the "danger signals" given by either the youngster's ego or superego are too weak, or the seductional involvement is too great for them to have any effect. In those cases, where ego or superego are still close to being "brought back," the signal of the adult seems to be sufficient to put them back into action so that they can directly take care of the impulsive upsurge which constitutes the problem. It would be fascinating to make a study of just what type of behavior can most successfully still be handled by signal interference and for what type of behavior signal interference seems to be too weak or entirely counterindicated. It seems to us at this stage of the game, however, that another question would be more relevant, namely, not so much for which type of vehavior but under what conditions signal interference is indicated or counterindicated. Our interest in this problem is naturally great. At this point we would like to make a few remarks based on the more ample material we have accumulated:

Signal interference is counterindicated when the excitement has increased to such a degree that the impulse quantities involved are greater
than the natural ego and superego power of the youngster can usually
cope with.

Signal interference is counterindicated when a disturbance in the relationships between the child and the signalling adult has occurred to
an important degree. In short, the adult or counselor to whom a child
is related in a friendly way at the dinner table may simply, through his
signalling, get him to stop drumming with his spoon. While, at the
same time, the counselor whose fury the child tries to provoke by misbehavior may frantically wave his disapproval signals, but may only increase the temptational challenge of the behavior involved.

Signal interference is counterindicated where the behavior has a much
more complex pattern so that it serves pathological goals rather distant
and unreached by the youngster's ego or superego pattern altogether.
The attempt, for instance, to ward off a severe fit of aggression by
signal interference after the working up to it has gone too far would
be naïve indeed. On the other hand, it is obvious that signal interference rather than any other interference can be used in a variety
of situations where the above conditions are not yet serious, and that
the ample use of early enough signal interference saves many complications.

In work with hostile and aggressive children this saving is a special advantage because signal interference, putting the load of
actual stoppage of the behavior on the youngster's own ego and
superego, avoids the usual frustration-aggression or interference-
aggression which more direct forms of interference elicit. Therefore, the greater the amount of heavier forms of interference which
can be replaced by signal interference with disturbed children, the
more of an economy in terms of avoidance of secondary aggression
quantities is guaranteed. On the other hand, it is unfortunately also
true that, in the early stages of extreme disturbance, the very fact
that the disturbance of these children lies in ego and superego functions makes the utilization of a wide variety of signal interference
less effective than with their less disturbed age-mates. The total
budgeting in terms of which youngsters can take what types of signal interference, and under what conditions, and of which cases interference strategy is indicated in at all is, of course, a most fascinating concern, mixing clinical with realistic and group situational
criteria in an interesting way. It might be worth while to add also
that these techniques mentioned here, and especially the one of

signal interference, seem to us to be of great value for the parent and educator of normal and well-adjusted children. The wise educator frequently learns how to make ample use of these techniques rather than those which involve more drastic complications in the inner economy of the child.

Tonight we were working with felt, cutting out banners for the boys' rooms. Bill soon began cutting his felt in broad, bold slashes. As I watched him, I observed that while, at first, he was cutting only his own materials, he was getting more and more excited and soon, either by design or accident, he would be catching up Mike's felt in his shears. I didn't want to say anything out loud for fear of attracting Mike's attention and arousing him, so I picked up my shears in quite a sweeping motion, hoping in this way to attract Bill's eye. He looked up and then I shook my head from side to side, pointing to what he was doing at the same time. This resulted in his asking me for help in making his design, after a moment of just sitting there while my gesture soaked in. (Entry: 4/13/47, Joel Vernick)

Danny was starting to get a little high at the table and the first manifestation of this was the exaggerated way in which he was getting up and reaching across the table for salt, milk, butter, etc. I knew from previous observation of oncoming temper outbursts that the next thing he would be doing would be to smash these items down very hard, leading from this to various kinds of spilling of items like milk and water and to breaking of salt shakers. At the same time I felt that open verbal "Verbot" would be counterindicated because there have been so many instances like this with Danny and it plays too much into the group scapegoating of him and the crowing on their part when he is openly reprimanded. So I jerked my thumb rapidly up and down, like a baseball umpire indicating a man out, implying "Sit down, brother, and stay in your place," and he pulled out of it with no further serious misbehavior. (Entry: 3/13/47, Fritz Redl)

3. Proximity and Touch Control

Every teacher knows how stages of excitement, anxiety, or restlessness are occasionally simply taken care of by increasing the physical proximity between child and adult. Just as the baby often stops crying when picked up, without waiting for the removal of the actual source of discomfort, the very young child sometimes can control his impulses toward disturbing activities if he sits close to the story-reading adult. If the distance is greater, his ego seems to be left helpless in coping with his frustration or his impulse onrush. It is interesting to note that, irrespective of age, some of the strongly ego- and superego-disturbed children for a variety of reasons have retained this response to proximity control to quite a high degree. We found that often the mere fact of coming close to youngsters or having them around or near the adult at the table would actually have a calming effect on the children. We want to make sure, by the way, that this proximity, as a calming ego- and superego-supportive device, is not confused with the proximity of the threatening person who is within easy reach of the youngster's head, ears, hair, or chin in an anticipation of punitive control. This would be a story of an entirely different sort and belongs in the section on threats and punishments. What we have in mind here is the peculiar, though not quite understood, fact that physical proximity seems, under certain conditions, to give some support to the ego and superego powers of the child which these do not receive if the adult who accents ego and superego demands for the child is physically too distant. For some youngsters a simple geographical proximity is enough. Of course, the concept of what does and does not constitute proximity is relative to children in different situations. In an organized game, the mere presence of the adult or the involvedness of the adult in it may be sufficient. In story-reading situations or dinner table situations, the demands on proximity for its control-supportive effect may have to be higher.

During the crafts program, I noted that Mike was starting to snap at Larry and that the latter was, in turn, beginning to look a little wild-eyed as he does before he has a squealing outburst coming on against somebody. (Mike is scared of all of the others but Larry, having quite definitely identified himself with the scapegoting that is being directed at him.) Accordingly, I shifted from the other side of the room so that I was considerably closer to the scene of action, prepared to interfere, if necessary, but not giving any other overt indication. This was quite simple because I was working on a model of the wallet which the group was engaged in making so that I could, so to speak, focus myself on the work itself rather than just stand there like a monitor observing them. It seemed as though just moving closer had the desired effect because Mike, looking at me sidewise, began to taper down his attack on Larry and finally half-heartedly began to pick up some of the craft materials which he had up to that time ignored. At this point I called to him, asking if I could be of any help, and he said he would like me to start his first stitch for him. This I did. (Entry: 3/18/47, Joel Vernick)

With some youngsters, proximity is not sufficient. Something like direct physical contact, which we call "touch-control," seems to be required. We have noticed sometimes that children, even of older ages, may retain the baby's original approach to what does and does not constitute security and ego support and protection against anxiety. Thus, putting the arm around the youngster's shoulder or patting him on the shoulder in a friendly way while making a limiting demand or accompanying the challenge to "come on, take it easy, snap out of it," by shoulder pats of a friendly nature may make all the difference between failure and success. Some youngsters seem to have specific disturbances along that line. We recall a child we had to deal with in camp who suffered a total loss of any self-control the moment adults were not visible on the scene of his action. In spite of a high degree of ambition to be a good boy and to counteract the temptations toward stupid and reckless destruction which seemed to pursue him wherever he went, whenever an adult was not visible, his personality was hopelessly flooded by his impulsivity. The moment, however, that any adult whatsoever was visible anywhere on the scene, without any implications of threat or danger of discovery, the youngster's ego seemed to gain enough support to control his impulses, to go to another adult for help, or to seek diversional activity in a substitute line. While not so extreme, many children with severe ego and superego disturbances fall into this category. At Pioneer House, it was obvious, especially in the early days, that we had to use whatever interference on a supportive basis we could possibly find. Thus, calming down arising excitement or stopping the aggressive outbursts which were really based on anxiety could be done by adult proximity or holding the youngster's hand in a friendly way.

Andy was stewing about Sam's teasing of him for his wetting but was unable to take it out on Sam, who is much more primitive and tough. He displaced his feeling toward Danny, calling him the "biggest piss-willie in the bunch." This proved dangerous because of Danny's own sensitivity in this area and because he too is more powerful physically than Andy. Soon Danny began to stalk Andy, who, much more agile, was beginning to enjoy this game of cat and mouse in which he was such a quick and agile mouse. Danny was on his way to a real tantrum and I felt that interference was indicated at this point. So I walked over to him and, sympathetic with his irritation, said, in a low voice, putting my arm over his shoulder, "O.K., Danny, I know why you're sore but

Andy is just doing that because he's burned up about Sam . . . How about just ignoring him so he'll stop?" Following this, I just stood there for a moment with my arm around him and he, swaying between further attack and letting the whole thing go as I was suggesting, finally said, "O.K., Fritz, but that bastard better watch it." (Entry: 1/14/47, Fritz Redl)

It is quite unlikely here that the verbal statement of the Director would have influenced Danny as it did if he had simply made it from across the room. Often, any one of these techniques is applied in conjunction with others. In fact, it will not always be possible, in presenting our illustrative incidents or examples, to avoid the fact that they were. In that case we have to leave it to the reader's judgment to figure out just how much of the effect is due to the one or the other involved, or to the peculiar pattern of their combination. This difficulty is certainly clear in the following incident:

I noticed that Bill was kind of stalling about going out to the wagon which was waiting to take the kids to school. Most of them were already in there. I walked over to Bill and, putting my arm lightly over his shoulder, said, "Walking out to the wagon?" and sauntered out the door with him. (Entry: 5/25/47, Emily Kener)

Needless to say, the housemother did *not* "push" him out the door. It is to be admitted, though, that we would be hard put to prove whether the effect was primarily due to her presence, her touch control, or to the impact of what she said. Having seen her trying to soothe or motivate Bill innumerable times, though, we have a justified hunch that the verbal encouragement in this case would not have been enough.

It is also obvious, however, that this technique of proximity and touch control has a variety of important counterindications. For instance, some children's relationships to some people are disturbed by either hyperaggressive involvements or by an undue amount of direct libidinous demands. In those cases proximity and touch control complicate rather than ease the problem. For instance, the youngster who has to accept behavioral limitation from an adult whose role as interferer he accepts but with whom he is personally at odds at the time will find it easier to accept signal interference by that adult than to have the temporarily hated adult touch his shoulder or put an arm around him. Or, the youngster whose hostility to other children is stirred up each time he feels the secure possession of the beloved counselor and whose need for adult affection has a very sensual tint had better not be approached through touch control in this area of his problem. Otherwise, his holding the counselor's hand, his getting support in control through affectionate adult relatedness, will only stir up his libidinous demands toward this adult and therefore increase the hostility against the rival child which the very counselor is trying to subdue through touch control at that time. It is also obvious that there are a variety of group psychological cautions which this technique of proximity and touch control implies. Often enough, in Pioneer House, we might realize that if this or that adult would pay more exclusive proximity attention to a specific child, some of his disturbed behavior could be easily controlled. At the same time, it was obvious that such a technique could force us to pay the price of a complication of the jealousy of other children or in the status relationship of a specific child in the group and that such a price of group psychological complications was not worth paying.

The technical advantages of the use of proximity and touch control wherever hygienically feasible are obvious. Like the two previous techniques mentioned, it avoids the secondary implication of producing frustration- and interference-aggression against the adult which, with adult-hostile children, is a technical advantage of enormous weight. It also involves the possibility of working "quietly" without making a special issue about points so that the basic ongoing activity is not so much disturbed by this type of interference as by some of the ones which will be listed later. In order to safeguard its technical advantages with highly ego-confused and superego-disturbed children, it is also obvious that a sufficient number of adult personnel, a sufficient amount of flexibility in program, and, of course, a sufficient smallness of the group are primary prerequisites. Many of the classes, for instance, in schools which contain highly emotionally disturbed children should be of a much smaller size than they are, not only for instructional reasons which are obvious, but for reasons of possibility of keeping the emotional level of children through proximity and touch control in a learning-favorable state of affairs. This becomes entirely impossible if the adult cannot be where his supportive role is needed most.

4. Involvement in Interest Relationship

Very young children seem to know most about the basic processes involved in this technique. It seems that they can hardly see something that interests or fascinates them or which is new and which they feel happy about without pulling the adult who happens to be on the scene into a process of involvement. They constantly have to point out the window and tell the adult, "Look," and force him to come to watch what they see. They have to run up to the adult at regular intervals to show him what they are doing, what they are playing with, or to make some comment or other, or ask one question or another. This behavior implies more than just a friendly relationship to adults. In fact, it is obvious that the adult often gets impatient and that children continue this procedure in spite of it. It does mean that the coping with new experiences, with the seductions or anxieties developed around them, is easier if the adult is pulled into the picture and somehow involved, so that the child meets the new or fascinating situation with the adult rather than alone. With disturbed children such a need may continue far beyond the years of early childhood. Most educators, especially those who are considered "naturals," make ample use of this possibility. The child who seems to get bored or disinterested or anxious about the task he cannot do well sometimes will perk up even though the adult just asks him a few questions about what he is doing or gives him a chance to explain. A youngster who seems just about to make an illegitimate use of a tool or piece of equipment sometimes is easily diverted into continuing to use it in the legitimate way if the adult at this moment shows interest in the task he has started on. In short, ego-disturbed children seem to need a more constant revival of the vitality of their interest fields by direct adult participation than children otherwise would. This is what requires, of course, such continuous adult vivacity, what is such a serious strain on adult nerves and is so productive of fatigue, and what makes the availability of sufficient and sufficiently rested adults an absolute condition for clinical work of this type. This technique of engagement in interest relationship, of course, cannot cope with heavy doses of impulse push behind the youngster's behavior, with more severe anxiety attacks, or with more pathology-reinforced behavioral patterns. It does, however, often enough serve as a means of avoiding otherwise dangerous or strategically undesirable conflict-loaded life situations. The youngster who is just about to use the new toy gun in a way which soon would lead to conflict with the other children is sometimes easily diverted by the adult's interest in having it shown to him or in having pointed out to him its uses and its advantages. The possibility of a skillful avoidance of emotional upset around dinner tables and other strained life situations through involvement in interest relationships is a well-known device to any large family as well as to the educator and clinician. While it seems to be a simple technique, there are obvious problems in finding specific indications and counterindications for its workability.

On one occasion our Housemother bought the boys some shoe polishing kits which they had all requested at an earlier time after having seen such a kit at the Director's home on a visit. There was a frenzy of shoe polishing. The boys, although at first quite enthusiastic, soon began to gripe because they found that the polish was rather lumpy and pasty and wouldn't yield what they considered to be a good shine. Rather disorganized behavior just this side of having the brushes and polish thrown around the room then began to occur. At this moment, the Director, who had just come in from a meeting, walked into the room. Noting their upset and the reason for it, he said, "Oh boy—new polishing kits. Hey, how about a shine?" This revived them from their frustration doldrums and they all clustered about, waiting for turns to smear polish on his shoes. They got quite gleeful when his shoes, too, got rather dull and bumpy looking. Then he was able, because of their lightened mood to show them how to rub the polish in such a way that it would spread more evenly, following which they turned back to working on their own shoes, this time with quite a good deal of success and satisfaction.

At dinner, tonight, Mike began to describe a situation that had occurred at school today in which their teacher had taken a boy out of a game of "murder" ball because the boy had insisted on tripping other players near him. He was hugely delighted by the discomfiture of the boy and, in telling the story, out of his exuberant hostility, began to weave in little fantasy obscenities like "and he said to the kid I'll kick your ass if you do that again, and Pete said shove the game up yours." Then he began to imitate, with obscene pantomime, the whole episode for the amusement of the group, and I knew from past experience with him that this would fan out into a larger pattern of obscene clowning so disturbing to the others that he would eventually have to be removed from the table. So I said to him, "Say, Mike, what the heck is murder ball? I never heard of that game. Could you tell me how it's played?" This diverted him away from the particular episode and he began to describe the game quite legitimately. The group then joined in and the rest of the meal was passed in hilarious, but quite acceptable, recounting from the others as well as Mike of some of the funny incidents that had occurred at many different times when they had played the game, which is, by the way, a rather primitive version of dodge ball. (Entry: 12/14/47, Paul Deutschberger)

5. Hypodermic Affection

By this rather artificial term we mean the fact that sometimes all that is neded for an ego or superego to retain control in the face of anxiety or impulse onrush is a sudden additional quantity of affection, the lack of which seems to be disastrous. Older and more normal children can work for long stretches without the need for direct affectional signals from surrounding adults. Younger and more disturbed children cannot do that. It is not only the need for the interest involvement of the adult in what they are doing but the need for constantly reiterated affectionate dosage which is perfectly natural for them. Children with severe ego disturbances may have trouble accepting the more traditional forms of affection or even admitting their need for them. However, the unconscious need pattern frequently is still in a very similar stage to that of the much younger child. In order to maintain any workable engagement in an activity program among the Pioneers, for instance, a constant flow of direct affectionate relationship of the counselor to the various children involved was essential. Sometimes the attention that was sought or needed was of the type mentioned in the point before, an attempt to engage the adult in an interest relationship. At other times the interest-related contact was obviously only an excuse for seeking an additional affection supply. This could be seen especially strongly when the youngsters had to cope with some increase in jealousy, in anxieties about adult acceptedness, and in frustration-aggression because of incidents of sickness and special care needed for one or the other of the Pioneers. At other times, we soon had to learn that some of the most hostile and aggressive attacks from youngsters could be assuaged more easily by an increased affection on our side rather than by falling into the trap of responding to threat with open limitation or counterthreat. The youngster, for instance, who becomes provocative because of the sudden anxiety that he is not liked will calm down more easily if the adult ignores the provocative content of behavior and gives him sympathetic support for the problem he really has at hand.

Tonight, Donald had one of his typical hysterical attacks in which he became upset over sneering remarks made by Andy about his mother's picture, which Donald keeps by his bed. First he attacked Andy and really tried to mangle him but, when prevented by the counselor from carrying this out because of his really murderous savagery, he suddenly broke away, locked himself in the second-story bathroom and threatened to jump out. Joel (counselor) got him out of there by talking quietly to him and assuring him that we all liked him and that it would be foolish for him to act this way and then simply waiting him out without further pressure or propaganda. Sobbing violently, he came out and, at the sight of Andy, again flew at him, and then suddenly veered away in midstream and dashed toward the living room window this time. I stopped him and took him out on the upstairs porch, saying very little but just holding him close to me. From time to time I would say, "O.K., now, O.K." still keeping my arm around him. He did not verbalize at all, but just stood there sobbing. Gradually, his sobbing diminished and I felt the tension go out of him and finally, after about twenty-five minutes, he stood quietly. I said, "Are you all right now?" and he nodded. We walked back in and he picked up a book in which he buried himself for about thirty minutes. Then he wrote a letter to his mother. (Entry: 5/14/47, Fritz Redl)

Since last night, Larry has been down with a severe attack of bronchitis with fever and it has been necessary to keep him in the medical isolation room adjoining my quarters. This proximity to me has had a definite impact on the sibling jealousy load of the rest of the group. Danny was impossible at breakfast and I had practically to dress him in order to get him to go to school at all. Andy was especially gripey and sarcastic and called me a "dirty whore" for not having pancakes for breakfast. Mike and Bill have just regressed to a diffused aggressiveness which is far beyond what their usual pattern now contains. This evening, their acting out became more focused and showed strikingly how related their aggressiveness was to Larry's illness and increased contact with me. Bill and then Mike complained of headaches and I deliberately gave them exorbitant attention around the area of the complaints, taking their temperatures solicitously, and rubbing their heads with witch hazel before bed. Danny scratched his foot and I bandaged him prodigiously, again playing purposefully into the fantasy of injury because of its meaning in relation to Larry, while at other times I might have tried to get him to behave more realistically toward such a slight scratch. And to cap it off, just before bedtime, I gathered the group together for a special double snack of ice cream and cake and also to decide on a "surprise" menu for tomorrow morning's breakfast. I explained to them that, for this one time, everybody could have individual breakfasts and that the cook wanted their "orders" tonight and, presto! tomorrow morning they would be on the table. This really broke their reactive disturbance to Larry's illness and intrigued and delighted them. Bedtime went excellently after that. (Entry: 2/18/48, Emily Kener)

Needless to say, this is not a palliative for temper tantrums of all types or for destructive and aggressive behavior all over the place. There are other forms of aggression and destruction which would not only not subside at the offering of increased affection quantities but would rather be increased, or, at least would take place regardless. It is again one of the most important challenges for practical and specific research to find out more about the exact indications and counterindications for the usage of hypodermic affection in the manipulation of surface behavior. Which sulk is shortened by the friendly response of special affection gratification from the adult, and which is intensified and increased, with the aggression of a youngster doubled, if an adult makes such overtures, seems to be one of the most practical and important issues to be studied in detail. The idea that special doses of love, in themselves, dissolve or cure tendencies toward temper tantrums or negativistic behavior is, of course, clinically entirely unrealistic and can only be called a naïve illusion. The idea that affection works in an assuaging way even temporarily in *all* moments of excitement or aggression is equally erroneous. It is, however, a fact that occasionally the very supply of an additional hypodermic of affection which the youngster otherwise would not have had coming at that time may be just the item needed for the youngster's ego to be able to cope with the problem at hand rather than go to pieces under its impact.

6. Tension-Decontamination Through Humor

One of the greatest surprises during the many baffling experiences at Pioneer House was the discovery that, after a certain amount of total ego improvement, even the most severe and obviously extremely pathological temper tantrums of a specific child suddenly could be avoided with a well-timed attempt at "kidding the youngster out of it." We want to make sure, by the way, that this statement is not misunderstood as implying that temper tantrums should be cured by being avoided. On the contrary, the successful completion of a large amount of even extreme temper tantrums seems to be an essential condition for a treatment approach with certain types of pathology. But, sometimes the special situation in which the temper tantrum would take place would have so many secondary involvements that it would be a strategic advantage to avoid it, at least at that time.

The reason why a skillful approach by the technique of "humorous decontamination" would work and the conditions under which such effect is secured are still a puzzle to us. Speculation about the basic machinery involved may differ depending on the basic theoretical framework from which the problem is tackled. Our hunch is that we probably deal with a combination of several factors:

(a) We demonstrate the invulnerability of the adult, who, by his display of humor, shows himself to be so secure as to be unassailable by either the problem he is confronted with or the destructive impact of the child's intention.

(b) The child, through the humor of response, is saved the extra guilt feelings or fear by which he was just about to be overcome in the process of attack or the production of problem behavior. That means that the retaliation which he fears or the guilt which he feels suddenly is visualized as unnecessary because the intended destructive or hurtful effect did not take place.

(c) The possibility of face-saving is extended, especially in cases where youngsters work themselves up into a demonstration of attack or toughness over and beyond what they are quite ready to live up to, so that the offering of a humorous means of avoiding these implications is experienced as a great relief.

(d) In some cases, a humorous reaction may actually make it possible for a youngster to get such intensive satisfaction out of the "funniness" or "wittiness" of the moment that this overbalances whatever other emotional processes are keeping him tied up at the time. In this case, "humor" would work like a "diversion" through a newly induced program activity.

We think there are more complicated factors in the picture. However that may be, though, for the practitioner it is essential to know that under certain, though well-prescribed, conditions, the mere "humorous reaction" to problem behavior in a specific child may actually, through its tension-decontaminating effect, stop it more efficiently than any other approach could have done and, on top of that, with less production of secondary complications. Illustrations for this are numerous.

Danny came at me in his euphoric, boisterous way, with which there is always a liberal sprinkling of sadism, and began to slap at me, saying, "Yah, old man Wineman, old man Wineman (slap, slap), how'r ye, Wineman old boy, etc., etc." These moods frequently follow some tense moment with the group where for some reason or other Danny may withhold the aggression he might otherwise express toward the child with whom he has been feuding or arguing over some possession. Sharp, aggressive interference like "Hey, cut that out, it hurts" may lead to increased attacks from him so I decided to try to cut it humorously, saying, in great mock pain, "Hey, my left kidney, watch it boy—that's my bad one." So he said, "O.K., how about your right one, hah, hah," slapping prodigiously, and I replied, with what I tried to make a mock, piteous whine, "Oh, didn't you know—they gypped me. I only got one." Off he went crying out, "Ho ho, he only got one, he only got one, ho ho," and tore out to the station wagon where the group was getting ready to go off on a trip. (Entry: 4/18/47, David Wineman)

At dinner, tonight, there was an enormous amount of obscenity and cursing, especially from Joe and Danny. Typically, the more they displayed this style of defiance, the more their guilt and anxiety drove them to greater excesses and yet, short of a group ejection which would have been fatal at this stage of the game while we are in our first month with them, there was no direct interference device that would cut it short. Finally, after a vehement "goddamit Fritz, pass the bitchin' butter" from Danny, with a resounding thud on a table for emphasis, I passed it and suddenly, pounding the table myself, said, "Now goddamit, you pass *me* the bitchin' salt" in as close an imitation of Danny as I could muster. The group did a double take and then burst into screams of laughter, saying, "Oh, Fritz, you had us fooled for a minute. We thought you was really sore, hah, hah." The rest of the dinner went much more smoothly because every time somebody would begin to swear someone else would refer to me. Far from exploiting it, it was as though my action provided them with a prefabricated pattern for an aggressive joke, for they all imitated me imitating Danny and in this way did not go beyond the level of really good-natured teasing of me and Danny, which he could bear because I shared it with him and which, in general, gave the group atmosphere a real shot in the arm. (Entry: 12/10/46, Fritz Redl)

Mike came in to see me in a mean and gripey mood. He complained about his teacher at school, saying he wasn't going to go "no more" because that "bastard" made him stay in the room when all he wanted to do was go downstairs to the bathroom, etc. I tried to get him to ventilate a little more steam but suddenly and unpredictably he closed up and instead threw all of his energies into prowling around the room, at the same time making demands for some special items that he saw, like my eight-day clock which he wanted to take with him. Finally he got to a case of cigarettes I keep for visitors and, taking one, said at the same time, "I'm gonna take this fuck'n cigarette," putting it in his mouth. I replied, "I guess you'll need this fuck'n lighter, then," passing him my lighter. He quickly grinned and said, "Here," tossing back both cigarette and lighter to me. With this, his "ornery" mood seemed to be dispelled. (Entry: 5/18/47, Fritz Redl)

We want to be sure, however, to avoid the implication that all funny reactions should be considered humor. The difference between genuine humor and the totally wrong and aggression-increasing use of ironic sarcasm, cynicism, etc., is of great importance. It can be well described but shall not be gone into in further detail here. We also want to avoid the implication, which might be drawn, that any tense or difficult situation could be successfully handled by humorous reaction. This is, of course, not true. In fact, there are a variety of conditions under which the same youngster would react only by an increase of his aggression or anxiety if confronted with a technique of "humorous decontamination of tension." The criteria for the decision as to under which conditions a specific youngster will be relieved in his tension and therefore be able to stop negative behavior under the impact of a humorous reaction by the adult, under which other conditions a humorous reaction will bring only increase of confusion or total disorganization in its wake —the differential discrimination between those criteria is one of the most important practical problems in clinical work with disturbed children. We could actually draw, for each of our Pioneers—and this would change, of course, in different phases of treatment— something like a formula of favorable or unfavorable conditions for the use of humorous decontamination techniques. Details about this would lead us far beyond the scope of this discussion.

7. Hurdle Help

Some of the most intensive outbursts of aggressive behavior or anxiety attacks are not necessarily part of the original natural pathology of the children but are often a result of the clash of the original pathology with specifically frustrating obstacles connected with some problem-solving situation. Some youngsters throw their most vicious or dangerous temper tantrums, not out of a clear sky, but when they run into a block on the way to an attempted goal. Others may go to pieces in a diffused aggression or anxiety attack around similar situations. In those cases, the most ego-supportive thing to try, and also the practically most valid form of interference which will stop this kind of behavior if that should be indicated, is a technique which we might bluntly call "hurdle help." School situations contain a variety of easy illustrations of the need for such a technique. A youngster, for instance, who is facing his test paper and getting more and more desperate, may the next moment blow up in a frustration attack, tear up his paper, run out of the room, slam the door in confused aggression, and therefore produce a discipline problem for the teacher and the group. If approached a minute before that outburst takes place by the teacher, and if given just the little help which he needs to get over the hurdle at which he is stuck, the same youngster is often able to continue his problem-solving task without the complications of the pathology described before. Needless to say, this hurdle help does not treat the youngster. The behavior of the teacher constitutes no therapy for the basic problem involved. But whenever, for strategic reasons, it becomes necessary to avoid the behavior which otherwise would be the result of a hurdle problem, this technique of hurdle help can easily take care of it. In the same way we noticed with our youngsters that many momentary crises which threatened to make hopeless frustration-hash out of an otherwise valuable program activity could often be avoided by the use of this technique.

Danny, having become twelve years old, has had to be moved to a new school, since it is the policy of the old school where the children have gone to date to keep them only until twelve years of age. I took Danny over to his new school today. He was quite visibly anxious and embarrassed about his size, pointing out that he "didn't want to be in with all of them babies," and I tried obvious reassurances like, "They're not younger than you, just smaller." There was little more I could do than this plus some marginal discussion about his feelings about leaving the old school, since he knew the teachers and kids there so well, etc. The teacher and principal, however, were quite cooperative about the situation and when I explained Danny's plight to them, with Danny himself putting in that he just wouldn't go in, they called out the biggest and heaviest boy in the class and introduced Danny to him. Then they said, "Say, Danny feels a little funny because he's so much bigger than most of those guys. Want to measure and see how you and he compare?" This the other youngster did, with great diplomatic skill. This really pulled Danny out of it completely and he went in quite gaily at this point. (Entry: 4/16/48, David Wineman)

Both Mike and Andy were engaged in making flower holders. Andy quickly made a receptacle that resembled some of the ashtrays that the boys made on another evening. His was quite smooth and he took a good deal of time in pointing out how smooth it was. Quite naturally this called Mike's attention to Andy's ability. Therefore, each time a crack appeared in his asbestos receptacle, he would lump it together and with much swearing make some remark like the following: "The god-damned thing won't even stay together." After lumping it together several times, he finally started on a receptacle like the one Andy had been working on. Andy called him a copy-cat for doing this. I said something to the effect that it really didn't make any difference and that sometimes, if people had a pretty good idea about how something should be made, it wasn't really too terrible if the idea were imitated. I even pointed to my imitation of some of the things that the boys had done before. Since Mike kicked up such a fuss over his inability to make these receptacles, I got hold of a dish of water and worked with him in smoothing the asbestos and piecing it together whenever a crack appeared. This seemed to take care of the problem for the time being and he began to relax and continued under his own steam. (Entry: 3/19/47, Pearl Bruce)

Needless to say, this technique has its flaws. First of all, it can take care only of frustrations coming from an actual problem-solving block and not from other pathology; the youngster who has to throw a temper tantrum because he is jealous of the other child's production will not be stopped from having it by simple hurdle help. At the same time it is also obvious that the technique of hurdle help has its limitations for hygienic reasons. Excessive use and too reckless offering of hurdle help in all cases might produce a smoother performance and avoid emotional complications but would involve the damage of giving the child so much overprotection that the chance of running into a new challenge is practically excluded, or of making him overdependent and unable to meet situations on his own. On the other hand, hurdle-help techniques may become the most important rescuers from an otherwise rather disturbing incident. The same thing, of course, is true for the group as a whole.

If an adult notices that a chaotic frustration-diffusion of everybody attacking everybody else is a result of the inability of a group to handle a task which they have tried to approach, then some reasonable hurdle help may solve the problem and offer a really ego-constructive experience. Thus, for instance, the youngsters may plan a project the basic nature of which they could well be able to enjoy. At the same time, the attempt to distribute their roles to handle the financial problem involved, etc., may lead the group toward hurdles for which they are much too confused to find an answer. The result could be disinterest in the project or total personality disorganization of the group. In such cases, it would be the task of the leader to take over the supportive and organizational function, to make the basic project lines for which the group is ready possible and through this offering of hurdle help in other phases of the task avoid the amount of conflict behavior which otherwise would break it up. The educator usually has a great stock in trade of tricks of this type up his sleeve. His problem lies along the line of overestimating the long-range therapeutic value of temporary hurdle help. The clinician does not run into that danger and seems rather ready to underestimate the possibility of stopping or avoiding even serious momentary complications by this seemingly simple supportive device. The evaluation of indications and counterindications for advisability and limitations of this technique forms a practical issue.

8. Interpretation as Interference

By this is meant the attempt to help a youngster understand the meaning of a situation which he has misinterpreted, or to help him grasp his own motivation in an issue at hand. Furthermore, the way the term is used here involves the application of interpretational elements, not for the purpose of long-range clinical treatment, but simply for the purpose of stoppage or production of surface behavior. The following may be an illustration clarifying the point:

In preparation for the roller skating program for this afternoon, the first one the group has gone on, I told Andy that he should change from his blue jeans to his regular school pants since the rink is insistent on dress pants and will not admit children dressed in blue jeans. Andy accused me of being mean and not wanting him to go skating, and I said that I had telephoned ahead of time to find out about the clothing the usual skaters wore. He called me "a goddam liar" and derided me and said that I was just a mean old bag and I didn't want him to go skating. So

I said, "O.K., I guess we'll have to call up and find out on the phone again, if you think I'm just being fussy and mean," and, after stewing a minute, he waited while I called and spoke to the rink manager who clarified the question decisively. Andy changed and went as soon as it was clearly demonstrated that this wasn't a whim on my part. His extreme behavior had obviously been motivated primarily through his misinterpretation of my "fussiness" about his clothes. With reality put back into its rightful place, his behavior became unnecessary and could be discontinued. (Entry: 1/18/47, Emily Kener)

Needless to say, in order to take effect in more subtle and complex issues this technique requires a certain amount of acceptance of the adult and of ego improvement. This could only happen later in treatment. An illustration of this, in its employment to cut off internal motivational contributions in a child's behavior, might be the following one:

For the past week Mike has been sabotaging activities in connection with his rivalry with Bill for Andy's affection and interest. His pattern has been to get temperamental, especially at crucial moments. When the group is getting into the station wagon to go on a trip or when already out on a trip he will involve the counselor in having to handle his unacceptable station wagon behavior. Through this he will make him stop the wagon and delay the ongoing activity. This intensifies the scapegoating of him by the whole group, which he then uses as ammunition for reprisal behavior as well as for complaints to me. This in turn fulfills his original desire "to queer" things for Andy and Bill as well as to get even for the scapegoating. Finally, he is now deliberately creating scapegoat incidents against himself. Today, he insisted on taking along a hunting knife on a group trip. This, in accordance with long-established policy already well accepted by Mike and all of the others, is not permitted, since for obvious reasons hunting knives can only be used around the house. Still Mike persisted in thus holding up the show and the group was beginning to get whiney and threatening toward him. I suddenly called him aside and said in a voice too low for the others to hear, "Look, you know darn well you don't even want that knife. You're just going to get all the guys against you and that's what you want so you can keep up your complaint to me that they are mean to you. Now look how you're starting the whole thing yourself and then you are going to say that the other guys are picking on you . . . Why don't you go ahead now and not give them that chance to say that you're stopping them from having a good time on the program. I can't keep on protecting you if you always give them such a good chance for being angry with you . . ." He glared at me for a moment and then handed over the knife and got in the wagon. (Entry: 8/16/47, David Wineman)

We are aware that the term "interpretive interference" might be misleading. The way in which it is used here is purposely different from the straight psychiatric or case work implications of the same term and the level on which we move at this point is much more clearly circumscribed. To avoid more serious misunderstanding, we might point to just a few of the issues implied: If we say interpretation, we do not mean anything that is comparable to the use of the term in psychoanalytic treatment, where an attempt would be made to tie up a youngster's behavior with deeply unconscious roots or experiences from the past. We also do not imply what the case worker might think of in reading this term: telling the youngster, for instance, that he is acting that way because he is really jealous against the brother at home, etc. Wherever this type of interpretation is implied, an entirely different situation is meant. We mean interpretation here, not as a treatment technique, but actually as an interference technique. We mean it on a level in which it implies only making it possible for a youngster to correct confusions he had about situational involvements from the outside which he had reacted toward or motivational involvements from within.

Needless to add, there are ample indications as well as counterindications for the usability of this type of technique. For instance, if we had used an approach like that on Mike even a few weeks before we did, we would not only not have avoided the display of pathological problem behavior but would probably have doubled its intensity and its duration. This means that a careful appraisal of which type of interpretational interference the youngster is ready for at any given time is a condition for the use of the technique. Furthermore, it is obvious that a variety of behavioral expressions would not be influenced at all by a technique of this sort. The youngster, for instance, who is happily giving vent to his fury against an adult whom he hates at the moment, would find little reason to stop his happy temper tantrum by being told he is angry at the adult or is really angry at something or other. He is angry, wants to be angry, wants to give expression to his anger. This is all that he is interested in. That means that the technique is limited to some situation where there is a possibility of the youngster's different reaction in case of a correct appraisal of reality, where the display of his behavior is primarily due to something akin to "misunderstanding." In those cases the removal of the misunderstanding and the facilitating of a correct cognitive appraisal of the situation involved take the props away from under the disturbing behavior which otherwise would go ahead full force. We might also add, of course, that not all very heavy impulse quantities once set in motion can be stopped through interference of this type after a certain point has been reached. It is of a preventive nature rather and has to happen at a time when the relationship to the person or to reality is still strong enough for cognitive corrections to sink in. By the way, we might also add that this "interpretation" does not always have to be given through words. However, we shall give this item more ample space later and shall, therefore, only mention here the importance of this possibility.

9. Regrouping

Sometimes the source of increased and practically or clinically intolerable problem behavior comes primarily from the group psychological constellations or the interplay between the individual's pathology, group atmosphere, and other group psychological factors involved. In those cases, very often the simple device of a change in the group psychological constellation does away with problem behavior which otherwise would have needed a considerable consumption of time and display of counterforce on the part of the adult and secondary conflict production on the part of the child before it could be discontinued. This term, regrouping, is used here in a rather broad sense for reasons of shortness of space. We have a large variety of most fascinating and specific problems in mind and a large number of specific techniques are involved in the problem we are trying to raise. At this point it may be sufficient to mention that we think of regrouping primarily on three different levels. The first is total regrouping, which means that a youngster is excluded from an institution not necessarily because of the intolerability of his own behavior or his inaccessability to treatment but because of the untenable complications which the clash between group psychological needs and his own pathology produces. Such a step occasionally becomes important and must be carefully distinguished from any punitive kicking out. It results from a realistic problem inherent in all group therapy. On the second level, we mean by regrouping a shift in group composition within the institutional limits. Thus, we know that quite often at Camp a youngster who, in Cabin No. 7, may, because of the peculiar constellation there, be stirred up into an intolerable display of persecution fantasies and sibling rivalry, may also show the same tendencies if moved into Cabin No. 9 but only to a degree which can be coped with and without as much impact of disturbance on the rest of the group. This means, then, that, far from really treating the problem, we simply reduce the temporary intensity of a specific problem behavior from one which remains strategically too unmanageable to a more manageable one. While this seems to be therapeutically a rather modest attempt, for anybody who has to cope with the practical complications of multiple life situations of many disturbed people in a group, the potentials of such a technique will be quite impressive. Needless to say, the problem of regrouping involves a variety of special subproblems such as, for instance, the youngster's readiness for removal, the new group's acceptance of his addition, and the whole strategy of timing with reference to all details. A third level on which we think of the technique of regrouping is in terms of distributional changes within a given group. That may mean, for instance, simply a change in project assignment so that a youngster whose participation in the project with three of the children leads to unbearable and strategically undesirable complications may be able to participate in the project with two of the others with much less unmanageable friction. Or we may mean a change in subgroup formation around activities. Here the group membership remains constant but subgroup factors are manipulated. Thus, in a team selection, some youngsters may be able to take the challenge of the competitive team arrangement with some reasonable chance for survival in the game depending upon whose side they are on and whom they are trying to beat. One certainly would try to avoid adding fuel to smoldering subgroup hostilities by pitting them against each other. Again, we may mean by regrouping a different distribution of seating around the table, different distributions of children around supervisory adults, or the attempt to separate geographically certain program activities from others as compared to having all youngsters in the same group activity.

Joel (counselor) and I took the boys downtown today to shop for suits. Ordinarily we would have had staggered shopping tours in which I took individual boys on different days. But a suit is too emotionally meaningful an item for us to expect each boy to wait while the others are served ahead so that we decided to take them all together. Initially, the boys were quite cooperative and really rather holiday-like in their mood. But the closer we got to the department store, the more their anticipation of the event itself began to produce aggressive and impulsive outbursts. Mike and Bill especially started a mutually supportive chain reaction between them. Mike would grab Bill and begin to tickle him and say, "Does the suit fit?" Bill would make mock protest but, when we would quiet Mike, Bill would seduce him into it again by flicking out at him. Several times we stopped the station wagon because the noise and confusion were dangerous in the heavy traffic. Andy, Danny, and Larry did not get involved to the same extent that Mike and Bill were disturbing each other so that, when we finally got downtown, Joel and I quickly concurred on splitting into two subgroups: I would take Andy, Larry, and Mike, and Joel would shop with Danny and Bill. This worked out all right for my group because, without the stirring-up from Bill and his appreciative reaction, Mike soon quieted down. Joel reports equal mildness from Danny and Bill. (Entry: 9/15/47, Emily Kener)

In the baseball game tonight, Andy, Bill, and I played Joel (counselor), Larry, and Mike. My team was wrecked by the current conflict which Bill is having in his whole relationship with Andy. After many months of gradually wearing out his "good brother" image of Andy by encouraging Andy's sadism against him and after beginning to hate him in turn, Bill has now reached the point where his aggression toward Andy is almost conscious. Tonight, aware of Andy's competition tension, he kept making sloppy plays, missing balls, and flubbing his chance at bat far beyond the range of just normal missing, especially since he is agile, fleet, and a pretty good ball player. Andy played right into his unconscious design by getting furious with him and tormenting him for it. The pattern gradually snowballed until it looked as if Andy simply would not be able to refrain from attacking Bill. Finally, at one point when Andy screamed at him in fury at another mistake, Bill said, "O.K., if I'm not good enough for you, I'll quit, you bastard." Joel (counselor) suggested choosing up teams again and making it Larry, Bill, and me against him, Andy, and Mike. Larry griped for a minute, saying, "Look how lousy Bill is playing tonight," but then, probably prompted by an inner sensing that this was just the way Bill would play with *Andy*, he said, "O.K., let's do that then," and we resumed our play to wind up with a fairly good game. (Entry: 9/18/48, Paul Deutschberger)

On the way back from our two-day overnight at the E. farm, the boys were fatigued and reached a kind of hilarious state of excitement which particularly involved the three sitting in the back seat, Danny, Mike, and Andy. Andy took off his shoes and started waving his bare toes around and poking and prodding Danny, who was sitting on Mike's right. This in turn set off Danny's sadism and he began to lash out at Mike, warning Dave (Executive Director who had accompanied us and was driving) that he was "gonna beat Mike's butt in." Andy and his toe wiggling were the key to the whole reaction and Dave tried to quiet him, asking him to stop, but he was in too great a pitch of excitement to do so. For a few seconds he would quiet down but soon was off again, and finally Dave told him that he should come up front and change seats with Larry. He refused and we stopped the station wagon. Dave told Andy that he was just excited and that we knew he wouldn't be able to stop if he stayed in back because he got too much of a kick out of setting Mike off, but that, if he came up front, we thought he'd be O.K. Andy got out of the wagon and insisted on walking a block in his bare feet, and, after this final flare of exhibitionism, got in the front. Larry went in the back and this terminated the whole episode for, without Andy, Mike and Danny fell asleep and Larry talked quietly with me about some of the things we had seen at the farm. (Entry: 4/5/48, Vera Kare)

It seems that regrouping is an especially self-evident device when we try to deal with an attempt to avoid or interrupt incipient "contagion chains." Under what conditions this is a way out and under what others it would be definitely inadequate or even counterindicated is, also, a problem far beyond the scope of this presentation.

10. Restructuring

No matter how well defined a life situation is or how fortunately a game or activity may start out, after a while something may "go wrong." The children, for instance, may enjoy listening to a story but the frustration of passivity, noiselessness, and quiet posture get in the way. The competitive challenge of a game may be satisfactory for a while. Suddenly its overstimulating effect on some of them produces problem behavior which spoils the fun for the rest. Or, the fascination in a number-guessing contest may hold them for a period. The fact that some of them are passive while only two participate, however, soon becomes too much of a load on the rest of them. In short, it will frequently happen that a life situation or program structure which originally was well planned and took care of the existing need balance suddenly becomes out of focus or that new elements which enter in create an imbalance.

It is well known that the most immediate reaction to such an imbalance by normal children, to say nothing of disturbed ones, is problem behavior of all sorts. One of the techniques for avoiding the type of problem behavior which is really the result not of the original pathology of the children but of elements in a situation in which they are is what we call "restructuring." [2] By this is meant the abandoning of the activity pattern or life structure in which they were imbedded at the time when it became insufficient and the substituting for it of a temporarily more desirable and "well-matched" structure. Wise and unpunitive educators have long made ample use of this technique. Thus, the teacher who notices that her group of children is becoming restless because they are sitting still much too long may, instead of "bawling them out" for their restlessness and starting off on a campaign of innumerable little acts of revenge, blackmail, bribes, and punishments, simply take care of the resulting problem behavior in a happy spirit by changing the activity, allowing them to get up and stretch, or throwing a chance for happy laughter into the picture which will drain off energies otherwise too heavily frustrated. In work with children of our types of disturbance, the technique of restructuring can also be used as an actual device in the preventive avoidance of extreme behavior which we know to flow from certain inadequacies of life situations for them. Thus, a safer technique to avoid one youngster's extreme temper tantrum at a moment when we can't afford it than holding him is to anticipate the duration limit of a structural exposure and to change the structure before the extreme breakdown happens. On this basis, the timing of competitive games, the exposure to more or less sublimation-demanding life situations and their change, in themselves may become something like a preventive interference technique.

We took the group to the Greenfield Museum this afternoon. Although there was quite a bit of interest on their part and they had been there once before and wanted to return, it was evident, once we were in there, that it was not going to work out. Instead of looking at the different exhibits they started climbing into them (into old planes and locomotives) and soon a chain of incidents had occurred which involved forbidding interference from the attendants and also from me beyond what I knew the group could take. I think they were more aggressively disposed because of the coming Christmas dinner, gifts, etc., which

[2] The term "restructuring," originally used in perception psychology, was transferred by Kurt Lewin, Ronald Lippitt, et al to the field of social psychology and appears in many of the writings of this group.

might explain why we were able to have a successful trip three weeks ago but not today. There are a number of temptations for them in the exhibits themselves and the nice, shiny wax floors. So I called them together after we had been there for about thirty minutes and suggested that I had a surprise for them: how would they like to pile into the wagon right now and spend the rest of the afternoon tobogganing at Rouge Park which was only about fifteen minutes ride from here? This met with wild acclaim and they tore out into the wagon. Tobogganing worked out beautifully, although I am sure that, if I had originally said "No Greenfield Museum, let's go to Rouge," they would have accused me of not wanting to go. (Entry: 12/22/46, Joel Vernick)

Today, after school, I was doing a craft project with the group. Bill, the first to be bored, ran out; the others, too, soon lost interest. After about twenty minutes Bill came back in yelling, "Look what I got. Boy did I have fun. You guys should have been there with me." Bill was carrying a dressmaker's frame that was partly burned. Andy came up to admire it and Bill tipped it up, saying, "She doesn't have no pants on—(pats it)—no pussy either." This seemed to act as a signal for both Andy and Mike. They started to dance around and jeered and laughed, making coitus movements. I had quite a time warding them off when they tried to jump on my back. Larry in the meanwhile chanted excitedly, "No pussy, no pussy," and the others poised themselves to jump on me again. I said, "Look, can't Bill bring a dressmaker's frame in here without all of you starting to act off the beam? O.K., so you're tired of doing crafts and Bill starts talking dirty about the frame. Do you have to try to jump me? Why don't you guys take the frame out in the backyard and see how far each of you can heave her. Then we can have some inside games. I have an idea about having a mock track meet. Want to try that after you play with the frame outside for a while?" This channelized their aggressive energies and they whooped gaily out in the yard with the frame. Tiring soon, they came back in and we had a pretty good time in the mock track meet before dinner. (Entry: 12/5/47, Betty Braun)

This is another one of the cases, by the way, in which the effect produced is obviously due to a combination of techniques. The counselor's "ignoring" of their sexual intent directed at her, her nonpunitive reaction combined with an unmistakeable brush-off of their behavior, had their share in the effect. Yet we are convinced that the suggestion of more realistic—and previously experienced—ways of program change had its impact, too.

These illustrations may suffice, for many of our other examples, especially those involving programming, are also applicable at this

point. Of course, restructuring, like any other interference technique, also has its negative side. At best, it only avoids the momentary results of momentary situations, and has little to do with the
basic pathology at which our long-range treatment goals are aimed.
Then, an overdosage of restructuring easily tempts the adult to become evasive, looking for skillful diversion tricks rather than tackling
some of the other underlying factors which might demand more of
his effort than restructuring does. We also would, in the long run,
certainly want to avoid the possibility that the children might come
to expect to get off scot-free regardless of what they ever do, just
because the adult in charge of them enjoys ingenious diversion
more than the struggle of confronting them with limitations and
subsequent talks. Also, the type of problem that, at its best, can be
eliminated by restructuring, naturally is limited to the case where
the ongoing structure and its being out of focus with the children's
basic needs or disturbance pattern were to blame to begin with.
Thus, a temper outburst coming from increased competition-anxiety
or frustration through a too difficult game task might well be
warded off this way. But no amount of restructuring would avoid
the kind of tantrum that is basically an expression of a child's confusion between the present and his traumatic past, or that has its
foundation in interpersonal conflict far beyond the usual severity.

   Within these limits, though, and for the adult who is taxed heavily in his ingenuity by the strain of tweny-four-hour-a-day life with
aggressive children, restructuring is certainly one of the devices
that can sometimes be used to cut down the total output of crisis
behavior to a tolerable and manageable sum.

11. Direct appeal

   One of the most frequent mistakes of either unskilled or aggressive educators is to think that they always have to interfere by drastic means, by stopping, prohibiting, threatening, punishing, even in
cases where youngsters themselves have quite well-developed controls, an appeal to which would do the trick. With disturbed children, of course, this avenue is partially blocked. The children we
talk about, by the very definition of their disturbance, will show
only a minimum of approachability through that technique. Because, obviously, if we want to appeal to something that could function as an inside control for the youngster's behavior, the thing we
want to appeal to ought to be there to begin with. With the chil-

dren we talk about, many of the avenues of appeal so usable with normal children are not in operation. For instance, as long as youngsters have not the slightest feeling about what is or is not proper behavior in public, an appeal to their feeling of shame, embarrassment, or decency in connection with sex language would be futile indeed. Or, as long as youngsters consider an adult an enemy to be outwitted or cheated or triumphantly evaded, an appeal to act reasonably so as to make it easier for the adult is wasted. And as long as youngsters have no relationship to the future or little perception of the consequences of their act, an appeal to be more quiet or sit down and plan so as to have a chance to go on a trip later is so much futile effort.

It is interesting, however, to discover that, at least soon after the first improvements in ego functioning and the first repairs in superego developments have taken place, a wide area opens itself up for appeal even in work with highly disturbed children which is easily ignored by the adult under the impact of daily battle fatigue. Convinced of the uselessness of some of the avenues of appeal open with normal children, he may underestimate and not recognize areas where the beginning use of appeal could be made. It was interesting, for instance, for us to notice that even with youngsters who basically still were engaged in a wholesale battle against what they considered hostile adults, in certain moments of temporary relaxation, caught off their guard so to speak, a friendly appeal for consideration and tact often could be immediately effective. The same youngster who a short time ago had to be physically prevented from indulging in a rather vehement act of rambunctious destruction soon after the first attack was over might really show a very positive reaction to the counselor's warding off of some extreme behavior with the plea, "Please, not now, Danny, I'm really tired. This noise now bothers me." In other cases, where an appeal to adult relationship or a concept of the future consequences for the individual would be impossible, an appeal related to consequences in terms of immediate group effect could occasionally work. For instance even our youngsters, when they felt reckless, wild, and hyperactive, might react to an appeal to "please cut it out now, that really holds us all up," at least for a short time.

On the way to school today, Larry and Danny were in an isolational mood, speaking very little, each wrapped in his particular daydream of the moment. Mike, Bill, and Andy formed a trio in the group interaction scheme, with Mike and Bill operating heavily on an obscenity theme and trying all the way to seduce Andy into it. At first, of course, they were just individually disgorging filthy language, paying little attention to each other. Then each began, in interludes of quietness on the part of the other, to improvise on what the other had just said. If Mike would end on "shit" Bill would take it up and elaborate it into "Yeah, shit my dick," etc. Andy, however, was not responsive to the obscenity invitation although quite friendly to them otherwise and soon, noticing this, they began a concerted drive to ring him into it. Observing that neither Andy nor Larry nor Danny was responsive, I decided to frame an appeal around this basis, suddenly saying, "Hey, what's the matter with you guys? Can't you see that the other Pioneers have gotten over this dirty language stuff by now?" This had a rather sudden effect which surprised me, for they quit and Bill even went so far as to reassure me along psychiatric grounds, saying, "O.K., Dave, now I got it out of my system so I won't have to do it any more." (Entry: 2/16/48, David Wineman)

Mike had to be removed from his sleeping room tonight, as on so many nights, because, in his usual fashion, he was both erotically aggressive toward Larry, putting his foot on Larry's bed, giggling and laughing hysterically, and at the same time lashing out at his own pillow and fighting off his imaginary enemies, muttering and cursing at them. I took him downstairs where he continued to act out the same pattern in relation to me as he does with Larry in the sleeping room, running his foot up my leg, etc. After the real anxiety attack passed, he became plain "pesty" and I finally said, "Come on now, Mike, let's cut it out. I've been here since 7:30 this morning and I'm dog tired. How about going upstairs now and quieting down, huh?" He stood still for a minute and then quite soberly said, "O.K., Dave, I'll do it for you." And he did, going up quietly to his room and going to sleep without further ado. (Entry: 3/17/48, David Wineman)

It is important, again, to gauge the area in which a youngster may be potentially ready to allow an approach by direct appeal to work, the conditions under which such an approach is at all possible, and the major reality issues involved in the timing and selection of this in contrast to other situations where more direct action is indicated. On the other hand, it is, of course, clinically valuable, provided an equal action effect can be obtained, that even simply realistic needs for interference be met by direct appeal, if that is possible, rather than by other more frustration- and battle-producing interference techniques. The most frequently used bases for appeal which adults employ in the daily battle with child behavior can be listed as follows:

Appeal to a personal relationship ("Please don't do this, I don't think this is fair to me. I've been nice to you." Or, "Listen, you don't have to act like that, remember we are friends." Or something similar.)

Physical reality implication ("Say, you can't do that. That's dangerous, you know. This and that might happen.")

Undesirable consequences inherent in the act ("Listen, if you saw the wood recklessly, you'll break it and then your gun won't hold.")

Outside role sensitivities ("Say, we can't get away with that. You know people won't at all stand for this behavior in the bowling alleys.")

Superego demand and value sensitivity ("Come on, you don't want to be like that." Or, "You really wouldn't want to do that, would you?")

Group code value ("I don't think the kids would think that is fair.")

Narcissistic pride ("Oh come, you don't want to run around like that with all the other people looking at us.")

Appraisal of community consequences ("Listen, if you get caught for this, you know what will happen.")

Awareness of peer group reaction ("You can't expect the other kids to like you if you continue messing up their fun.")

Hierarchical limitation awareness ("Well, I guess I can't stop you, but you know that Fritz won't let you get away with this." Or, "You know I can't make this exception. We counselors are not allowed to spend that much money on a trip.")

Personal considerations ("Please stop banging on the door, I really need my sleep right now, I've been up all night.")

Pride in personal improvement ("Oh come on, you don't have to act that silly any more, you know better now.")

It is obvious that each one of the previous illustrations involves a whole host of technical problems demanding specific criteria for and against using this type of appeal. The importance of a clinically realistic and wise mixture of appeal choices becomes one of the most burning practical issues in work with disturbed children. Many of these forms of appeal are also used as part of a long-range policy which we shall discuss later. At this moment we are interested in what we call the technique of "direct appeal" primarily as an actual interference technique to stop undesirable, or produce necessary, surface behavior for a variety of reasons. In areas in a child's life where potential sensitivity exists and valid control power is attributed to any one of those appeal potentials, they can actually be used efficiently for the direct manipulation of surface behavior. Needless to say, wherever appeal channels are open for use, they involve a technical advantage over some of the techniques which we shall describe later, which they share with some of the previous ones, namely, the avoidance of direct frustration-reaction and interference-aggression, of face-saving problems, of status complications, etc. On the other hand, it is important to realize that the weight of any one type of appeal may vary greatly with the issue involved, the excitement to which the youngster is exposed, or the temporary confusion of the group in which he may find himself. One of the most puzzling observations for workers with disturbed children is the great variation in the openness of youngsters to different types of appeals. The same youngster who may be highly considerate because of his temporary crush on a counselor may be totally inaccessible for even a reasonable consideration appeal in a moment of group psychological intoxication or the riotous excitement produced by subgroup mischief. It is also interesting to consider the fact that some of the appeals can be used in individual relationships only and are entirely ineffective in a group situation, and that with others it works the other way around. Which one has more individual or group psychological usefulness may change from group to group, of course, and even from situation to situation.

12. Limitation of space and tools

The confusion of "public opinion" on this issue unfortunately has thrown even the professionals into a hopeless state. There is a wide-spread inclination to make a philosophical either/or issue out of what obviously has to be a strategically planned decision from case to case. For, depending on people's sentiments and personal outlook on life, "limiting and taking away" has either been made the sign of the wise "reality toughness" of a responsible educator, or has been viewed as the undeniable symptom of punitiveness, lack of feeling for children, or psychiatric naïveté about deeper meanings. At Pioneer House, we had ample opportunity to witness this confusion in our visitors—and sometimes in ourselves. Our educational friends who might drop in on a rather wild scene would often have trouble hiding their incredulity about our "weakness and stupidity" in not protecting toys by locking them up, or in not taking away a gadget which the youngster could be expected to use the wrong way soon. On the same day, we might produce unmistakable expressions of horror in a psychiatric or clinical visitor when we dared to admit that "we had taken away the flashlight from Mike last night," or when we confessed that some drawers and rooms were kept locked. It was also clear, however, that we had, in the beginning at least, trouble with ourselves and our own upbringing. Many staff meetings and supervisory conferences had to deal with such questions as: why are you ashamed that you "had to take Bill's knife away" yesterday? All the evidence shows that this was a most realistic move, and the way you handled it took care of all the antiseptic cautions in the books. Or we had to admit to each other that yesterday's deprival of Joe's knife was due to our own anxiety rather than being the result of a clinically wise and really needed move. For the practitioner cannot take refuge in "general policies"—for him the problem of space and tool limitation becomes an issue of daily strategy. Without being able to describe even a fraction of our thinking and experience along that line, may it suffice to offer the following preliminary glimpse into the problem.

The technique of "limitation in tools and space" can be thought of on two entirely different levels. One is the level of "avoidance": we can lock up tools and toys and rooms or we can surround their use with a variety of "conditional strings" and "tabus." Which of the two is preferable and in which case, and which areas and tools or toys should be surrounded with such "limiting policy," constitute a most practical and fascinating issue far beyond our present scope. Suffice it to say that, with all our basic policy of "symptom tolerance" and strategic leeway for misbehavior so as to exploit it for learning later, we definitely think that there are some clear-cut indications showing when limitations in space and tools are very important, indeed. Leaving loose cash around unlocked, for instance, may at times simply mean to seduce unnecessarily children whose pathology is heavily geared in the direction of such temptations. The injudicious leaving around of some tools and toys under certain conditions in Pioneer House simply invited group intoxication and riot which in no way were beneficial on any account. The specific decisions along that line can become very crucial, indeed. Here is just one illustration taken from many: Aware of the hunger and curiosity of children for some access to drawers, rooms, and desks of adults who are important in their lives, we knew we would have to provide some gratification along the line of "messing around" in some adult's desk or drawer, or fiddling with the gadgets on his desk while engaged in an interview. At the same time, undefended access to all adult possessions would have meant a simply silly lack of caution, knowing the seductive challenge this would imply. So we arrived, in the case of the housemother's room, for instance, and this is one of the strategically most important areas in the children's life space, at something like a "zoning" policy: There would be a drawer which the children could open and fiddle around in at any time when she was in her room with them. They could put in or take out whatever they wanted, or at least ask permission to do so. There would be another drawer, which the housemother would not object to their opening and rummaging around in somewhat, but which she would not let them put things in or take things out of. It would contain a variety of things adults keep in their desks, some bookkeeping records, and what not. If the children's curiosity were stirred up, they would be allowed to explore that drawer, look at everything in it, convince themselves they weren't really interested in it and nothing special was hidden from them, that it was all "adult stuff" in there, and put it back. There were other drawers like that. Some, however, were simply locked, and the children could not get into them just because they felt like it. They were told so, reasons were given, comparisons with their own need and right to have some of their things locked were made, and feelings around this issue, however strong, were handled each time they arose. We hoped, thereby, to develop a certain ego-awareness in those children of various "levels" of privacy and accessibility of people's belongings and lives, and frankly exploited behavior and feelings around this policy for interview work of all types.

The other level on which the question of "limiting space and tools" is important occurs when a child who is using a tool or space wrongly refuses to yield to all other influence techniques mentioned before, so that we simply may have to block his entrance into the room, or take away the gadget so seductively breaking down his own controls. This level seems to be the most controversial issue in education-psychiatry discussions. As we have said before, we hope that we are not in danger of being mistakenly regarded as being overinterfering adults who want to save ourselves trouble by taking away toys from children just so that they don't abuse them. We would like, however, to make it quite clear that we are convinced that, under certain conditions, taking away something from a child may be a very wise and worth-while interference technique. In fact, not ever allowing ourselves to do so would ultimately actually pauperize the life space of these children to an impossible degree. For, by exposing them to certain situations, allowing them the use of certain toys or tools, we obviously invite trouble. Without inviting the kind of trouble that comes from the overstimulation aroused by an excitement-producing gadget, we could not develop the program we need so badly for other reasons of therapy. If exposed to the type of program they need, children will, however, invariably run into situations of "overstimulation" or "seduction" through temptational lure, or "group psychological intoxication" as described before. Sometimes we can predict such risks and avoid them. Sometimes we can't. In the latter case, to cope with the confusion which would be bad for the child or his group, especially if the involvement or excitement is beyond the stage in which other approaches still work, taking away the gadget around which his problem of control seems to focus right now is not only a realistic but also a clinically wise step.

On the other hand, it is obvious that we must be fully aware of the great complexities of "antisepsis" which surround this issue. For it is true that "taking away" often means, to the unconscious of the child, much more than we may realize or want it to mean. This is especially true of certain gadgets and toys more than of others. And we also know how the whole issue of taking away may be used by youngsters as evidence that we don't like them, so that such active interference in the use of toys or tools is clinically much more dangerous than many other interference forms. We think that sometimes these considerations may be sufficient to counterindicate against using this technique. In other cases, the very way in which the adult acts while taking something away from a child, and the total policy of life which governs his relationship to the child in other moments, can be geared in such a way that this marginal effect of "taking away" can either be avoided or taken care of adequately in "postsituational follow-up."

Let us use a few illustrations of this point. Sometimes it may happen that the counselor reading a story to the children at bedtime is disturbed in his attempt to do what most of the group want very badly by one youngster who cannot resist the temptation to switch his flashlight off and on into the eyes of the other children. It would be stupid, for a variety of clinically obvious reasons, to avoid such problems by a total policy of not allowing children to take their flashlights to bed. On the other hand, it would be unwise to surrender to any such situation automatically by giving up the experience for which the clinician had a variety of reasons to begin with simply in order to avoid a more drastic interference with the one youngster's problem. Or it may be unwise to let the youngster continue with behavior which will bring the wrath of scapegoat revenge from his roommates down on his head at a time when we are trying to make him more acceptable to them. That means that it may happen that the adult may have to insist that the flashlight not be used, that it be placed in the youngster's drawer where he can get it again in the morning. The counselor may even, if the excitement has gone beyond the point of preventive interference, have to take the flashlight away for the time being and thus avoid its use. It is important, however, that the worker in a clinical situation be well aware of criteria in favor of or against any one of these procedures and of the symbolic meaning and the potential damage which are involved in an enterprise of that sort. This means that, even though he may have to interfere this sharply, he will create conditions and situations for this interference which will avoid the confusion it may raise in the fantasy of the child. He also will make it possible to manipulate the unavoidable damage to be done now in a subsequent interview situation. Among such assurances against misinterpretation by the child are: the friendliness and lack of punitive affect with which the adult interfered; the patience with which the adult put up with minor misbehavior before such taking-away-interference finally became necessary; the attempts he made previously to help the youngster stop his disturbing behavior through cajoling or appealing, without recourse to threat; the reassurance the youngster has received from previous life with this adult that he will get his flashlight back again, that the adult does not frown on the pleasure he receives out of it but tries only to stop its momentarily disturbing use; the total lack of impatience or triumph in

the act of interference itself; the implied sympathy with the youngster's feeling about the interference after the act, and so forth.

In other cases, in a momentarily dangerous situation produced by
the reckless flashing of a knife by a youngster in excitement, even
such hygienic considerations may have to be temporarily excluded.
This means that the knife may have to be taken away from such
a child. At the moment, the youngster will consider such interference as hostile rejection, mutilative tendency on the side of the
adult, or what not, but in that case, again, subsequent interview,
the total atmosphere in which children and adults live together,
will offer a sufficient and adequate counterbalance for the dissolution of whatever wrong feelings were produced in the process at
hand. The most important issue is that all interference which limits
severely and drastically the use of tools, space, or equipment be
totally free of the implication of adult aggression, punishment, or
revenge. The way in which the adult acts in such situations must
make it either perfectly clear now or easily interpretable afterward
that his act of depriving is nothing but temporary control-support
for the youngster's or the group's benefit and implies neither rejection of the child nor retribution or punishment in any way whatsoever. Needless to add, also, the timing of deprival has to be clinically realistic and free of punitive overexposure, the reassurance of
the deprival being temporary has to accompany this act of deprival,
the interpretation of the reasons for and the meaning of the interference has to be made clear verbally or by the affectionate accom-
paniment of the adult's behavior. Under the conditions described
above, an occasional severe interference in the use of tools, equipment, or space may be an unavoidable, even a reality-clearing and
only partially confusing, experience in daily clinical handling.

It is our impression that the adult group leader who knows that
in an emergency he can make a reasonable and wise use of effective
and clear-cut techniques of this sort will feel happier and freer the
rest of the time with the manipulation of relatively risky but treat-
ment-valuable and desirable gadgets and will also feel free from
excitement, revengefulness, or aggression in the moment of interference itself. Rather than consider interference an unfortunate
accident which is really alien to clinical principles, we ought to
make its marginal use under hygienic conditions a well-taught,
worth-while protective and reality-geared device. The workers at
Pioneer House were encouraged to take great care to establish an

especially good, happy, and child-fun-identified relationship toward the very tools or gadgets which might later on become more dangerous and be most liable to demand extreme interference of this sort. With such a "friendship with the dangerous gadgets" established, the moment of interference hits the child and the adult in a much more opportune mood. This means that the adult who takes away a knife or flashlight from a child who knows the adult viewed it with suspicion and did not want him to have fun out of a gadget like that to begin with will much more easily be viewed by the child as a hostile interferer of a retributive type. The adult who has shown the child that he is basically interested in the youngster's happiness derived out of a reasonable use of a toy or gadget will be able to handle even an excited moment of sharp limitation in the child's life without the flavor of undue hostility and with the implication of this being a temporary measure of control rather than a planned hostile act by the adult. Even though the momentary excitement or pathological tendencies may suggest to the child a temporary interpretation of that sort, we find that it is usually easy to live down or talk down or listen down in later planned situations the temporarily negative effect of an interference technique as drastic as this.

This afternoon the boys were playing most of the time with some new water guns that had been given to each of them by the director of the Home when he returned from an out-of-town trip. They had several counselor-supervised battles in the shower room. Stripping down to trunks, they gaily sluiced each other in ambitious imitation of cops and robbers. It went pretty well without mishap of a serious nature. Before dinner they were rounded up and encouraged to dress and get ready to come down to the dining room. They all cooperated pretty nicely in this routine and when it came time to go down they all tucked their guns in their belts and started to trek into the dining room. I said, "Wait a minute, guys—how about checking your artillery with me just for dinner?" They all squawked about it and I said, "Aw, come on, you've all had a swell time this afternoon with the guns but that was in the shower room. Why spoil it by taking them into the dining room where somebody is sure going to get the idea to dip his gun into the water pitcher or milk and start firing at somebody else, and then there'll be real trouble. Might as well let me keep them in the office for dinner." Then Mike surrendered his, saying "I want it right after dinner, Dave" and I said "Sure," following which the whole group handed over the guns and went in to eat. (Entry: 10/17/47, David Wineman)

While I was reading to the group tonight during the bedtime period, Larry kept switching his flashlight off and on. Finally the other kids began to complain about it, saying justifiably that it was interfering with the story and that Larry was getting away with breaking a rule about using flashlights in bed anyway. It was his brand new jumbo size flashlight that he had gotten for Christmas and I was leery about taking it away from him because of its obvious symbolic meaning. Along with this it was also quite clear that the play with the flashlight had some kind of masturbatory meaning for him. He would duck it under his blanket in about the genital area and suddenly bring it out and flash the beam the length of the ceiling, this act being repeated rhythmically. As soon as Danny complained, Larry got very aggressive, saying that nobody was going to take "no flashlight from him, no sir," and he turned over and lay belly down on the flashlight to protect it from being taken —which I had made no move to do, by the way. Soon, however, he started blinking it all over again. So I said, "Come on, Larry, we can't let you do that. I insist that you at least put the light in your chest and leave it there until morning. Otherwise I may have to take it and keep it for you until then myself because everybody is getting gypped out of the story on account of your playing with it now." Grumblingly he got out of bed and put it in his chest, climbed back in again, and I finished reading the story. (Entry: 1/18/48, Barbara Smith)

The boys were back in my quarters after school today for their milk and cookies treat and, after they finished, Sam and Joe suddenly became imbued with the notion of having a wrestling match right then and there. So they stripped to the waist and proceeded to grapple with each other. Laughingly I interfered, saying, "Hey, hold it there guys—upstairs in the play room is the best place for that. C'mon we'll get mats out and have a referee and make it a real honest to goodness match." (Entry: 1/18/47, Emily Kener)

13. Antiseptic Bouncing

This term, "antiseptic bouncing," may seem quite shocking to anybody who is even mildly identified with the basic principles of progressive education, to say nothing of "therapy." We hasten to add, therefore, that the term "antiseptic bouncing," is purposely overdramatized in this paragraph for the sake of color and, we might add, frankness. We might have found a more clinically sounding term as, for instance, that of "situational elimination." However, we still feel that if we used that phrase we would dodge the issue. For, basically, it amounts to the same thing. We also hasten to add, however, that "bouncing" has the term "antiseptic" as an adjective affixed to it. In short, we do not visualize an angry adult throwing out a youngster with a display of hostility, aggression, anger, and triumph, but we do have in mind the fact that, under certain circumstances, the removal of a child from a scene of conflict is the only way to cope with the behavioral implications involved.

The situation in which the use of this technique suggests itself often has the nature of an "emergency"—it seems that the child's behavior has reached an intensity or his loss of control or his stage of excitement has reached a peak for which the usually effective ways of stopping him don't seem to be feasible. This, however, is not necessarily so. Often "antiseptic bouncing" suggests itself as a rather wise move to be considered long before any form of "crisis" has developed, primarily as a preventive step.

The criteria which would speak in favor of removing a child from the scene of the problem can easily be listed:

1. Physical danger

This hardly needs any further explanation. It just so happens that children with extreme quantities of hatred and destructiveness occasionally work themselves up into such a state of excitement that all usual perceptions of danger limits go overboard. The next minute, unless stopped, they will surely reach the limit beyond which the safety of other children or themselves will be risked. Such a situation may be the result of mistakes made in program planning to begin with or it may be the unavoidable risk one could not predict. Either way, behavioral stoppage may become paramount at the time.

2. Irritation through the group psychological scene

Sometimes, a youngster may work himself into such a state of tension with the rest of the group or some of its members, or the ongoing activity may be so overstimulating for him, that it is quite obvious that he cannot be brought to calm down as long as he remains involved in the ongoing contagion chain or exposed to the excitement around him. In that case, taking him out may calm him down much more easily. This is often the case after an exciting fight, or in a threatening or overexciting game, or after a personal flare-up constantly newly engendered by the visualization of the scene or personnel that caused it.

3. *Uncheckable contagion effect*

This seems to be the reverse side of the point made before. Sometimes the presence of a youngster or his behavior keeps a group stirred up to such a degree that there seems no chance to get it calmed down somewhat as long as he is acting up or even around. The classical example of this is the well-known situation where a particular youngster may work himself into such a state of "giggleomania" that, no matter how hard he tries, he cannot stop it, while at the same time each new outburst of his has disastrous effects on the group. Camp counselors will know how easily this happens even among the most cooperative children. The rest of the group may be just about ready to relax and fall asleep. One youngster keeps them in stitches by his giggles under the blanket, which he cannot stop no matter how much we plead or threaten. In this case, often enough, the whole problem is solved if we sit outside somewhere under a tree with him. In our friendly presence and removed from the overstimulation of the group scene, he soon calms down. By the time we walk back with him to his cabin the rest of them are also sound asleep. Needless to say, neither threat nor punitive issue is involved. Sometimes, of course, the situation is complicated by the fact that the particular youngster's behavior is a purposive one. A skillful "ringleader" can keep a whole group in turmoil. This may reach a point at which his separation from the others may seem the easiest way out.

4. *Need for a face-saving device*

Youngsters sometimes work themselves up into stages of intoxicated hilarity which may have to be checked. It may so happen that a particular youngster may be ready to give in but cannot possibly afford to do so openly without losing face or being considered a cowardly traitor to the cause of group mischief or a "teacher's pet." In that case, taking him out for an extra talk actually saves face with the group, and also makes it easy for him, in friendly contact with the adult, to accept the meaning of our stoppage without being "on the spot." The group, too, can "give." Had he stayed there, they would have been ashamed to "budge first" to adult demands, and would have feared his subsequent reproaches of being "yellow." Such youngsters are often even grateful for being "bounced." In fact, they sometimes invite that solution when they can't help themselves in any other way.

5. Limit rub-in

Occasionally, taking a youngster out of the group may be needed not because his behavior is so extreme or can't be stopped at all but because the issue around which it happens demands a clearcut demonstration of limits by the adult in charge. If, after ample tolerance of deviation, a certain really important issue, as, for instance, not stepping on the gas pedal of a moving car, has been made quite clear, the youngster who right then and there dares the adult by doing it again does endanger the morale built up around the issue just before if he can continue the tabued behavior unchallenged. Occasionally, other forms of "limit rub-in," like stopping and talking it over, have already been used up or are unusable at the time because of excitement. Then it may be wise to draw a clear line by temporarily removing from the scene the youngster who cannot accept even the minimum condition of a certain vital issue. Needless to say, all the adult has to demonstrate is that "this behavior will not happen after we have made that rule." There is no need to become angry, punitive, or show personal feeling against the wrongdoer at all. On the contrary, the more the firmness of "guarantee of behavioral stoppage" is insisted on, the more salutary an affectionate dealing with the offender and ample interview follow-up individually and on the group basis will be.

So much for the "bouncing" side of the picture. We had better remember the adjective which we tied as an absolute condition to this procedure: no matter why we think we need it, removal from the scene still has to be *antiseptic*. That means, while solving a temporary problem on the one hand, it must by no means be allowed to create damage somewhere else, or to interfere with our real clinical goal. In order to be sure of that, we might list the risks we invariably take with the use of such a technique:

CAUTIONS AND COUNTERINDICATIONS:

1. Protection of rapport

We wouldn't want "removal from the scene of a problem" to destroy the personal rapport we have so carefully fostered with the individual child or the group. This means that we want to be sure that the child knows we are only stopping behavior which we couldn't have stopped otherwise, or that we are trying to help him avoid worse trouble. Or, at least, if he doesn't know right now, we want to be sure that we can easily "interpret to him" by word or deed soon after what it was all about. By no means must this technique of removal from a problem scene be confused by him or us with punishment, revenge, or rejection. The same is true for the group. Watching an adult exclude a child from a situation sometimes gives a peculiar tint to his group leadership which would be a bad price to have to pay. For this reason, we relegated this role only to the top personnel during the first months at Pioneer House, so that the group-leading counselor or housemother would not be loaded with the counteraggression brought forth by such incidents. It is essential, therefore, that all such situations be kept entirely free of anger, aggression, and, especially, the implication of disapproval of the particular child as a person. It is amazing to see how well a staff can learn to keep the "tenor" of an incident hygienically clean. If, at any time—with the exception of moments of extreme physical danger—we could feel that the disturbance in rapport caused by bouncing would have been too serious for a particular child, we would rather have had the mess produced by his onthrust than touch a technique as costly as this. We were encouraged, however, by the sight of otherwise quite hostile children soon catching on to the difference between such "control interference on a strictly behavioral level" and real punishment or rejection by us.

2. Effect on other children and the group

Removal of a child may be quite an interference in the group process. On the most simple level: you can't bounce the baseball pitcher if you have no substitute without facing an activity frustration of the whole group. On a more complicated level: removal of one youngster often would have brought on "solidarity identification" with him by the rest, or would have produced "fear of loss of love" in some of the other children, even though the particular child to be bounced could have taken it perfectly well in his stride. In such cases, it is obviously counterindicated. Sometimes the effect of too much of the wrong type of removal from the group has a sort of "characterological" ill effect on a group. Seeing Joe being bounced—which *he* may understand while *they* interpret it as "being punished"—may give them the feeling that the "black sheep" is out, and may on that basis produce an anxious overidentification with the adult and increased rule obedience but at the price of lowered toleration leeway for their own group members. This would be deplorable, indeed, and it means that we cannot bounce a child no matter how well he would react to it if we aren't sure we can also interpret to the group what "really" happens in such a case.

3. Considerations of status effects

Removing a child from the scene of a group activity also may do something to his "role" in the group, and that has to be as carefully considered as other factors. This works in two opposite directions. Removal from the group may be "face-losing" under certain conditions, and may invite scapegoat formation or at least lowering of prestige in the child's subsequent social life. Or, removal from the group, especially in the case of a child who has great skill in exploiting such situations for his own benefit, may be very status-increasing, may create the halo of a "hero in a subversive cause" around the child's person. Neither of the two effects is desirable, and either one of them would be sufficient reason to look for another way out.

4. Necessity for total antisepsis

One of the severest cautions—and often counterindications—against this technique of "antiseptic bouncing," lies in the question: can we manage it well, *are we equipped to do it antiseptically?* For, far from being a simple device, it is one of the most complicated maneuvers which can be carried out. The following are the *conditions*, without which we are not in a position to try this technique at all:

a) POSTSITUATIONAL PROGRAMMING AND CONTROL. It isn't enough to "bounce" a child from the situation which is too hard for him to handle. You also have to ask yourself: what is he going to do? You can't send him out of the room when you know this means he will run away, find a good excuse to mess up the other children's room, or cower in a dark corner with an anxiety attack. We have to know what kind of situation or activity a youngster needs in order to get over the immediate after-effect of his being bounced, or what kind of activity he should engage in, provided his bouncing was so unnoticeable to him that the removal itself is not an issue. In our case, that means: some adult has to be with him—preferably the best-related one. A place has to be selected which avoids the previous overstimulation and is either conducive to calming down or offers substitute activities. The activity has to be of such a nature as to fit the youngster's momentary state of mind and emotion without being considered a coveted privilege by the rest of the group at that time. If he is excited, we may need to stay with him until there is restored in him whatever control system he has available as his "normal self." If an exciting scene has preceded the problem, the place where he calms down should be away from any interference or noise from the activity from which he has been removed, without being negatively status-loaded. We cannot list all the innumerable special considerations here. Suffice it to say: unless we know what we can do with him, and who will do it, "bouncing," no matter how well indicated, is ruled out as a technique. We hardly have to emphasize the need for personnel which this involves. It is obvious that the group leader cannot leave his involvements with the rest of the group, and elaborate policies and precautions have to be made all down the line. Removal from the scene is possible only in the best-staffed and most amply staffed treatment home. By the way, whoever remains with the group must also know that he may have to pick up whatever effect a child's removal may have had on the rest of the group. This may involve group or individual interview, program restructuring, and a variety of other measures.

b) HANDLING POSTSITUATIONAL AFFECT. The very fact of removal itself is often what the particular youngster needs special help on. A wide variety of policies and techniques may have to be planned, depending on the case and treatment phase in question. Sometimes it will be necessary that the child's favorite counselor be freed to stay with him for a while. He will then gauge carefully just which approach would best assuage excitement as well as "interpret" the realism in the situation to the youngster. Timing of staying out of or being reintroduced into the group has to be handled with great care. We paid a bitter price for any "too late" or "too soon" mistakes along that line and could write many pages on this issue alone. In other cases, it is very important that not a counselor but a person representative of the "overgroup" policies of the institution itself be with the child.

It was often essential, for our strategy, for instance, that the director of the home be tipped off invisibly and do the removing, seemingly without the cooperation from the youngster's natural counselor at the time. He could then spend time wearing down the youngster's emotional stir-up around the issue in time-consuming interviews in his office, or even in a tantrum that could not be escaped. At other times, the strategy was for the counselor to bring things to a head by telling a particular youngster that, since nothing seemed to get across, he would have to ask somebody else's help or advice. Sometimes, a sort of "free floating" policy of "unnoticeable pickup" or even encouraged "self-bouncing" was instituted. The housemother or somebody else might be tipped off to wander around, engage a child who was close to the breaking point in an activity, or challenge him to help her in her room at some chore, or what not. After the earlier trial and error, we found it helpful to take the housemother out of direct activity leadership programs at certain times and use her as a "self-bouncing" device instead. After the children had come home from school and were engaged in some program the strain of which we would expect to get too much for some, she would stay in her room, engaged in writing letters, sewing, etc. The children would know they could at any time leave the ongoing activity if it became too threatening for them, and, without losing face, wander into the housemother's quarters. She would get them there in all stages and moods. Some would really be like "self-referrals," who, when coming close to a blow-up or breakdown, would simply wander off to chat or sit with her, or fiddle in her desk drawers for a while, in order to rejoin the group spontaneously when they felt ready to do so. Others would throw a tantrum in the group, but, before being bounced, would wander off to the housemother's room in order to vent their gripe, in bitter complaints, against the counselor, the directors, the house policies. Volumes could again be written about the varying ways in which such situations have to be handled and the possibilities which such arrangements involve. Sometimes a youngster would really be removed from the group game, but would be "dumped" on the housemother to be taken care of, rather than have the original counselor or the director stay with him. To make a long story short, the question of just what is done to make the best out of a bouncing situation clinically is a most relevant one.

Only with all cautions guaranteed can it be considered as a valid stoppage technique at all.

c) Exposure to Total Treatment Home Climate. The most important condition for the use of bouncing, though, is a surrounding atmosphere of happy adult acceptedness as a basic requirement. For, whatever we say, exclusion of a child from a situation or activity is still a heavy "interference" in his life, and is experienced as such. Only if the rest of the life space is soaked with affection, understanding, and acceptance, can the youngster learn how to have his momentary frustration-aggression soaked up by the general atmosphere. This means: in order to afford a technique like "bouncing" as an efficient behavioral stopper, the whole world of "treatment home atmosphere" has to be built up first. Without this framework in which to happen, any individual act of bouncing becomes invariably another source of aggression, hatred, hostility, or evidence of the "rejective" character of the surrounding universe.

With all these cautions given, however, we can firmly say this: strategically planned and well-handled, the removal of a child from a too confusing problem scene can be a very expedient, but also clinically clean, device. It is *not* true, under those conditions, that it destroys rapport. It can even become one of the most valuable tools in the total job of "reality interpretation."

At camp, as well as in Pioneer House, we made frequent use of this technique. We soon lost our original clinical softness about it, but also learned how to respect its intricacies and how to study them.

Sometimes we used it simply because we had made bad mistakes to begin with and now needed it to avoid worse mistakes to follow. Sometimes we used it very wisely and with a good deal of pre-planning as one of our aids in the long-range job of ego support. Sometimes, we feel, we couldn't have taken on the job we did with the children who hate so much without knowing that this device was usable, provided that we knew what we were doing. The following illustrations may be expressive of our planning as well as our plight.

In the sleeping room of Henry, Andy, and Joe there was a great deal of difficulty tonight. Joe was belligerent toward the counselor and kept calling her "pussy face," and opening his window to try to get on top of the sun porch although it was freezing cold. Andy, seduced into great excitement by this behavior of Joe's, began to call out "Pussy face, hee haw" and exposed himself. Henry carefully exploited the whole situation, skillfully keeping it going by egging the other two on whenever there was a lull in the activities. Several times I went into the room to quiet them down, and the counselor would start reading again, but no sooner would she start than either (a) Joe would begin to call out "pussy face" and go for the window again or (b) Andy would take up the same theme in his abandoned erotic way or (c) in the absence of either event Henry would skillfully lead one or both of them into the behavior all over again, just by little signals like snorting or laughing in inappropriate moments. I finally went in and sat with them while the counselor tried to read. At any point I could have threatened to call off the story but didn't want to use this device unless absolutely necessary because later they would misuse this paranoiacally: "You bastards never let us have a story and that's why we won't quiet down, etc., etc." My physical presence in the room had enough effect to quiet them for the remainder of the story, but, as soon as the counselor left, they started getting restless all over again. So I stayed in the room. No open break was made by either Henry or Joe for a few moments and finally Andy, unable to restrain himself, resurrected the "pussy face" theme all over again. This time Joe was the seducee. He jumped out of bed, ran around the room wildly, and then dived under the bed, from where I had to retrieve him. Andy was by this time so wildly excited all over again that I decided to remove him from the room because he had "refueled" the contagion chain by his outburst and was still keeping it up and I thought the other two might now have a chance to quiet down without him. I removed him from the room and took him downstairs to sit with me in the living room. As soon as I went over to him and said "Let's go," he began to screech that I was being unfair, calling me "mother fucker" and "bastard," to which I did not reply. Instead I urged him to quiet down so that he could return to bed. Almost by the time we hit the staircase he stopped screeching and said, "O.K., let me walk, I'll go myself," so I held his hand loosely and, when we got downstairs, he sat down quietly on the couch beside me, making no effort to run away. In about twenty-five minutes he became sleepy and I asked him if he thought he could handle himself if he went back. He mumbled, "O.K." So I escorted him back to bed. The other two were practically asleep by now and Andy dropped off shortly afterwards. (Entry: 2/1/47, Fritz Redl)

Tonight at dinner most of the group were in a wild hypnomanic state. Danny was on his way to one of his euphoric outbursts of aggressiveness at the table in which, the more he eats, the more he breaks and smashes things. Larry was aggressively excited, too, with a lot of wild baby talk and smearing of food plus wild giggling. Joe and Sam were full of obscenity and were poking at their neighbors on either side (Andy and Harry), making great demands and criticisms about the menu and cursing the housemother and cook. Andy was hyperactively involved in all of this and jumped around, threw food, and imitated both Joe and Sam incessantly. Henry was the coolest of the lot and enjoyed the acting out of the others as though it were a special side show for his benefit, which, on the part of Sam, Joe, and Andy, it was, at least in part, since he is the undisputed leader of the group. He registered his enjoyment and approval by appreciative and supportive remarks, also through open encouragement of their antics as well as by joining in at safe moments when he couldn't be accused of starting it. For instance, after they called the cook a "pigfucker" because there was no chili on tonight's menu, he reflected appreciatively, "Yeah, the goddam bastard—at home we got chili twice a week." At another time, when Andy was temporarily out of food to throw, he shoved a carrot in his hand. Finally I banged on the table for emphasis and said that the meal would stop right here for a while if they couldn't all quiet down. For a brief two or three minutes this had some effect, but soon Henry let out guffaws and said his favorite, curiously unobjectionable, but arousing word: "Horsefeathers." Now obviously, "horsefeathers" is a very mild expletive that doesn't even rate in the lowest order of Pioneer House or any other kind of obscenity. But tonight it was enough. Backed by Henry's high prestige and the group's perception of his signal acceptance of their previously wild behavior, it started the ball rolling again. Almost immediately Andy began acting up again, and couldn't refrain from throwing a piece of bread across the table at Larry, who started to wail and complain that now Andy was throwing stuff at him and he couldn't eat, etc. Joe and Sam, too, started their routine all over again, picking up pieces of food, saying "Shit" disgustedly, and throwing it down on the table. It became quite clear that Henry was with great skill and finagling keeping the whole thing going and that, with him there, I didn't have a chance to quiet the group even though what they were doing was much more objectionable than anything he was doing. So I determined to watch for his next openly supportive move and then bounce him. It was when he picked up the water and motioned to Andy saying, "Hey, look at this, Andy," and then set it down again. Andy began to pick it up. I got up and quickly took Henry by the arm and led him out of the room, saying, "That will just about be enough for tonight." He struggled and tried to free himself and said, "What the hell am I doing, you dirty bastard?" to which I did not answer, and marched him into the office where I sat down with him, telling him that I wanted him to cool off. He was indignant and accused me of being unfair and said, "Those other guys are raising hell and I get blamed." I pointed out to him that he was keeping it going and he said, "I'm not to blame for what they do." So I said, "How about shoving that carrot in Andy's hand before, huh?" To this he replied, "Well, the goddam fool didn't have to throw it, did he?" I said, "Listen, you know darn well that you were looking for every chance to keep those guys, especially Andy, Joe, and Sam acting wild, as long as you yourself did not get in too deep. Then after I got them quiet for a few minutes you started it off again with your 'horsefeathers' crack and then picked up the water jug, showed it to Andy, and expected him to pick it up, too, and probably heave it. Now we don't have to take that and we won't. If the other guys are wild and out of control themselves, that's too bad and we don't like that either, but we won't have one guy keeping it going just for a joke." To all of this he didn't say much but got sullen and disgusted and finally asked what kind of joint this was where a guy couldn't even eat his supper. I said I wasn't eating either and was trying to work this out with him. Then I offered to set him up with the rest of his supper in the living room if he thought he could handle himself. Muttering assent, he went out with me to the living room where he ate the rest of his meal in that black silence which we have come to recognize as a typical Henry sulk which just has to be waited out. The group, on the other hand, except for a few isolated outbursts which quickly petered out, got through the rest of the meal fairly well. (Entry: 12/13/46, David Wineman)

14. Physical Restraint

The "children who hate" and at the same time show severe ego disturbances will invariably be given to violent fits of rage, accompanied by a total loss of control, from time to time. They will hit, bite, kick, throw anything within their reach, spit, scream, swear, and accompany all this by disjointed and meaningless movements of lashing out at things or people "without apparent reason." In short, their organism will show a totality of destructiveness with a totality of abandon comparable only to the fits of rage of the little baby in the crib. Such behavior may turn up "spontaneously" from "within" at any time, or it may be the reaction to something in their surroundings that "brought it on." What "brought it on" may only feebly be related to what they express. It is sufficient to have them frightened, insecure, reminded of an old trauma, or to have them exposed to any one of the previously described situations of "excitement, temptation challenge, group psychological intoxication."

The worst thing about it, however, is that, in such moments, the child also loses—temporarily—all relationship he has had before to the adults around him and the ego is suddenly stripped of all channels of communication. This makes us powerless. Neither fear of consequences or of law, nor authority, nor respect, seems to have any effect, and even the ties of love and friendship, where they have been developed, are out of commission. In fact, this is the hardest part to take: the adult so proud of his successes in establishing a "good relationship" of some sort with the "children who hate" will suddenly see it gone completely. The child will lash out at his most beloved counselor as he would at the most hated policeman. Just who says what doesn't seem to count any more, at least in the more extreme stages.

The implications of this for the practitioner are simple: such cases sometimes constitute an emergency. If, for a variety of reasons, the behavior involved cannot be afforded or is counterindicated for clinical reasons, only one thing will stop it: interference through action.

Assuming we are stuck with it and cannot, for a change, allow the youngster to run through the twenty- to fifty-minute orgy of disorganized attack, we may have to hold him physically, either to remove him from the scene of danger and involvement, or to prevent him from doing physical damage to others or himself.

For the "progressive educator" and, especially, the clinician trained in psychotherapy, this is a hard lump to swallow. He has as many feelings of hesitation and guilt about being "forced" to use physical restrictions as the naïve and punitive educator has temptations to be lured into acts of triumphant revenge. The only comparable situation the normal educator and parent ever get into with the normal child may happen when a youngster is very young: we can easily imagine a most loving and progressive mother dashing out after her two-year-old who is just chasing after a cat with abandon and comes close to running off the curb into traffic. No matter how unpunitive, she will certainly have to stop him, if by no other means than by picking him up quickly and carrying him back into the house, even though he may be kicking, biting, hitting, screaming, in the sudden frustration and panic of his interrupted pursuit of the wrongly located goal.[3]

The difference between the reasonable and the punitive mother will not lie in what she does in such an emergency, but it will be clearly visible in how she does it and what she does afterwards. We want to make it quite clear that what we are calling "physical restraint" here has nothing whatever to do with "physical punishment." Since there is so much confusion about this in lay thinking and even in the theories of professionals, we had better say a word about this. We are against the application of physical punishment in any form whatsoever under any circumstances. Even for the normal child we reject the idea that physical pain will "teach" the youngster, that the entrance to the character of a child leads through the epidermis of his hindquarters, or that physical pain will solve things by giving a child the chance to pay for his sins and thus end his guilt feelings. The implication of physical punishment is always, no matter how mild a form is being used, that physical violence will "change" a child, or will motivate him toward a more social approach to life, people, and values. Sometimes it is admittedly meant to be a "behavior stopper" only, but even then we can show the enormous price we pay for such a technique in terms of its poisonous by-products, even should the surface goal be achieved.

No, this is not what we have in mind. In all our work with the children who hate, in our club projects, at Camp, at Pioneer House, no adult will ever strike a child, nor will a child ever be sent to somebody for punishment of a physical type.

We had, however, to become experts in physical restraint. The difference is easy to see. Seizing a child in order to take a knife out of his hand in an emergency, moving him quite forcibly to another room away from the scene of hysterical involvement, or even holding him in an extreme temper outburst, is a clear-cut job of antiseptic manipulation. There is not even an inkling of punitiveness involved. The adult can afford no counteraggression nor an ounce more of counterforce than is necessary to achieve the goal of re-

[3] An interesting and important contribution is found in an article by Milton Wexler, "The Structural Problem in Schizophrenia: Therapeutic Implications," *The International Journal of Psychoanalysis*, Vol. XXXII, 1951, pp. 1-10, in which he shows with great clarity the ego-supportive implications of protecting schizophrenic patients against the expression of their violent impulses through the use of a variety of limiting techniques, including physical restraint.

straint. He has to remain calm, friendly, affectionate. He will not respond to the wild lashings with arms and tongue which the child indulges in with counterviolence or rebuke nor will he, at that level of loss of control by the child, enter any argument the child's delusional system may suggest. He will, rather, continue to talk soothingly to the child in a low voice, using primarily content-empty wordage meant to calm the waves of excitement. He will answer the child's screamed insults by a quiet, "Take it easy, kid, everything is O.K. Nothing to worry about. Everything will be all right again just as soon as you calm down. You will be over it any time now, just take it easy, nothing to worry about, everything is all right." Details may vary from case to case. Sometimes quiet waiting it out is to be preferred. At no time will the adult "take the child seriously" in his wild behavior—that is the very strategy of it. He will neither threaten nor blame, encourage nor insult, lure nor bribe. The attitude he tries to convey, put into a mixture of the child's language and our own, would sound like this:

"Listen, kid, this is nuts. There is not the slightest reality reason for you to act that way. You are clearly off your noodle. We like you. There is nothing to fear, but there is also nothing to gain by such behavior. You didn't get us mad by it, for we know you can't help it right now. But we sure hope this will reduce as time goes on. We aren't holding it against you, either. You can't 'make up for it.' You needn't; this behavior is too crazy and unreasonable for any such thought. We want only one thing: get it over with, snap back into your more reasonable self, so we can communicate with you again. Right now you don't even see who is with you doing what. Remember? This is not an ogre out of the past or a figment of your delusions. This is me, the guy who likes you and is here to help. Right now he is helping you only in one way, by taking over where your own dopey ego left its business undone. Since you can't block that screwy behavior from within, I am taking over until your ego is back on its job again. That's all. No hard feelings. Don't think of it even. It's all water over the dam. You will soon be able to do without this screwball stuff."

Needless to say, we do not use such words during an attack, though we might convey some such philosophy to the child and his group later, when their ego is back in commission again, in a post-situational interview. But we do whatever we can to convey this basic approach to such fits during, before, and after, as a general philosophy of attitude toward them in the whole institution.

It is amazing how this policy has paid off. By "not taking it seriously" even in its obvious destructive intent we have been able to pinpoint the irrationality of such behavior to the youngster's ego in relatively short periods of time. Nothing that makes any sense can be done during the attack anyway, since during that time the child's ego so obviously has gone AWOL. So we can try to prepare the ground most strategically for our subsequent interpretation of such behavior in terms of its irrationality and senselessness through "postsituational reality rub-in." We do not *want* the child to think he will be rejected or punished for this type of act. This would play right into the hands of his pathology. We want him to "turn away from such behavior himself in the disgust of a rational personality," and to identify with our approach to it as something that has no place in his life. Only thus do we get the cooperation of part of his ego in the long run, in our attempt to help it kick this pathology out of its system. As long as the ego of the child, after the attack, can view such behavior as though it were part of its regular equipment and might really influence us the way it wants to, or lure us into "taking it seriously," it is still preserving its pathology defense. The job of "re-educating" the child to this different approach to his own symptom, and of getting the same idea across to the whole group, is of course an elaborate and time-consuming one, and happens not during but between attacks. In order for it to succeed, all our behavior during the attack, however, has to be foolproof, so that there is nothing on our side to back up the youngster's own triumphant, self-commiserating, or paranoid interpretations of the event. Our behavior during the attack is in no way dictated by humanitarianism or sentimentality: it is simply the logical conclusion of a concept of "total warfare on the youngster's pathology," of a consistent "strategic" approach.

We might as well admit that it is not easy for the adult to remain consistent and to "take it" under the impact of hatred and aggression, of blows and scratches that really hurt, of narcissistic hurt caused by the loss of relationship and power over our patient during the attack, and of natural disgust with pain, counteraggression, and simple fatigue. We are happy, though, about the universality with which staff can learn not only the strategic importance of a nonpunitive attitude during periods of physical restraint—a sometimes somewhat "saintly" attitude to their own predicament—but also a certain skill in predicting timing, form, intensity, and duration of such attacks in the children, and about how they can learn to gauge their own behavior during the attack accordingly.

Frankly, it took us a while to get over being somewhat "ashamed" of having to hold a child, until we finally discovered the full impact of the real strategic issue behind it. We soon learned that only some of these extreme situations are the result of "something we missed" and could have been prevented at the time by wiser programming or by a quicker predictive hunch. We soon saw how some of them were not only unavoidable but most salutary indeed. Going through these attacks of the children in an antiseptically clean way would enhance our total treatment strategy tremendously, and what we suffered while going through all this was amply repaid by the wonderful usability of such strategically prepared ground for our techniques of the "clinical exploitation of life events" of which we shall hear later. The real problem lies, of course, in the obtaining of relevant criteria for the question not only of how to handle "holding" with a particular child so that it remains antiseptic, but of just how to know when such an interference technique is indicated, or counterindicated. We have to forfeit the fascination of developing details about this here. It may suffice to point back to the previous section on "antiseptic bouncing."

With some modifications, the basic points to be made are the same. In the use of physical restraint, too, we shall want to think of such criteria as these: physical danger, irritation through the group psychological scene, uncheckable contagion effect, need for face-saving devices, limit rub-in. And here, too, counterindications will lie in such factors as these: personal rapport disturbance, effect on other children and the group, considerations of status effect. Just as in the other case, the antisepsis of this technique does not only lie in what we do during the attack, but contains items like these: postsituational programming and control, postsituational handling by the adult, exposure to total treatment home climate, and so forth.

Space allows us to single out only one of these items for special mention: the problem of "therapeutic rapport." It seems that especially the psychoanalytically trained therapist has compunctions about this point. "But what does this do to your rapport with the youngsters?" he may ask. "Any such scene must wreck whatever you have built up in the meantime, for good." Fortunately, we can assure our reader that this is not so at all. The reasons for this are too detailed to be dealt with here. Suffice it to list just a few of them: Our children are different from the usual middle-class neurotic to begin with. Our therapeutic role also contains a different mixture of ingredients than is planned for the straight "interview in my office" design. The very skill involved in handling these situations "antiseptically" and having them followed up by post-situational program and life situations as well as by special interview work, the interweaving of all such events into a total life design of a treatment home, the very walls of which breathe a consistent "treatment atmosphere" and every person in which, from the janitor through the psychiatrist to the cook, meets the children with the same policy of strategic affection—all this makes it possible to maintain and develop the type of rapport we need, in spite of events as basically "untherapeutic looking" as these fits. The "rapport-destroying effect" of such incidents is unavoidable only if they are badly handled or happen in a punitive atmosphere. Under our conditions, the ill effects of these situations last little longer than the attacks and their mood hangovers themselves, times during which the child's ego would be unrelated anyway.

There is one more thing which we would like to stress: it is important for a treatment home to take these things seriously and to give much time and thought to such "superficial" seeming incidents as the holding of a child during a tantrum, rather than to consider these things as "unavoidable accidents" basically not on the agenda of our clinical task. We view every phase of our life, even the ones described here, as a challenge to our total strategy, and deserving of all our attention as heavily as every other part of our treatment design.

Just before "lights out," the boys and their counselor were deciding which bed story they would want her to read tonight. Mike demanded a new story. Larry insisted, and the rest of the group in his sleeping room agreed, that they were supposed to continue the story they had been reading. Thereupon, Mike, in all defiance of reality, began insisting teasingly that his story was the one they *were* reading last night. For some reason this infuriated Larry, who said Mike was lying and was going to spoil everybody's fun. Finally, Larry was so vehement about it that he challenged Mike to a fight. I tried to talk Larry out of it since it was just before "lights out" and we have an inflexible rule: no fights for any reason before "lights out." Larry, however, had worked himself up to such a state of temper about it that, heedless of my insistence that he could not fight Mike now, he flew at him and tried to wrestle him off the bed. So I had no alternative but to take him out of the sleeping room. He immediately put up a tremendous resistance, kicking, biting, and scratching. He then became completely rigid and his arms and legs stiffened. His facial expression was distorted with a staring straight ahead look; meanwhile he was screeching at me that I wouldn't get him "no further" (we were at the head of the stairs leading to the lower floor of the house), which he backed up by getting an adhesive hold on the floor and adjacent wall, to which he stuck like a stubborn tree toad. He seemed to be getting more and more terrified by the tempest of rage he was unleashing and yet completely incapable of giving it up. While holding him with one arm I began to pat his head and soothe him, saying I wanted him only to quiet down for a while and then he could go back to bed. I wasn't mad at him and was holding him only because he got so wild against Mike when I couldn't allow it. Finally, as he seemed to lose some of his rigidity and struggle I said, "Come on now, you're all overheated and upset. How about us going into the kitchen and getting a glass of water and talking this whole thing over, huh? What's the sense of keeping up all this fighting with me?" And, to show my good faith in the deal I was proposing, I took my hands off him completely. He got up immediately, went into the kitchen with me, and converted to loud verbalizing about how "he wasn't gonna take this stuff from Mike no more, no sir, boy." He was very responsive to my further attempts to reduce his upset and finally went off to bed quietly enough in twenty minutes or so. (Entry: 8/3/47, David Wineman)

At dinner tonight, the whole group was wild and upset. There was much obscenity and Danny, sitting next to me, got wilder and wilder as the meal progressed, piling food higher and higher on his plate (and inside him too!) and yelling anal terms all over the place. When dessert finally rolled around, he had just about worked himself up to his highest pitch and, refusing to wait for anyone else to take anything, began to grab for everything in sight. I interfered and said, "Wait a minute, we have to have turns at taking dessert. Let's wait 'til it reaches us. Wait until it comes to you." This was too much frustration for him. He jumped up, shouting curses, and straightaway threw one of his temper tantrums, throwing things, swearing, hitting out wildly, ready to run amuck. I had to take him by the arm and lead him into the office. In the office, he began to yell and kept it up for a full thirty minutes, at the same time trying to bite me, kicking my shins, where he drew blood, struggling all the while, of course, to free himself. He also scratches like a sharp-clawed cat and he marked my wrists up quite a bit. All in all, he is very hard to hold for some thirty minutes of this. He shouted: "Mother fucker, bastard, cock-sucker, dirty bastard cop, you're hurting me, leggo my arm, you fucker, I said LEGGO my arm, you bastard, you fucker, dirty sonofabitch. I wanna go home, you have no right to keep me here youse fuckers. Yeah everybody else gets to eat except me, cocksucker, bastard, I wanna go home, I wanna go now, right now, ouch, you're hurting my arm, let go my arm, cocksucker, I said LEGGO MY ARM, goddam fuck'n Pioneer House, I want to call my mother, go home, etc., etc., etc." Through all this I held him firmly and answered all of his insults with constant assurance that I would let him go as soon as he quieted down. "O.K., Danny, take it easy, come on now let's quiet down . . . I'll let you go as soon as you quiet down . . . I'll let you call your mother but you have to quiet down first . . . If you would stop yank-ing like that, your arm wouldn't hurt . . . I have to hold you when you're upset . . . I'm not mad at you but I have to hold you until you quiet down . . . O.K. now, take it easy . . . Come on now, easy . . . Quiet down . . . Stop trying to kick over the desk and knock the typewriter down on me . . . Quiet down . . . You see I have to hold you when you're this wild . . ." Gradually, after thirty minutes, he began to stop screaming at me and trying to hurt me, and then I loosened my hold on him, and he sat down on a chair and glowered at me for a full ten minutes. I just sat there with him; he was no-where near the talking stage. Finally he said, "I'll be O.K. now if you let me out," and I said, "O.K.," and we both left the office to-gether. He asked if he could have his dessert now and I said "Sure, they probably saved it for you. If not, we'll get you a substitute." (Entry: 12/12/46, Fritz Redl)

15. Permission and "Authoritative Verbot"

It may puzzle the reader to find these two techniques listed under the same heading, since they obviously seem to belong at opposite ends of the same line. Open permission as an encourager of be-havior seems to be the exact reverse of "authoritative Verbot," by which we mean a sharp and clear statement that this piece of behavior is intolerable. For the practitioner who undergoes training in the daily practice of survival with disturbed children, either one of the two techniques certainly deserves a section of its own, and their technical ramifications are enormous. For the purpose of describing their potentials in such an abbreviated list as this one is meant to be, they might well be handled in the same section.

When we refer to "permission" here, we do not mean the larger issue of a policy of "permissiveness," its clinical advantages and limitations, which we discuss in other places.[4] We use the term here to refer to a specific act on the side of the adult which is meant to influence surface behavior only right here and now. The use which this technique of "permission" can be given falls into three categories:

1. We sometimes openly "permit" in order to *start a piece of behavior* which we want and which might otherwise have been blocked, or at least in order *to take the sting of anxiety or guilt* out of it. This use of permission is well known. It may be openly verbal, or implied in the adult's attitude or general policy. In arts and crafts, a child, for instance, may have hesitations about getting to work on a wood gun he planned to make, because of the fear that the inadequate results might draw criticism from the group leader. By openly encouraging and "permitting" enthusiastic experimentation without too much worry about whether materials are wasted or not, the group leader gets the youngster going full force, and allows him to enjoy his exploit without the compunctions of perfectionist guilt or shame.

2. The technique of "permitting" can, however, also be used for the opposite end, a fact which seems to be less well known. By "permitting" something openly, we sometimes really stop it faster than by any other technique. This effect is usually limited to the case where a piece of behavior was meant to irritate, antagonize, or try out the adult, or to express an attitude of rebellious defiance. If permitted openly, such an exploit loses all its attraction to the child, and the activity is stopped right away, with none of the accompanying "frustration-aggression" which would have been tied to a more direct form of limitation. In the beginning, for instance, we could often watch the youngsters "surreptitiously" picking something up that belonged to the adult, just waiting for a response of fury and a Verbot. Instead, when we could afford that, we made it clear that we didn't mind at all: "You can try out that lighter, as long as you just watch out that you don't break it." The youngster would soon lose interest and put it back where it belonged.

3. The most fascinating use of permission as a technique of con-

4 See p. 58.

trol, however, is made when it is applied not to stop an activity we couldn't prevent except by extreme means anyway, but to "take the triumphant rebellious sting" out of it, and through that *keep it on a manageable level*. In this way, the technique does not bring about absolute stoppage of the behavior, but decontaminates it of its negativistic sideline, and at the same time keeps it within tolerable limits. To use a crude illustration: a youngster may be engaged in a milder form of name calling or some semi-aggressive "horse-play" directed toward the adult. By humorously permitting a certain level of it, or even entering into it up to a certain point in mock action, the "triumphant sting" is taken out of it, and it soon peters out without swelling up to the intensity it would have reached had it been left alone, and without one's having to wrestle with the secondary by-products of sharper interference forms.

During the evening program tonight, we were doing some finger painting and water colors. Bill was rambling around and, in a rather subtle way, trying to lure Andy out of the activity. But the latter was quite fascinated by the effects he was getting with his water colors and so was quite impervious to Bill's seductive wiles. I suggested to Bill that I would be glad to help him mix his colors and that the other guys were getting a lot of fun out of working with the paints. Why didn't he come over? But, no, he didn't want to and so the pattern dragged on for about another fifteen minutes or so, with Bill finally making open overtures to Andy: "Hey, Andy, let's go out and shake some cherries off the tree," or "Hey, Andy, c'mon let's go out and sell some flowers to that old lady next door and make us some money." But Andy adamantly stuck to the painting and ignored Bill, partly now getting some sadistic gratification out of thwarting him. Bill, in final desperation, began to chase around the living room and jump off and onto the couch and then, crouching up on the fireplace mantle, jumped from there onto a nearby lounge chair, giggling and whooping. He now began to displace against me the aggression meant for Andy because of the latter's ignoring of him. This behavior was against house rules which discourage the use of the living room for such activities but I felt at this moment that an open command to stop would play even more into Bill's hands. So I walked from the dining room, where we were doing the painting, into the living room and said, "Oh boy, look at the stunt man. I guess you found yourself something to do, didn't you?" This was rather unexpected, for Bill had thought I would interfere, perhaps even chase him. But he went along with me and said, "Hey, Barbara, catch me" and jumped from the mantle into my arms. I held him for a minute and he brushed my cheeks with his open hand in a mock slap, saying "Hi ya, mammy," and then leaped down to the floor, now appearing to have had a mood change for the better. The others still being absorbed in their painting, I danced a little jig with Bill and then he had the idea of turning the record player on to listen to some of their new records. I went back to the finger and water color painters in the next room. (Entry: 5/13/47, Barbara Smith)

This evening the group had, as a program innovation, a "picnic supper" in my apartment. It was the first time they had ever been there, and they were quite boisterous and excited, but still in a somewhat positive way. The minute they hit the place they were all over it like a blitz. They got into every conceivable nook and cranny; they examined my closets, the bathroom, my wardrobe. They had to use my hair tonics and handle my shaving equipment. They poured over my desk, every drawer of which they yanked open and shut and went through like a horde of frantic termites. They breezed through my pipe collection and carried it triumphantly like battle trophies into the living room. They were touching, feeling, smelling, in a mad outpouring of tactile and other sensory investigations of every single item that could be dislodged and moved. My attitude was one of deliberate *carte blanche*, realizing that I had made a mistake in having them in that early in the game to begin with, and now wouldn't stand a chance to prevent serious collective aggression against my domicile if I took a restraining approach. And, of course, I didn't want to have this visit end up in a scene of group bouncing, either. The funny thing is, this very desperate effort of mine to "permit" and even enjoy what was going on anyway seemed to have a really restraining effect. They handled literally dozens of fragile and breakable items—little jade elephants out of a collection I have and curio pieces of china and glass. My guitar and accordion changed hands dozens of times without anyone ever deliberately mishandling them. Nothing was broken during the whole evening. Yet these same children had, during the previous thirteen days at Pioneer House, destroyed ninety per cent of the toys and other equipment. I am now convinced that real damage would have been done had I been frightened by our previous experiences and tried to lock up or protect my possessions with open effort. Had I tried any one of the other ranges of interference techniques, the evening would have ended in disciplinary mayhem with tantrums being thrown all over the place. Not that I want to pretend, in retrospect, that the idea itself of bringing them to my house that early in the game was too well timed. (Entry: 12/14/46, Fritz Redl)

It is important, of course, to remain realistic about the possibilities and limitations of this technique of "stoppage or decontamination through permission." It can, as the examples show, be a great help, but, of course, there are limits to its use. It must never be applied in too open contrast with what we really are able to "accept," and its too liberal application might easily be confused by the children with actual permissiveness or total license, or might be interpreted as a sign of weakness, fear, or disinterest on our side.

By the technique of *"authoritative Verbot"* we mean exactly what the term implies. We simply say "NO," and we say it in such a way that it is clear that we mean it and we don't soften it up by arguing, explaining, or what not. We simply imply: "This has got to be stopped. We can't have it. That's all there is to it, and right now we don't care whether you understand or like it at all. It's got to be stopped, that's all." We said: we *imply*. If we would say all this explicitly it would take away from the very nature of the technique suggested here. Of course, not all our "No's" are of this nature. Some of them really belong in the section of "signal interference": while the spoken word is only a short "No," the total context of the situation is so clear that everybody knows or has just shortly ago discussed all the reasons why such behavior is unacceptable anyway. Then, the "No" only serves as a signal reminder of a larger policy that has already been worked out. In the present item, we really go one step beyond that. We seriously suggest that occasionally a simple clear "Verbot" of behavior, the reasons for which may be far beyond what can be explained or got across right now, may do a great deal of good. We have often been amazed at how it works. For, even in cases where youngsters are engaged in openly adult-defying conduct, if that adult suddenly comes out with a clear-cut limitation demand, it may take the youngster so much by surprise or assuage his own beginning unconscious anxiety about his exploit so well that he actually does stop, even though we wouldn't have believed it possible. The "hygiene" of saying "No" is an important issue, of course. Such "authoritative Verbot" must be free of hostility, anxiety, or anger on the side of the adult. It must happen in a basic atmosphere of acceptedness and tolerance, as an exceptional rather than a usual gesture.

It is sometimes accompanied by changes in gesture, physiognomy, or tone of voice. Occasionally, it makes a great difference from which "status source" the "No" is issued. Thus, we would find that, in moments when the group leader who was involved with the children in an aggressive scene could not have stopped them any more except by sharper interference techniques, the "overgroup representative," executive director or director, appearing freshly on the scene, could still stop things by nothing stronger than a clear-cut "No, that doesn't go, stop it." A planned manipulation of hierarchy and role distribution in our interference tactics was one of the most important items in our stock in trade at camp as well as at the Home. Whatever the details might be, we soon learned that we could save ourselves some of the much more conflict-producing interferences if we learned how to predict when whose "No" would be most effective.

Among the cases in which the use of this technique seemed most effective were the following:

1. If the youngsters were engaged in their misbehavior not so much because of uncontrollable impulsivity or pathology, but more because of the temporary "excitement" engendered, and because of a lack of reality-awareness or the feebleness of their value danger signals from within. In those cases a clear "No" seemed to snap them back to a previous state of control which they would have been capable of had not the addition of the excitational stimulation been present.

2. If the youngsters were just about to go farther than they really would have wanted to, so that they actually were pleased by or began to ask for a stoppage by the adult. Our "No" then saved them guilt feelings, anxieties, or loss of face.

3. If, in spite of the impulsive and pathology-conditioned mayhem, by some miracle the basic relationship to the present adult was still intact, so that signals coming from him would still be meaningful and challenge them toward unconscious cooperation.

4. If the "No" was surrounded by a situation whose impact was clear enough in itself (like the danger in station wagon traffic misbehavior) and had often been handled more explicitly before.

5. If the youngster's behavior needed to be stopped, while the issue itself was much too complicated to be taken up at the moment, and the youngsters were dimly aware of this. An example of this was given occasionally when our youngsters were engaged in some of their naïve and basically harmless sexual excitation, which would lead to sex language being bandied about gleefully—and, for a change, without aggressive intent—or to hopping around in the nude in a small child's enjoyment of narcissistic exhibitionism. Sometimes outside circumstances made it necessary to curb such

activity, even where it was not possible to explain why. Once, for instance, the youngsters had to be stopped from exhibiting themselves gleefully at the window to innocent passers-by, enjoying the mild shock or curiosity reactions thus produced. The whole mood in which it happened was relatively harmless, but we thought we had reasons of a community relationship nature to interfere. Short of using heavy interference means, which we didn't want to for clinical reasons well understood by the psychoanalytically trained educator, all that would be left would be arguing. But how would we argue with them? Any appeal to decency or morals would, at that stage of the game, have been wasted effort—you can't appeal to something that isn't there. To threaten them with what these people would do to them or that they might call the police would only stir up their already overdeveloped antagonism against "those people" and "the police," who represent law and order to them, a hatred which we did not want to stir up. And to impress them with the fact that these people might not find such behavior nice or might object to it would have been just grist for their mill—that was exactly what they wanted to begin with. We were pleasantly surprised, therefore, when we noticed that the youngsters gave up their activity when we simply said: "Stop that, we can't let you act that way." The clarity of our interference signal, coinciding with a vague notion that somewhere there was more to it which we couldn't or wouldn't raise at that moment, sufficed to bring the scene to an end.

It is clear, of course, that "Verbot" would have no power once excitement had trespassed a certain degree, where clearly traumatically derived pathology was rampant, or where a total loss of reality relatedness had already occurred.

As I came into the housemother's quarters tonight, I was confronted with Danny hitting viciously at Larry, while the housemother was trying to pull him away but unsuccessfully so because of his bulk. Danny was yelling at her: "Keep your hands off me, you dirty whore. I'll kill the bastard." "Oh, oh, what's the matter in here, off the beam again Danny?" I asked, and he, for the first time aware of my presence in the room, dropped his attack on Larry and said, "Goddamit Fritz, every time I wanna talk to Emmy private this motherfucker has to butt in, etc., etc." After being permitted to ventilate his gripes for about fifteen minutes, he calmed down, and then I played checkers with Larry out in the living room while the housemother talked quietly with

Danny about his clothing, which was what he wanted to do in the first place. (Entry: 4/14/47, Fritz Redl)

At 12:15 A.M., I got a call from the housemother that the kids were rioting and running all over the place clad only in shorts. This behavior included sallies out into the really frigid snow-covered Second Boulevard to fill pails with snow so they could make snowballs to throw from inside at passing traffic. The total staff was alerted but nothing seemed to work, and so I dressed hurriedly and tore down by way of frozen and deserted Hamilton Avenue to the Home. When I got there, they were acting according to specifications over the telephone and Joe, Andy, and Danny especially were "higher than kites." Joel (counselor) by this time had corralled Sam, with whom he has an excellent relationship, and was half talking, half protectively holding him so that he wouldn't get into any more mischief. Emily (housemother) was trying to calm Larry, who was absolutely manic with excitement but who was not daring enough to get into active participation and was screaming as though he were beside himself. When I parked my car and started on the double toward the house, Joe and Andy, who at that precise moment were dashing out to the sidewalk to get more snow both yelled, practically in unison, "Oh, oh, there's Fritz," and tore up into the house, not forgetting to bolt the door against me in their mad dash, so that Emily had to let me in. The boys were now upstairs dashing around. I went up there, bumped into by Andy in the dark as I entered. I grabbed him unceremoniously while I bellowed out to all others within earshot: "I want you in bed right now." Thank God, the magic of hierarchy worked, and there was a rustling as they all tore out of their hiding places and into bed. I marched Andy in, and stayed around for another full hour. Aside from a few upsets in the two rooms which were quickly handled, they dropped off to sleep without much trouble. (Entry: 1/15/47, Fritz Redl)

Pearl Bruce and I were co-counselors today and, after school, tried to interest the boys in some active games indoors since it was freezing cold outside. They were in a wild and primitive mood, however, and our program efforts fell seriously short of reaching any mark. Soon, Andy and Joe began sexual teasing of Pearl and me and got really quite mean about it. Andy lashed out at Pearl viciously when she sharply told him that she did not want him to jump up and hit at her breasts. In one of these exchanges between Pearl and Andy, Dave (Executive Director) who was making systematic fifteen-minute inspection tours of the house because of the wild mood of the boys, walked in on the situation and sharply ordered Andy to keep his hands off Pearl. He dropped them immediately and then began a whining attack on Pearl and me, "Aw, they never let us kids do nothin'." Finally, he went downstairs to Dave's office to talk to him. (Entry: 2/5/47, Vera Kare)

There is one more issue, however, which we had better emphasize in order to be sure to avoid a severe misunderstanding: we are talking only about the occasional trick of getting kids to stop something by simply forbidding it, and thus, so to speak, "swaying them off their feet" temporarily, without having to use interference techniques as drastic as the original situation seemed to suggest. This is very different from, and has nothing to do with, a policy of solving life problems by "authoritative Verbot," instead of involving the children in an understanding of what is going on, creating self-participative insight into the reasons why their behavior cannot be tolerated, or even by direct appeal and reasoning of all sorts. We would strongly oppose any such policy of autocratic restrictions, firmly believing in the intrinsic value of cooperative planning, challenge to value sensitivity and insight, symptom tolerance, and, of course, democratic group leadership. In fact, we are convinced that the nondamaging use of the occasional "authoritative Verbot" is possible only if the rest of the lives of the children is built on the other policies just mentioned as far as their disturbance degree allows. We consider "authoritative Verbot" as an interim interference stopgap only, and want it clearly understood as such. It must be followed and surrounded by a wide range of other techniques.

16. Promises and Rewards

Along broad lines, parents and educators are quite familiar with this approach. It is based on the assumption that children are under the impact of the "pleasure principle" and, while education aims at reducing its impact somewhat, they can be expected to remain under its influence up to a certain point for the rest of their lives. The idea, then, is that it is sometimes possible to influence their behavior by the granting and promising of "pleasure" in its widest sense.

These techniques can be used both for initiating and stopping behavior. We expect a child to do something the value of which he would have trouble seeing at the time, the doing of which is fraught with displeasure and strain, if we can dangle some special gratification luringly at the end of the line. Or, we expect he may stop indulging in pleasurable behavior now by making something like a deal with him: you forfeit this momentary fun, in compensation for which you can expect an unusual pleasure dose at the end.

Educators and parents also usually realize, in their more serious discussion, that this whole approach isn't quite so simple as it sounds and that many pitfalls must be avoided along the line. We know, for instance, that there is an intimate relationship between promise and reward and that things go wrong if it gets out of focus. Promises which aren't lived up to, or which go beyond what we want to come through with after we get to the reward stage, are dangerous indeed. And rewards which add an unusual dosage of "extra" pleasure seem to tend to fixate the children on the pleasure principle rather than help move them away from it, or, in other words, may involve the danger of spoiling, coddling, getting soft. Besides, it obviously makes some considerable difference as to just which life situations are used for promise as well as reward. The place of such techniques in a child's life is not easy to work out: nothing is worse than a "perversion of motivation," where what originally was meant to be a "marginal incentive" for an extra output of effort becomes a main attraction, so that children are motivated by profit thinking only, to the exclusion of all more realistic as well as more decent motivational challenges.

It might be fascinating to follow this trend down to its specifics —only, it wouldn't belong in a book like this. For we have a surprise coming right here and now: The very technique which seems so common and well known in educational practice is nearly unusable for the children about whom we write. Since the reasons for this throw additional light not only on our children, but on the nature of this educational tool itself, we might list them briefly.

But first we must note this: promise and reward are not really so simple as they sound. To use them wisely at all, a variety of rather basic ego functions has to be well intact. In short, the use of promise and reward, while helpful as a marginal educational tool for the normal child, already presupposes that a child's ego is in pretty good shape.

This becomes clear when we analyze just what happens in a case of promise and reward, and compare this with the list of ego disturbances which we have presented in *Children Who Hate*.

1. Relation to future, ability to interpret the present in correct relationship to one's own past:

In order to make any constructive use of a promise, it is obvious that a child must be able to apply what might be an issue in the future for the purpose of present impulse control. In order to react to a reward as reward rather than as just a "bit of luck," he must have the ability to single out in a present experience those factors which are really due to a combination of his own merit and adult kindness.

Neither of these prerequisites is given in our case. We could never use promise and reward very much with our children. Had we promised anything, that vague future pleasure image would still have had no power over their present acts, and had we "rewarded" them, they would have happily enjoyed the reward, without the slightest logical and causal link-up at all, as "so much good luck."

2. Inability to "deserve"

Promises make no sense, educationally, unless the reward is tied to the proviso that the youngster keeps the conditions of the promise—that he "deserves" the reward, that he earns it. With our youngsters, this very condition would have thrown us into a hopeless mess. For, of course, they would have made any "deal" with us, but because of the short-livedness of their intention and their actual inability to keep any good resolution in the face of momentary frustration, impulse upsurge, or temptational challenge, they would have constantly been in the position of having broken their contracts. By the time moments for reward would have come around, they would only have been confronted with the fact that we didn't come through with something that was mentioned before. With their usual unrealism about their own contribution to the destiny they suffer, they would have gone raving mad at us, as though *we* had broken the contract by sheer meanness. This means that our life with them, already full to the brim with conflict and confusion, would have had a considerable measure of such chances to get fantastically angry at us added to it.

3. Sibling rivalry and inability to accept unequal time distribution

Promises and rewards cannot always be identical in timing, quantity, and deservedness. Once you start with such a system, it will be unavoidable that one child sometimes gets something at a time when the other one doesn't. Had we given them, in the earlier days, for instance, the chance to earn money for a chore, the mere fact that one of them got his money for the chore today, while the other one might have his chore and its reward coming tomorrow, would have led to hopeless confusion, sibling rivalry, and fights. For the mere visualization of one of them having or getting something at a time when the others didn't used to send them into fits of paranoid delusions. Even in normal families the inequality of reward levels because of "deserving" and age levels sometimes constitutes quite a problem—in our case it would have caused mayhem.

4. Fatalistic and business deal concept of life

Up to a high degree, our youngsters operated on a *fatalistic and "business deal" concept of life* anyway. The idea that there might be other reasons than profit for behavior, on the adult's side as well as their own, was hard for them to accept. Introducing into our life with them too much of the same principle would have lessened the possibility of inserting motivational ties, rather than helping us do so. In making too many "if you do or avoid this, you will get that" arrangements with them, we actually increase their delusional power against us. For all they have to do now is not to live up to the conditions of the deal, and then they have a chance to get furiously angry at us at any time for not coming through with the proceeds. On top of that, they need only to increase their demand potential in order to make any "promise" seem miserly and then become angry at us for not "promising" what they really wanted in the moments of their most unrealistic absurdity of demand. We already had plenty of problems along that line to begin with; it would not have been advisable to use techniques which were liable to add to them.

5. Gratification grants without strings attached

The most stringent and important reason, however, why we would hardly use promises and rewards very much lies in the *basic*

design and function of the Treatment Home. It might be summarized under the term of the need for *"gratification grants without strings attached."* These children need affection and full gratification of their needs, ample symbols of adult acceptance and love,
as so much *medicine* in order to recover at all. To tie any set of
gratifications to the condition that they *perform well* would be like
promising a child cough medicine provided he goes without cough-
ing for a day. In short, whatever they got from us they had to get
"anyway," because they needed it either for the experiential and
program value attached to it or as a reassurance of our love meant to
counterbalance their hostility-eager misinterpretation of life. And
gratifications just for the sake of having "rewards" could not be
introduced into their lives when they were not ready to take them.
In short, if they needed an overnight trip because we felt that that
was a good medicine for them, we couldn't have said: you can go
on that overnight trip if you are good boys today. It was rather the
other way around. We hoped the overnight trip might be one of
the experiences helping them to get to the stage of being good boys.
And if they weren't ready for one, we couldn't have "promised" an
overnight just to reward them when we knew that such an experience was going to make hash of our strategy of ego support.

There was one interesting observation, however, which we could
make and which is related to this issue. When we really had made
some progress with them, the "need" for promises and rewards itself
often became lessened simply because they seemed to skip a phase.

In the beginning, for instance, we could not allow those children
any participation in household chores. The reasons ought to be obvious by now: it would have led into so much confusion and secondary conflict that chaos would have resulted. Of course, it would
have been easy to lure them into it by special reward grants. But
such procedure would have been clinically as unwise as anything
could be. By the time their ego recovery had advanced far enough
for them to accept minor household chores like bringing food and
dishes in and out of the kitchen and to perform them, they also
were motivated enough to enjoy such participative activity for its
own sake. They were eager to perform some of this and asked for
it, so promise or reward would have been entirely out of place. And
the stage where a marginal use of promise and reward techniques
might have been reintroduced in their lives in connection with

"surplus tasks" we unfortunately never reached, because of our premature closure.

In summary, we can say that, strange as it may seem, with children of our type of disturbances "promise and reward" is not a feasible technique. In a wider meaning of the term, of course, the pleasurableness of an experience would be occasionally used as a "propaganda item," to soften the necessity of an unavoidable step. We might fight their disgust with the job of packing bedrolls by reminding them of the fun they would have as soon as we got going. Or we might try to get them over some of the wildness during a "planning session" around a trip or party by dangling before their eyes the fun of the final event and the need to get there. But this would always be done casually, not as a condition on which the future event would depend. As specific techniques to start or stop behavior, the two techniques could not be used.

17. Punishments and Threats

The issue of punishment is probably one of the most befuddled ones in educational practice as well as in educational thought. The confusion in public opinion between punishment as an educational tool and as a simple outlet of adult temper, cruelty, wrath, and revenge is indeed a spectacle to behold. Even in more professional educational circles the confusion about issues of punishment is amazing. Controversy about different taste patterns, the pitching of philosophic and religious convictions and opinions against each other, usually takes the place of rational thinking, technical speculation, or reality-geared scrutiny of actual effects. The problem of how to evaluate which punishment was effective and what criteria are available to measure the subsurface effect of punishment, which need not coincide with its surface operation, seems to be especially undeveloped.

Unfortunately, mental hygiene and psychiatry have, as yet, contributed little to clarify the issue and to produce more specific research. Even these two fields have confined themselves to a general warning about some of the most tangible pathological effects of badly handled punishment and abuses of it, but have done little to clarify the wide variety of risks as well as advantages of well-handled or normally usable punishment practices. On top of that, so little thinking has been done about this issue that even professional educators, mental hygienists, and psychiatrists frequently will produce as naive punishment beliefs and habits of their own conviction as any nonprofessional person might muster in a hot debate. There seems to be a total lack of organized research, especially where the problem of punishment is raised around issues of group leadership.

It would be fascinating, indeed, to tackle this problem and its relationship to other problems of discipline and to long-range problems of education in specific terms. We had to do this, of course, in order to arrive at any amount of reasonable criteria for the clinical evaluation of this tool. For the purpose of the present description, we have to forfeit the pleasure of producing our specific material on the issue or what is supposed to be a section would turn into a book. We shall, therefore, limit ourselves to listing the points which seem to constitute the main implications of punishment for the clinical scene.

I. Basic Theory

Our basic theory of the mechanism which is supposed to be at work in a situation of punishment can easily be condensed into a few lines. Both punishment and threat—the two are interrelated in the same way as promise and reward—are obvious appeals to the pleasure-pain principle. This time the emphasis is on the "pain" end of the line. At this point, of course, we mean by "pain" not physical pain but simply the application of an unpleasant situation —or the threat of such an application—with the hope that it will help the individual to control impulses which otherwise could not be domesticated. Thus, all punishment, basically, strives after supplying the individual with additional aggressive energy for drive control. The conditions under which such control becomes effective are the following ones:

a. The punishment situation must be experienced as something unpleasant.

b. Frustration or aggression produced by such an experience of "pain" must be related to the real issue at stake and not confused with the person who inflicted it.

c. The aggression generated through punishment-inflicted pain or unpleasantness must be internalized and directed toward that part of the personality which produced the problem to begin with.

d. The aggression produced through punishment must be internalized in such a way that it will effectively control the impulses in question rather than produce defense, anxiety, aggressive stages, or self-recrimination and withdrawal.

The mental hygiene problem in punishment always involves the following questions:

a. Which experiences produce what type of aggression?

b. Under what conditions can aggression be produced in such a way that, rather than being thrown back at the outside world or the source of punishment, it becomes an internal act?

c. Under what conditions can a cognitive awareness of the meaning of this pain as punishment rather than as hostility from the outside world be guaranteed?

d. Under what conditions can the quantity of aggression produced actually successfully domesticate impulse energies rather than produce confused anxiety or aggression or other negative results?

e. Just what will the individual do with the surplus aggression which is not involved in the actual domestication of the behavior to be controlled?

Thus, for instance, a specific form of punishment could be called successful if the youngster feels it as unpleasant enough to make him angry, if he realizes that he, himself, produced the real problem instead of getting angry at the person or the society which inflicted the punishment, if, at the same time, he is able to use the aggression thus produced for a successful domestication of his impulses rather than for a general state of fury, sulk, aggression, hostility, anxiety, or guilt. Punishment fails, even though the surface behavior effects may be guaranteed, if something goes wrong in connection with any one of the points just mentioned.

This means, then, that the infliction of punishment presupposes a rather complex functioning of the individual's cognitive and control system for which it is meant to be an energy-supplying support. Whenever such a system is not functioning with reasonable reliability, punishment is liable to have disastrous effects. Remembering the description of the basic ego machinery of the children we talk about, we have little difficulty in seeing that this complexity of ego-functioning needed to make punishment a successful experience is certainly missing. In fact, we must say that most of the children we talk about are as incapable of dealing with so complex a mechanism adequately as of dealing with the other more complex situations of their lives. The application of punishment in their case is therefore totally unacceptable, certainly in the early stages of the repair job, and must be considered a marginal potential only at such a time when they are pretty close to recovery anyway. In short, even as a tool to manipulate surface behavior, punishment for the children we are talking about is counterindicated. A marginal use of it can be gradually inserted to the degree to which they have recovered normal ego functions. Certainly, at its best, punishment is a marginal control technique or a technique to be used for additional "reality rub-in" in later stages and not a technique for repair.

II. Intimate Relationship to Motivation and Time

Punishment, as well as threat, has as intimate a relationship to the child's *concept of motivation and time* as the techniques described under the title "Promises and Rewards." In order to be perceived adequately as an educational act rather than as a willful, hostile act of rejection and aggression by the adult, it is important that the individual punished is able to:

a. Correctly perceive the intention of the punishing adult.

b. Connect the present unpleasantness with the internal contribution made by himself in a previous piece of behavior.

c. Tie up the present experience of punishment with a clear structure pattern so that it can be used later on as a deterring factor in a moment of temptational challenge.

It is obvious, from the very description of their pathology, that our children, certainly in the early stages, fulfill none of these conditions. Far from being ready to perceive the unpleasantness-inflicting adult as a friendly agent, they are liable to attribute negativistic motives, even in the best of harmonious relationships to the adult surroundings. They approach punishment, therefore, with such a host of projective, hostile delusions that even the most wisely planned acts of punishment would have little chance to penetrate through their defense. They would react to even deserved, and wise, and kind punishment as though it were the hostile act of an enemy, and use it, therefore, to increase their counterhostility without question.

Also, our children usually react to any unpleasant experience as a momentary stimulus coming from the outside, and accordingly project all aggression which they feel in its wake to this outside pain-producing source. They are not able to relate the displeasure which they feel right now under the impact of punishment to anything that they have done before. Like most anti-social delinquents or "psychopaths," they react to punishment as a hostile act from the outside world, repressing entirely any contribution which they may have made to its occurrence, considering it only as an excuse for their further retaliation or compensatory pleasure seeking. Thus, they pervert the logical chain between guilt-causation, pain experience, and reaction to punishment into the opposite. Punishment is to them not the end of a chain of causation but the beginning of one. This means that they consider it as an excuse and an alibi for all the subsequent behavior which in their eyes is justified as revenge for unpleasant experiences to which they were exposed because of the fault of people around them. At the same time, little can be hoped from punishment experiences for "learning for the future." By the very nature of their ego disturbances, which we have described more in detail before, they are unable to make such resourceful use of their own past for future behavior. Confronted with a similar temptational situation next time, the chain starts anew, and previous unpleasant experiences either are not even remembered, or, if remembered, are met by one or the other or a combination of the defensive devices described under the title "The Delinquent Ego and Its Techniques." [5]

III. Ability to Take Pain and Frustration without Being Confused

Another one of the primary conditions for the constructive effect of punishment experiences is *the ability to take pain and frustration without being confused by them.* This, however, hits the very area in which these children are most disturbed. Their frustration tolerance is so low, their ability to remain reasonable under the impact of unpleasant experiences is so undeveloped, that any experiences of punishment would hit them without any ability to cope with them. This means, for instance, that the withdrawal of a privilege, even when it is considered fair and deserved, would expose them to the untenable situation of suffering frustration, to which they would react with the usual display of increased pathology. Any exposure to nonactivity for any length of time, as, for instance, being taken out of a game as punishment to make them realize that they

[5] See *Children Who Hate*, pp. 141-210.

don't deserve to participate in such pleasurable activities, would confront them with the problem of boredom, of lack of structure by which to bind their aggressive energy, and would therefore lead to new attacks either of anxiety or of aggression in increased form.

IV. Problem of Sibling Rivalry

The same item of *sibling rivalry* which we have mentioned as a barrier to promise and reward also functions here. The mere visualization of other youngsters, happily engaged with an adult, while a specific youngster is in a special punitive exclusion situation, will develop in a child such envy and such hostility toward the adult and the other children involved that a tremendous outburst of sulk and rage will be the invariable consequence.

In short, one of the prerequisites for being able to react reasonably to well-planned punishment is a certain minimum of ego organization. As soon as we deal with children in whom these very basic ego functions are disturbed, such a technique as punishment becomes inapplicable, not only for therapeutic, but for educational purposes, or even for the purposes of domestication of surface behavior.

V. Special Counterindications

In listing the reasons why the tool of punishment is unusable for ego-disturbed children, certainly in the early stages of their repair, we have not even mentioned a *variety of special reasons* which sometimes become additional counterindications for one child or another. Just to be sure that we do not forget them, we had better list a few of them right here:

Some children find exposure to the very life experiences which we find educationally desirable for them, or therapeutically important, uncomfortable, difficult, or even frustrating. Punishing their misbehavior in such situations by taking them out would in that case be unfeasible because in those instances what we consider punishment would not be punishment but reward, and the sequence would be reversed. In fact, we would offer the youngster, on a platter, techniques for withdrawal, escape, and return to more primitive lack of participation and challenge. Besides, some of our youngsters have developed their own delinquent technique of proving the hostility of the adult environment by provoking incidents of hostile relationships with them. In fact, they have an elaborate skill for forcing adults into forms of interference which they themselves can easily misinterpret as hostility or revenge and which then set off a new chain of counteraggression on this basis. This probably constitutes the most serious trap into which the educator is easily lured. The moment that we would cement such techniques by offering them the channel of punishment devices, we would actually furnish them with defenses and alibis over and above those they had already developed.

Furthermore, some of our youngsters have heavy masochistic trends or indulge in depressive delusional fantasies. They are already liable to misconstrue even inadvertent frustration as a purposefully produced hurt and then to deal with it by indulging in the feeling of being down and out, mistreated, hated, starved, not wanted, not liked, and so forth. For those children the application of punishment is especially untenable because it will only feed the delusional system in which they already operate.

It is obvious, by the way, and it is only mentioned for the sake of completeness here, that any form of physical punishment would be totally excluded in work with the children we talk about. Over and above the difficulty of reacting to "unpleasantness or pain" in the broader sense of the term in a well-structured ego-strong way, the application of physical pain involves the tendency toward very primitive and atavistic reaction. Even for normal children, it tends to encourage projection to the outside rather than internalization or, where internalization happens under the pressure of fear and guilt feelings, it produces the vicious circle of sado-masochistic pathology.

Altogether then, the clinician finds himself confronted by a peculiar problem. In one way, the behavior of the youngsters gives such open clues to the deservedness of punishment. On the other hand, the more the youngsters deserve it, the less possible is it to expose them to its process because of its bad effect on their ego disturbances. This clinical argument, by the way, seems to be the most difficult one to interpret, not only to the lay public, but even to highly sophisticated educators. The lack of the application of punishment is frequently confused with the philosophy of total permissiveness, ignoring the fact that punishment is only one of the seventeen techniques for the manipulation of surface behavior described here. On top of that, the general confusion about punishment being a good "teacher" of respect for outside reality seems to be so ingrained that the more special mechanisms involved in its correct perception and in an adequate reaction to it are entirely lost in the process. In fact, even well-trained educators seem to feel guilty or to feel as though they are neglecting their task of reality interpretation if they avoid the use of punishment techniques, in spite of the fact that many other techniques of reality interpretation and of the setting of limitations are much more effective and equally accessible to them.

In spite of all this, there is one area in which punishment, as a technique wisely handled, can prove helpful to the clinician.

This is when it is used as a *measurement for ego improvement* along the lines of the therapeutic goal. The moment when youngsters can take a tentative punishment arrangement without all the primitivism of reaction described before, it does mean undisputably that the ego function has increased in clarity as well as in dynamic power over impulsivity. This was especially fascinating to observe in the life with the Pioneers.

Searching for an area in which we might dare to experiment, only one offered itself as a logical choice: "station wagon behavior." The reasons for this are easy to see. The selection of this area for experimentation with a punishment threat seemed wise because of: (a) *The clarity of the danger issue.* For children who live in the "Motor City" the "realism" of danger in traffic is more easily demonstrable than any other reality of their lives. (b) *The advantage of tool-frustration.* If a youngster handles a knife carelessly while working on his favorite crafts project, it would be much more frustrating to say, "If you are that careless, you can't be allowed to make wooden guns," than to say, "This is a wonderful gun; we want you to make it and have fun with it. But, if you can't handle that knife more reasonably, we may have to stop you until you can be more cautious." It is well known that deprivation of the *actual gratification* hits the frustration budget more heavily than deprivation of a single "gratification tool." Thus, by picking station wagon behavior as an area for punishment-conditioning, we had a technical advantage on our side. If forced to a showdown, we could not be accused of not "wanting them to have any fun, like going places, driving to a movie, etc." We could keep up our open declaration of our approval of such pleasures for them, but could concentrate our punishment follow-up on the "tool" withdrawal only. This, by the way, assumes that our children don't really care for riding in cars very much, but would be hit if withdrawal of their transportation blocked them from pleasurable pursuits in other areas. With rural children, or less car-sophisticated youngsters of other cultures, this would of course be a different issue. In short, picking station wagon behavior for a potential "punishment issue" avoided two very severe technical problems. Yet, it still had too many others tied to it to be tried until very late in the game. For, even at a time when our youngsters would have "understood" the realism of such traffic-conditioned punishments, they still couldn't have coped with other elements in the picture. The actual frustration produced by transportation withdrawal would still have thrown them into chaotic confusion, and, if they had taken us up on the challenge, we would have been deprived of a variety of program resources without which we could not possibly have done at the time, for clinical reasons. Besides, since transportation was an issue involved in going to school as well as in pleasurable trips, they would have abused this opportunity to get our school-going policies all out of gear by simply producing station wagon withdrawal whenever they felt like playing hookey anyway. Also, if dangerous station wagon behavior would be punished by transportation withdrawal, individual differentiation could not be risked. This, however, would imply that the whole group might have to lose station wagon privileges because of one individual's daring behavior—and the implications of that can easily be seen. Or, individual differences would have had to be recognized, and the reader can by now imagine what it would have done to our sibling rivalry problem if the "good ones" had been driven to school or movie, while the sinners had to stay home or take the bus.

Therefore, for a long time it was still simpler and clinically cleaner to have enough adults around to "subdue" the youngsters who would go to extremes, or to engage them in enough adult involvedness or programming (e.g., group singing) to avoid total station wagon blowups entirely, or to remain specifically careful about timing of length of wagon inclosedness, or to become very cunning about the question of just who sat in front or in back and with whom. The use of a "Punishment" threat for this issue would not have been "simpler"—as so many of our educational as well as clinical visitors seemed to suggest—but much more complex and fatal to our clinical goals.

Late in the process of our life with the Pioneers, however, we could see enough of a gain in cognitive clarity as well as dynamic

force of their egos, and also enough of the development of a vestige
of a "group ego," so that we felt we might experiment with an exposure to a punishment regime connected with this issue. After a
week of especially wild and critical "station wagon" troubles, we
corralled the children for a group talk.

Exec. Dir.: The counselors report that you guys were pretty wild in
the station wagon coming home today. I want to talk with you
about it because this stuff has been going on for a long time now.
Sometimes it gets better and then it gets worse again. For the last
couple of weeks it's been pretty bad and it's dangerous. Any or all
of you could be hurt or killed in an accident that might be caused
by this kind of behavior . . . How come we can't cut some of this
stuff out?

Andy: Aw, Dave, it's those guys Mike and Bill. They get wild and
start throwing stuff around, and then everybody else gets all mixed
up in it, and then the counselors get sore and stop the wagon . . .

Exec. Dir.: How about you? I understand you were doing some of it
yourself. Is it really any excuse because they do it for anyone else
to get involved?

Mike: It's that goddam Bill . . . he starts it all the time . . .

Bill: Oh you goddam liar, Mike, you know damn well you took your
sandwich and threw it out the window this morning, didn't he
Andy?

Mike: O.K., ask Danny, he was sitting right next to me . . . Danny,
did I?

Exec. Dir.: Well, as always happens, everybody is blaming everybody
else. Look, we have known each other for a long time now. We've
been willing to take a lot from you guys. We weren't fussy and I
can't think of a single place where you could be living where they
wouldn't have cracked down hard and taken the wagon away and
maybe done other things along the same lines, but we never did
because we want you to have fun and enjoy yourselves and we
couldn't very well do that without the wagon. And we still can't
do without it . . . But this wild stuff simply has got to stop. Every
time I get together with you and try to figure out *why* it happens
we get no place. So we're going to have a new policy. Anybody who
can't handle himself in the wagon is not going to be able to use it
for a while. How long I don't know yet, but that's the only way I
can figure out to handle it. We can't let you endanger each other
and the grown-ups who are with you and we won't stop using the
wagon because some guys can't handle themselves. There's no sense
in punishing everybody . . . So each of you is on his own from now
on . . . That means: if you act up in the wagon in a dangerous

way and won't calm down when the counselor asks you, the very
next day you are out of the wagon. I mean for school and activities
too. Transportation to school will be by bus. That means getting up
earlier, eating earlier too, and taking the bus to school. If the program for that afternoon is using the wagon for some activity, then
whoever is out of the wagon has to stay home . . .

Mike: How about coming home from school?

Exec. Dir.: That's by bus too . . .

Danny: I ain't going to miss out on the wagon because of some other
bastards . . .

Exec. Dir.: I thought I made that clear. We're going to keep on operating the wagon. Nobody gets deprived for anybody else. Whoever
can't use it because he's that wild doesn't use it. Even if it means
that one guy is left, then that's what it means and that guy will keep
riding in the station wagon . . . Is everybody clear on this?

For a few days following this discussion things cleared up a bit,
but then Mike, Andy, and Bill again engaged in the same risky
behavior and we had to put our punishment machinery in operation. The incident occurred on a Wednesday. We told them, therefore, that, for the rest of the week, they would be "out" of the
station wagon. Thus Thursday and Friday mornings, we had extra
staff assigned just for their waking up, breakfast, and seeing them to
the bus. Package cereal breakfasts were used with a hot drink to
spare the cook whose heavy schedule could not be increased by
asking her to prepare two hot breakfasts. On one of these two days,
Friday, the group was taken out for a scheduled tour through an
automobile plant. The other two were engaged in activities around
the Home since they could not go in the wagon. They made the
trips to school and back without mishap and, although they threatened to play truant, did not do so. All in all, they appeared able
to take the novelty of clear-cut punishment without reprisal of any
kind and, after elaborate "rub-in interviews," stressing again complete unacceptability of their station wagon behavior, they were
readmitted to the station wagon on Saturday.

Of course, we couldn't even have risked any experiment like this
before we had the children in good enough shape to try. For, had
they taken us up on the challenge more seriously than they did, this
would have cut down our clinically so important program possibilities, would have created very great problems in home management,
and would, of course, have stirred up old pathology around sibling
rivalry as well as around the role concept of the adult.

There is another misunderstanding that the use of words might provoke: colloquial language sometimes also calls "punishment" what we would want to describe as "restitutional arrangements for the reduction of guilt, aggression, and shame." If a youngster, for instance, messes up all the other children's bunks during his attack of fury and revenge, and if the issue in all its implications has been cleared up satisfactorily on all sides—and both of these are very strict "if's" to which we bind this procedure as a condition—then it may sometimes seem wise to suggest that he participate in the clean-up. Such an act, however, is meant to be not something unpleasant to be inflicted upon him as a cure, but a gesture of getting back into their graces, or of "reestablishing his old relationships" with the group. Such "restitutional arrangements" can sometimes, if cautiously handled, be very helpful to the child and save him and the group a great deal of secondary hatred, revenge feelings, and aggression, or of embarrassment and guilt with all its by-products. It is to be remembered, though, that this is only indicated where it is important to *reduce* guilt feelings. In most cases with our children, we had to be so happy that they showed an inkling of guilt feelings about a misdeed that we would not have looked for techniques to help them "pay it off" as the easy way out.

The other judicious use of "restitutional arrangements" which looks, to the layman, like "punishment" but is far from it, is meant to help our task of "reality rub-in," or is a "challenge toward insight and value fairness" in itself. This, too, has as a prerequisite an already very advanced stage of adult-and reality-relatedness, and especially of frustration tolerance, without which it only leads into confusion.

During the fourteenth month of treatment, when Mike went through a special phase of "stealing" from the principal's office at school, from desks, from staff members, he also had taken a dollar from the housemother's pocket. For no previous incident had he been punished, of course, in any way. We felt that the special relationship Mike had to the housemother gave us a chance to combine our interview about what he had done with some form of "restitutional arrangements" as a special challenge to him, which we could begin to afford now:

Exec. Dir.: Mike, what do you think we should do about that buck you swiped from Emily?

Mike: I don't know.

Exec. Dir.: Do you think it is fair to her just to give up that buck?

Mike: No . . .

Exec. Dir.: Can you remember all of those other times you swiped stuff and it finally came out and we didn't do anything except to point out to you that we didn't think it was right to steal, that anybody who does steal as you do has a problem that he has to work out?

Mike: Uh huh.

Exec. Dir.: Well, what do you think now? Should Emily suffer the loss of her buck because you can't control yourself from stealing?

Mike: I'll pay her back from my allowance. How long will it take?

Exec. Dir.: Well that depends on how much you pay at a time . . . I think if you pay her fifteen cents a week, that would be enough until you're paid up. That way you'll have forty cents to spend and still be paying her back. . . .

Mike continued faithfully to pay fifteen cents per week and, when he had paid back sixty cents, it was arranged for Emily to "forgive" him for the rest because he had repaid so much in good faith at quite a considerable deprivation from the total fifty-five cents he received per week

It is obvious how tenuous and risky such an arrangement can be, and how crucial *precision of timing* is in such matters. We could never have dared any such thing until that time. Even then the timing problem would have counterindicated too frequent use of such "restitutional arrangements" to "rub in" a fairness issue very definitely, indeed. For the parent and educator, in general, we want to point to the importance of keeping such procedures most carefully "hygienic"—the slightest item going wrong there usually makes chaos out of what was supposed to help the child.

Turning now to threats, in colloquial terminology the word "threat" is used in a very broad way. It often refers to any "warning given" of a possible consequence, such as: "Listen, If you hit that nail as hard as that, you are going to bust the boat you are making." Or it is used to refer to behavior by the adult which is meant to "signal" an imminent conditional act of "tool interference, restructuring, or restraint." We might say, for instance: "If you guys are getting that wild up here in the living room, we may have to go down to the basement and play some other game," or, "You can't throw the big ball up here, only the little one. Remember our rule? If you can't stop throwing it now, I'll have to hold it until it's time for a game."

As long as we apply the word "threats" to such warnings about limits which will be necessary for reality or other reasons, there does not seem to be any harm involved and we have made ample use of such warnings. In fact the very techniques of protective interference, of signal interference, of direct appeal, and others, as well as the policy of preparing youngsters for interferences contemplated, seem to require them as part of behavioral hygiene. However, we want to make quite sure that there is no confusion between such "warning about impending limits to be set" and what is more commonly referred to as threat, as a precursor of *punishments*. Since, in this better and stricter use of the term threat we have nothing else in mind but preannounced punishments, it is obvious that such threats are entirely inadvisable, as long as the use of punishments is itself counterindicated. In this meaning of the term, therefore, threats could not be used with the children who hate, for the same reasons for which punishments would have muddled our clinical waters.

The fact that we didn't dare use "punishment" as a technique at Pioneer House, because of the ego disturbances of our children and because of the other clinical hazards it involves, does not mean that we didn't have a sizable problem of dealing with the *children's confusion* about this issue. They were about as bad in their misinterpretation of issues as any group of untrained adults might be— their own beliefs in the salutary effect of crude violence as "punishment" put our clinical wisdom to a hard test. And, like all delinquents, they would of course make ample and skillful use of their technique of "anticipatory provocation," and would try to lure us constantly into behavior which they could misinterpret triumphantly as "punitive." Yet, in the framework of a "total treatment climate" in a residential home, it is not difficult to create soon a "basic understanding" of what is going on—an "insight" which really can often be used to cement in the effect of what otherwise would have remained a verbally rather weak argument. It was only our total policy of nonpunitive acceptance which made it possible for us to get them to the point of even "understanding" a scene in which we might have to hold a child in a tantrum as not being "punishment," but simply "temporary outside emergency control" with no other issues involved. We are convinced that the more hardened techniques of "planned misinterpretation of adult behavior" which the toughie unfolds so impressively can never be "argued down."

But they can be "lived down" within the framework of a "total design."

The Limitations of "Techniques"—Cautions and Warnings

Frankly, this chapter on "Techniques for the Antiseptic Manipulation of Surface Behavior" might easily throw us out of focus, and we might as well make sure that we restore its correct perspective to our "long-range thinking," before we are through with it. The following "cautions" may guarantee it against being seen out of proportion to our total clinical task:

1. The seventeen techniques described here are not so separate from each other as the unavoidable limitations of writing a book have made them seem to be. Most of what we do in our attempt to influence surface behavior of children is actually a combination of a variety of them, and what is presented here is not at all meant to be complete or exhausting.

2. Some of the "names" used to describe these techniques also happen to be labels by which to refer to "long-range policies." Thus, "planned ignoring" seems very close to what we refer to in other places under the title of "strategic noninterference," and the adjective "antiseptic" or "hygienic" is used in both connections. For example, you can "hold a child" so as to stop him doing any damage. Or you may do so in the belief that this will "teach him something" about the realities and limitations of life. In both cases, the momentary situations look alike from the outside. Yet, it makes a world of difference whether we ascribe to a single act momentary stoppage power or the validity of a long-range clinical tool. In this chapter, we referred to all of these techniques only and exclusively in their role as "interference in surface behavior," with no other claims.

3. We have only taken our tools out of their boxes and held them up for a short inspection, with a few speculations about their potential properties and limitations thrown in. That is all. We have not as yet even raised the most urgent question of all: just what are actual criteria as to which one will or will not do what job under specific clinically goal-directed conditions? Of course, this whole chapter remains meaningless until such speculation and directions are added to it. In our staff meetings and training sessions, as well

as in our supervisory interviews, it was this very problem that kept us fascinated all the way through. Unfortunately, this is not the place to unpack all this yet.

4. There are two misinterpretations of this chapter which we are, frankly, most concerned to avoid: The practitioner who works with children in group and full-time life situations, which includes the parent and teacher, might be a little too happy about it. Knowing the vagueness with which questions of "how to interfere" are usually handled in literature, the seeming detail into which we go here might easily raise the false hope that such a "list of techniques" could be an answer to educational or even therapeutic problems. It is not meant to be. It answers nothing but the urgent demand to have a few concrete possibilities in mind in moments of "interference emergency." The clinical psychologist, case worker, and psychoanalyst, on the other hand, might easily be shocked by this chapter—and especially by the fact that we take some rather "crude" measures more seriously than he might be inclined to concede is necessary. To them we answer that it is far from us to substitute for therapeutic processes a bagful of interference tricks. We are also impressed, however, with the need to "know what we are doing clinically" when we have to interfere in behavior, and with the realism of the fact that, in daily life with the children who hate, emergency interference is a relevant issue, indeed. It seems to us that a "pharmacology" of hygienic interference techniques would be a better answer for both the clinician and the educator than the customary mixture of "therapeutic ideals" watered down by the crude mistakes which occur as "last resort measures because of the hard facts of life." We hope that this chapter will stir both the psychiatrist and the group-scene-geared practitioner into a more audible demand for more organized research on this issue.

IV
TECHNIQUES FOR THE CLINICAL EXPLOITATION OF LIFE EVENTS

IN the residential therapy framework there are two broad, basic variables which form a whole and are continually interacting with each other. The first of these variables is the child itself. The second is the milieu with which he is interacting and which, in turn, interacts with him. The fundamental premise of the milieu approach is that, through manipulation of the milieu variable, there is a resultant impact upon the child in the direction of modification toward a clinically desirable goal. Three aspects of the milieu variable have already been discussed in detail in previous chapters. These are (1) the aspect of total treatment design itself, which exerts a specific effect on children stemming from their perception of it, quite apart from anything else which is done within it, (2) the aspect of psychological hygiene, which acts, basically, to avoid traumatization of the child through specific techniques of handling child behavior, and (3) the aspect of programming which offers activity structures to help the ego achieve balance between impulse and control. All of these elements are indispensable to a properly designed residential approach to the type of ego disturbance under consideration. They are really conditions without which ego change cannot take place and some actual improvements in ego functioning are directly traceable to their presence in the treatment program. However, the tools which are most directly aimed at change are to be found in still another aspect of the milieu variable. This is the area of *clinical exploitation* of life events. In this phase of operations we try for "direct hits" against pathology. In order to demonstrate the interaction between milieu and pathology on this level, it will be necessary to do something in the nature of a process analysis, encompassing a large segment of clinical time, and defining symptom, techniques, and changes in the symptom picture. Before taking up this task, however, it seems expedient to show the techniques themselves in bas-relief. Following this, we shall take up a series of "skirmishes" with symptoms in chronological sequence as they occurred with various children, for the purpose of illuminating a long-range treatment profile.

Techniques

1. "Symptom Cultivation"

Simply because the adult in the treatment setting lives in close proximity to the symptom productions of the ego-disturbed child there is no guarantee that random clinical interference will be valid or efficient. There is no magic in geographical closeness to, or descriptive familiarity with, behavior. In order for true clinical exploitation of life events to occur, the total milieu must take over a task which for want of a better term might simply be called "symptom cultivation." For the therapeutic environment must actually "cultivate" symptoms in a variety of ways before they can be made available for still another kind of approach which is aimed at the removal of pathology. We might find an analogy in the field of medicine before the discovery of miracle drugs. In those days, if one had a carbuncle, the surgeon would apply heat to help it "ripen" before applying the lancet. The symptom complexes of the ego-disturbed child must be helped, similarly, to attain a certain intensity and quality for clinical interference to achieve a final maximal striking power. The various techniques which are employed in this process of symptom cultivation fall into two major strategies: (1) strategic noninterference and (2) exploitative interference.

A. STRATEGIC NONINTERFERENCE. The residential clinician is overwhelmed with symptom behavior from the very first moment a child enters the treatment home. However, in many instances these symptom productions are useless for purposes of clinical exploitation. Usually this is due to the fact that the total ego functioning of the child may still be too disturbed to permit any attempt to cope with pathology. In these moments, the residential clinician may find himself involved in various attempts to tone down symptom expression. At still other times, however, it may seem extremely important for a piece of symptom behavior to occur because, as the result of already achieved improvement in ego functioning and established rapport and security gains, a greater chance to cope with the symptom itself is promised. In such a moment, far from trying to soften or neutralize a symptom so that it disappears temporarily through various hygienic devices, a deliberate policy of *strategic noninterference* is followed. No action is taken to make the symptom subside. Thus the more vehement behavioral manifestations, formerly warded off because of their low clinical utility value, will now occur.

B. EXPLOITATIVE INTERFERENCE. Simple noninterference may not always be sufficient for adequate "symptom cultivation." Many times, in order for a symptom to manifest itself at the strategically necessary time and place, and with sufficient intensity for most advantageous handling, it actually has to be helped along through artificial acceleration from the outside. Just as the environment can be manipulated to soften and even temporarily neutralize a symptom, so it can also be made to lure or invite its expression. At such times, the residential clinician may follow the policy of *exploitative interference*, by which is meant that certain deliberate steps are taken to expedite and enliven symptom expression beyond what may be achievable through strategic noninterference. The same criteria for the use of this technique exist as for strategic noninterference, namely, it applies only to those situations or issues where a treatment chance is clinically visible. Since the various substrategies involved in exploitative interference do not necessarily vary from symptom to symptom, it is impossible to subdivide them into generic categories. Whatever the step taken may be, its essential characteristic remains constant: it is always deliberately meant to speed up symptom expression.

The following example may help to clarify some of the complexities involved in both strategic noninterference and exploitative interference.

Andy, one of the most deeply suspicious children at the Home at first, constantly read rejection into every move of the adult, even when the most gratifying things were done for him. Very slowly the impact of the total treatment design began to have some effect in "softening up" this paranoid ideology, but the potential for regression was very strong and misinterpretation of adult behavior to conform to case history expectations had to be watched very carefully. In this way, during the first summer, after about six months at the Home, the effect of sending the group to Camp Chief Noonday for a five-week stay was to reawaken in Andy insecurities about returning to the Home and staff that he hadn't seen and tested daily as to their affection for him. Upon his return, he lapsed into the same intense suspiciousness and aloofness he had displayed at the very outset of treatment. Since it was clear that this was an acute reaction and would disappear by itself within a week or so after he had reacclimatized himself to Pioneer House surroundings, one way of handling it would have been really to ignore it, all the while trying to show Andy that nothing had changed, that he was still loved and would be provided the same affectional supplies as had existed before he went away. Thus his fear of rejection would be groundless. On the other hand, it was felt that, while all of this should be done, precisely because he was already in better shape from the total ego viewpoint this might be a good time to try to point up this characteristic style of devaluating the adult world, to label more clearly "his problem" for him. This meant that special steps would be taken that his sulk might ripen into a clear-cut action which symbolized this attitude and could then be discussed with him. The detailed picture of how this was managed is seen in the following chain of events, taken from the recorded material.

Joel (counselor) and I took the group to Belle Isle today. When it came time to come out of the water for lunch, Andy, who had been in a sulk all morning that really started when we picked him up at camp, dallied, pretended not to hear, and stalled around before coming out to dress and eat lunch. Instead of putting pressure on him or coaxing, I let him stall until the very last minute because I wanted his behavior to take the most extreme form it could to force his sulk into the open. After lunch he was even more visibly upset and, as we went to visit the animal exhibits, he stalked along by himself, lagging about twenty feet behind us. At this point I began to structure the situation so that he might take even a more active turn in his hostility toward us. I told the group in a loud voice, Andy being within earshot, that I wanted everybody to stay together during the tour through the different animal exhibits so that, when the time to get our treat came, we would be in the same place, could all have our ice cream together, and then would wait as a group for about twenty minutes before we went in for our late afternoon swim prior to going back to the Home.

I stressed that, if we didn't do this and we gave everybody a treat at a different time, we might be so held up that the swim might not be possible. My thinking here was to the effect that, of all possible forms of rejection, Andy would prefer an oral one to consolidate his "paranoid" position and would have to delay coming to the refreshment stand in order to force my hand in not feeding him. If he did this, in spite of the clear-cut request on my part which was accepted quite reasonably by the group, then I felt I would be in a position to challenge his actions of today, to ask, "How come?" On the other hand, if he didn't come through and snapped out of his sulk, then nothing was really lost. Sure enough, before we got to the refreshment stand Andy "lost" us and, when we got there, still hadn't shown up. We bought ice cream for everybody and, to show the group that I wasn't just being "mean," I suggested that we wait five minutes for Andy to show up so that he could still conform to our "rule" and have his treat as long as we were still there. He appeared in about five minutes but, as soon as he saw us, he stopped and seemed to get interested in the porcupine exhibit which was close to the refreshment stand. I wanted to acknowledge his presence so I loudly again said, "O.K., better move on now, guys," and at the same time went over to the stand, bought Andy his ice cream and, holding it up, called to him, "C'mon Andy, here's your ice cream. Pretty hot. Let's get it before it melts, huh?" At this, he came over in tears and said accusingly, trying to spite his way out of it, "Huh, I thought you said you wasn't going to buy treat unless we was all together," and then, still squeezing as much sulk out of it as he could, went over under a tree and buried his head in his arms. I said, "Look, Andy. A whole day you've acted kind of funny, not cooperating, like not coming out of the water and staying away from the refreshment stand as if you are mad at me and Joel and the guys. Nobody is hurting you or saying anything to you and still you are acting hurt and upset. I want you to have your treat just as we always want you to have the things we prepare for you. You know that. Here's your ice cream. I wouldn't buy it for you if I didn't want you to have it. What's wrong today, anyway? Gee, before you went to camp you seemed to be over treating people as if they are enemies of yours no matter how nice they are to you." Andy looked at me and took the ice cream, then, without saying anything got up and went with me to catch up with the others who had gone ahead with Joel. As we walked I brought out, "Maybe it's kind of hard getting used to trusting us again after camp, huh?" He said he didn't know so I let it go at that. Afterwards he seemed a trifle less sulky and isolated and made no trouble for the rest of the afternoon. (Entry: 7/29/47, David Wineman)

In recapitulation, it may be seen that the withdrawal of any deliberate attempt to modify Andy's holdout in the water, which is a beginning acting-out of his suspiciousness and paranoid wish to be mistreated, is actually an application of the policy of *strategic noninterference.* Short of just being on hand for safety reasons and to make sure he is not left behind, there is no special handling. Later on, the executive director initiates the first phase of *exploitative interference* when he makes the "rule" that the whole group will have to be together for the ice cream snack, cementing this via the rationale that otherwise too much time will be wasted.[1] This acts as bait to Andy, inviting him to go to even greater lengths in his paranoid maneuver. If, by contrast, it had seemed desirable to soften his reaction, even this same principle of group management could have been easily effected by detailing one of the two adults to tag along with Andy. In this way he could have been "shepherded" along and have been with the group when the refreshment stand was reached. The whole issue thus could have been averted. But since the reverse was clinically desired, the "rule" announcement was the psychological precursor, together with the build-up occasioned through noninterference in the water behavior, to the final interview moment with Andy in which his problem is interpretively "rubbed in." "You are acting as if somebody is hurting you . . . We are really being nice to you . . . You used to act this way but seemed to be getting better . . . Maybe it's hard to get used to trusting us again after camp." A clarifying caution is needed here. This does not mean that there will now be a straight-line, uninterrupted chain of interpretive interviews with Andy in the future all around his paranoid ideology. This was only one moment when it seemed expedi-

---

[1] In *Wayward Youth,* Aichhorn offers some instances of beautifully manipulated exploitative interference performed in his Training School. In one instance he deliberately induces a child to run away by supporting the child's perception of the outside world as a more glamorous and gratifying place than the institution; this he does for the purpose of offering the child a reality contrast between the two, thus precipitating a state of conflict in which the child will be compelled to return to the institution, on his own, because it is innately more gratifying. This then initiates a positive transference to the institution which is necessary for further clinical achievement. In another instance he ingeniously lures a stealing symptom out into the open by the exposure of a boy to a tempting situation, following this by increasing the positive transference with subsequent production of guilt over stealing. At a high moment of transference he suddenly confronts the boy with his knowledge that he has been stealing and induces an immediate and anxious plea on the part of the boy for help. These cases can be reviewed in detail in Chapters Six and Seven of the book.

ent and clinically justified. There might be many more moments when a soft-pedaling of this issue might again be indicated. But this would be a beginning and many of these interspersed interviews in clinical time will eventually trace out the problem for him.

2. Interpretation through counterdelusional action

The treatment home offers the child an antiseptically prepared reality experience. It recognizes that the severe performance weakness of the ego-disturbed child must be met with a reality which above all things is hygienic and calculated to have a benign effect on the child's functioning. However, this is not enough. For the very nature of the ego disturbance being dealt with involves severe distortion of outside reality factors to the extent of actual delusional misinterpretation of the actions of the adult in many areas even when the adult and total climate are as benign as they possibly can be. In moments when the child may be acting out some of these delusional attitudes and ordinary channels of communication through verbal appeal are unnavigable, the clinical adult must convey the basically friendly ideology of the treatment home through what might be termed *counterdelusional action patterns.* When words don't work any more and when the perception that "this is a nice place where they really like me and want to do things for me" is rubbed out by the sudden outcropping of a case-history-developed hatred for the adult, a specific action on the adult side has to be expressed which argues, "This isn't so. How can you believe that in the light of what I am doing right now, this minute, which is just the opposite of what you are saying?" Such occurrences are an everyday event in the lives of children of such primitive ego structures as those of the Pioneers and the need to develop a consistent chain of gestural and action rebuttals for these delusions about the adult is one of the paramount tasks in the treatment environment.

During the treat in the station wagon Mike became wild and started throwing orange peels around. Dave (Exec. Dir.) asked him to stop this activity, stating that eating could not be allowed in the station wagon under these conditions, and immediately Mike handed the orange to me saying, "Here you fuckers, if you don't want me to eat . . ." Dave clarified that this had not been said, that he had only said that under certain conditions, i.e., throwing food around in the wagon, which made driving dangerous, we could not have eating in the wagon. He also pointed out that he had not told Mike to give up his orange but was warning him. "Shit," said Mike, "you bastards just want me to starve, you don't give a damn . . ." I again offered the orange to him, saying, "C'mon now, Mike, here is your orange. You know what Dave means, come on," and he took it without further comment, grabbing it and keeping a surly front for some thirty more minutes but uttering no more accusations. (Entry: 3/24/47, Pearl Bruce)

Mike, reacting to a safety rule with a delusional charge against the adult, will not yield his point after a simple verbal reassurance from either the counselor or the executive director. The counselor must concretely counter his delusional insistence by actually holding the orange in front of him, an action which becomes fused with her interpretive remarks and means, "You see, we really want you to eat. Here it is." It is important that Mike take the orange back and eat it for this means that his delusional argument is, so to speak, "swallowed up" with the orange itself.

One of the pet delusional arguments of the child whose ego is poor in performing the task of straight causal thinking is to misconstrue outer environmental events over which the adult has no control as a deliberate scheme on the part of the adult aimed against the child.

On the way home from school, when the station wagon jerked, Danny cursed Bob (head counselor driving) and accused him of wanting to kill him. This happened a second time, a couple of blocks later, when Bob had again to swerve to avoid a car, and Danny screamed at Bob in the very pitch of rage. I leaned over and told Danny he could sit on my lap, which he did willingly and grudgingly at the same time. (Entry: 10/1/47, Paul Deutschberger)

Here the action of the counselor in taking Danny on his lap is meant to convey: "Look, Danny, I am so concerned about your being bumped that I want to shield you with my own body. How can such adults want to kill you?" Even though Danny has directed his accusation against Bob, the driver, and it is Paul who handles it, the tendency of the child in the group climate is to lump the group-identified adults into one composite adult image so that the actions of one adult have implications for all other adults. Many such moments against which counterdelusional challenges from the adult side of the picture are directed make up a chain of reality reference points around which the case-history-enforced image of the adult as rejecting, cruel, or calloused can be neutralized.[2]

3. *Focusing experiences through the interview*

Interviewing in the residential setting with ego-disturbed children deviates considerably from the typical design found in the office interview practice of the caseworker or psychiatrist.[3] The main shift in emphasis is found in the space-time arrangements around interviewing *per se*. Interview by appointment is simply not valid with these children because certain moments in their experience in combination with certain behavioral issues which they create are more fertile for verbal handling than others and no appointment pattern could possibly previsualize which would be which. Thus, interviewing in the treatment milieu presupposes a mobility on the part of the residential clinician for *focusing experiences through the interview* in keeping with ongoing behavioral trends which may at any given moment display high clinical utility. The analogy may be made here to the investor in stocks who must watch ticker tape recordings and market quotations listings from different exchanges all over the fiscal community in order to know when to buy, when to sell. He acts in accordance with the indications of these data and he must have the initiative needed to act when it is opportune to "cash in" on his hunches. Beyond this departure from traditional space-time arrangements for interviewing there is still another, if more subtle, shift in emphasis in the residential framework. While not all interviews in the office setting are *interpretational,* there is a tendency to believe that it is this style of interviewing that holds the greatest promise for allowing ego change to take place. Life in the treatment home with ego-disturbed children, however, seems to impart a variety of functions to the interview approach, each appearing to have an autonomy and usefulness of its own in the approach to ego support and repair. When inspected quite carefully, these various functions differ from each other and from the interpretational interview which finally emerges in its own right as only

[2] The clearest and best described instances of counterdelusional handling of behavior within a residential treatment milieu are to be found in Bruno Bettelheim, *op. cit.*

[3] For a representative and informative picture of the use of the psychiatric interview method with more typically neurotic children, the reader is referred to Helen Witmer, Ed., *Psychiatric Interviews with Children* (New York: Commonwealth Fund, 1946).

one clear-cut interview function among many, with certain criteria pertaining to its application and usability. Thus, mobility for *focusing experiences through interviews* is important not only for those experiences which may lend themselves to interpretive handling, but for a variety of other experiences as well which may form the basis for other approaches toward influencing the ego. This refinement and subdivision of interview goal function actually is built around the peculiar breakdown in ego functioning of this type of child. This may be clarified further through classification of the various interview strategies that were used.

a. THE "RUB-IN" INTERVIEW. In part, the severely ego-disturbed child of the type we deal with in this study seems afflicted with a certain blindness or fogginess in his perceptual relations with outside reality.[4] In trying to cope with this aspect of ego disturbance in our work with the Pioneer House youngsters and other children with similar patterns in camp and club settings, using the interview for purposes of reality "rub-in" has seemed to be one avenue of approach. The "rub-in" interview has as its special function the task of making more vivid for the ego certain elements of reality to which it is customarily quite deaf and blind. The residential clinician, living in the same milieu with the child, can select certain issues which show his peculiar lack of reality awareness while they are still "hot off the press" and try to reinterpret the happenings involved so that the previous dimness with which the child approached the situation is replaced with some sharper cognitive awareness of what is involved from the point of view of physical and especially social reality.

This afternoon we went for a station wagon ride out in the country. When we stopped off for a snack at a soft drinks spot, Mike suddenly dropped to his hands and knees and started crawling on the floor. He wiggled his hips and made coitus movements along with this. Also he began to make high pitched noises and giggled wildly at the rest of the group. I asked him to get up, saying that nobody acted like that in public. After we got home, I had a talk with him. I rubbed the point in even more emphatically. He said, "What did I do?" I replied that there was nothing bad in what he did and, if he felt like doing that at Pioneer House for a "laugh," it might be O.K. But, I continued, people simply didn't act like that in public. (Entry: 5/2/47, David Wineman)

[4] See *Children Who Hate*, p. 122.

Mike's behavior in this instance, we would feel, is due to real social blindness "in the raw." If he had been more than usually upset about something or if the group had been intoxicated with wildness beyond control, it would have been different. In other words, we can see no specific determinant for this brand of behavior, which by the way was quite prominent in Mike's pattern, beyond the pure friendliness of his ego toward his impulse demands coupled with a very low threshold for social amenities. What is "rubbed in" in this interview is that there is a *sliding scale of acceptability* of behavior depending upon the situation that one is in. Thus, "in public, we don't act this way" is the theme of the "rub-in."

In other situations there is more pointedly an issue of reality consequences at stake toward the visualization of which the ego is blocked.

Out in the backyard this evening Danny swore loudly on various occasions, with his usual public address system volume, oblivious to counselor requests to stop. Finally a neighbor poked his head out of the window and bawled out just as loudly, "Hey, you better shut up or I'll call the police. You can't talk like that." At this point, Danny was asked to come inside and I had a talk with him.

Danny: I can swear all I want in my own goddam (more obscene modifiers) backyard.

Director: No, you can't. Didn't you hear the guy next door threaten to call the cops? What kind of spot would you and Pioneer House be in then?

Danny: I don't give a goddam.

Director: Look Danny, you have to watch yourself outside. The neighbors won't take it. Whether it's your backyard or not, it doesn't matter. The guy next door really will call the police if it keeps up. What will we do then?

Danny: Hell with the police.

Director: Well, what could we tell them? How could we avoid trouble if it gets to the point that the neighbors call the police? It is all right to say the hell with them now but how about when they show up? Think they'll take that kind of remark?

Danny: O.K., I'll watch it.

Director: I hope you can control yourself because it would be quite serious otherwise. (Entry: 6/15/47, Fritz Redl)

Here we can see that the main function of the "rub-in" is to try to make more vivid and dramatic for Danny's ego just how it would seem when the police do pull up to the front door of Pioneer House. This is really the reality consequence that he and we have to face in this particular situation. Basically, we are trying here to create some "richer rapport with the future" than Danny is usually capable of achieving. This, we hope, will act, in turn, as a brake upon his unacceptable obscenity, which will, if unchecked, involve future action on the part of the social environment.

In the application of the "rub-in" interview there are at least two clinical cautions that should be stressed. First, there is a temptation to take every mishandled reality issue that comes up and subject it to such interviewing. This would be disastrous for it would produce an undue amount of resistance and resentment and leave scarcely any free time for anything else on the clinical agenda. Secondly, the application of a rub-in interview, especially since it deals quite firmly and bluntly with the issue at hand, is most valid only when the rapport tone between child and adult is as positive as it can become. In moments of extremely negative rapport or transference, obviously, any attempt of the clinician to represent reality in this way will be regarded as a hostile act on the part of the "mean" adult.

b. THE "GUILT-SQUEEZE" INTERVIEW. The ego-disturbed child has great difficulty in the whole area of coping with guilt feelings.[5] First, part of the trouble is due to the thoroughness and efficiency with which the special "road block" placed by the ego in the path of guilt feelings does its job. Thus, even though a child may have some value islands internally intact which function to produce guilt in connection with specific acts of one kind or another, this is still not enough. The ego acquires a certain "tone deafness" to the notes of its own superego and the potentially forbidden act goes on. A second basic problem arises with respect to the inability of the ego to handle those guilt feelings that have been strong enough to get through the barrier into the ego. Experienced guilt feelings, in other words, "floor" the ego of the type of child we are describing. In these situations we usually see guilt as being met with aggressive responses and hostility against the outside. Our interviewing in connection with guilt issues of either kind has seemed to us to involve a kind of "squeezing" process in which we try either to squeeze legitimate but latent guilt feelings out into open awareness and to help strengthen their meaning to the ego

[5] *Children Who Hate*, p. 105.

or, in the case where they have already broken out and become diffused into aggression, to squeeze the aggression issue back into the original guilt picture that produced it.[6]

The function of the "guilt-squeeze" interview in helping the ego with the first of the problems raised above, namely, in permitting entry of a value issue into awareness is shown in the following brief action sequence:

Today was Bob's (head counselor) day off. Mike insisted upon going upstairs and waking him right after breakfast in order to get a toy plane that he had asked Bob to keep. His counselor told him that he would have to wait until Bob got up, but he was adamant and began to raise quite a fuss, saying he didn't care if he was awake or asleep. He was going to have his plane and that was that. I put it to him this way: "Don't you think Bob deserves a chance to rest up a bit? After all, he works plenty hard around here just so you and the other guys can have a good time. Do you really think Bob should be treated as mean as being waked up early on his day off?" Mike "gave" on this point amazingly well, saying, "I guess you're right, Dave." (Entry: 2/1/48, David Wineman)

In this interview it is clear that what we have done is to touch off an appeal to a latent value awareness that is already there to begin with but needs special support from the outside to emerge and become usable by the ego. The counselor's telling him that he can't do it is not enough for Mike. To any more normal ego this would already mean, "Listen, that would be kind of hard on the poor guy, wait until he gets up." But with Mike this has to be much more sharply focused than is possible by a mere implication. Our reader may ask at this point, "Suppose Mike doesn't 'give'?" We would still feel that such an interview attempt was valid. The value of the guilt-squeeze interview lies not necessarily in pressuring an admission of guilt, but rather *in strengthening a value awareness,* even if only for later reference.

In *Children Who Hate* we have depicted Bill, one of our Pioneers, in troubled straits because of his involvement in a stealing incident. The way in which this incident was handled by the counselor may serve to illustrate the second function of the guilt-squeeze interview, namely, that of shaping a guilt issue out of an aggressive

[6] Sigmund Freud early pointed to the relation between guilt and aggression in "Criminality from A Sense of Guilt," in *Collected Papers, Vol. 4* (London: Hogarth Press, 1924).

sequence of behavior that has been produced as a reaction to the guilt itself.[7]

Bill, who ordinarily is quite positive toward me, was quite rebellious when I reminded him that he wasn't supposed to hit golf balls over into the next door neighbor's yard. Instead of replying with his usual "O.K., Yo-Yo" (his and the group's pet name for me) and coming along with the suggestion, he snarled back at me, "Yer mammy," and deliberately knocked one over the fence. When I insisted that this was not acceptable and reminded Bill that I would now have to confiscate the club, Bill ran away, throwing the club at me. Five minutes later I found Bill trying to break down the office door with a two-by-four because he thought I had put the club in there. I relieved him of the two-by-four and asked him what was bothering him that he should act so "mean" this morning. Bill said that he was going to take "that club to school" or he wasn't going, and I said, "How come? You guys never get to take your golf clubs to school anyway." But Bill was adamant and refused to go along, so the group was taken without him. When I returned, Bill was even more upset and was angrily packing his clothes saying that he wasn't going to stay at this "goddam dump no more," etc. I said nothing but just stayed with him, finally bringing out that something must be bothering Bill and that I was sure it wasn't just the golf club. What was it? First, Bill said that nothing was wrong and then angrily threw out, "That goddam Danny, he thinks that he can shove everybody around!" I replied that I hadn't seen Danny do anything special this morning to Bill or anyone else. Was Bill sure that was it? Bill didn't answer and I said, "O.K., if you don't want to talk about whatever it is, I guess we'll have to skip it, but I think it would be better if you came out in the open . . ." Finally Bill, in a gust of feeling, said, "I didn't keep none of it and I ain't going to be blamed for it. Last night Mike went over to that old lady that lives next door and gave her some flowers. I was with him and we saw she had a roll of bills this big (rolls up his fist). Mike said for me to watch out in the yard this morning and he would go over and swipe it, and I did but I ain't got any of it and I won't get blamed for what he did. The wallet is hidden in the garage." (Entry: 5/13/48, Joel Vernick)

In this episode we see the counselor helping Bill to realize that his aggressive behavior of the morning in question is related to his guilt surrounding his participation with Mike in the stealing episode. Here the clinical goal is of a long-range nature. We seek to help the ego through many such sessions to become familiar with

[7] See *Children Who Hate*, pp. 107-108.

its need to escape from guilt and to make the guilt more usable as an aggression-stopping rather than as an aggression-producing agent. Should this be achievable, Bill will be able to come to the adult he likes and trusts most and confide in him instead of escaping into guilt-denial mechanisms.[8]

We should like to stress, before leaving our discussion of the guilt-squeeze interview, that its use must be guarded by the most stringent clinical cautions. It should be obvious that it will *never* be used in the case of a child who shows evidence of open guilt feelings about an act. Thus, it is not the style of interviewing that would be very much in vogue with the classic psychoneurotic child, who suffers all too often from too intense value sensitivity and guilt. For example, to try to stir up increased guilt feelings in a child who is already quite miserable because he cannot break his compulsion to steal from his mother's purse, who openly admits it, who says, "I know it's wrong, I don't want to do it but what can I do?" would constitute a serious clinical error since obviously his guilt is already so strong that, if guilt alone were to strengthen his controls against his act, he would not be in such straits to begin with. In such cases it is obvious that quite a different area of pathology than the one we are talking about in this section is involved and that piling more guilt on may prove definitely harmful, may force the child to become self-destructive or to draw serious punishment upon himself through frantic increase of misbehavior. We should use such a technique as the guilt-squeeze interview *only when we are absolutely sure,* on the basis of reliable observation of behavior and case history information, that we are dealing with well-entrenched defenses against guilt or with a real deficiency in the ability of a given child either to feel guilt in appreciably usable quantities or, when he does feel it, to have sufficient tolerance for it so that he does not immediately take flight into aggression as an escape with no residue of awareness of either the guilt-producing act or the guilt itself.

c. THE EXPRESSIONAL INTERVIEW. One of the most widely known and accepted functions of the therapeutic interview, next to its interpretive aspects, is that of providing a chance for expression of feeling. The value of this has long been recognized in almost all circles of life, from the layman who understands that "you feel

---

[8] For a theoretical discussion of the role of values in personality functioning see Daniel Miller and Max Hutt, "Value Interiorization and Personality Development," *J. Soc. Issues,* 5, (4), 1949, pp. 2-30.

better if you can just blow off a little steam" to the psychiatrists and social workers who talk about "catharsis," "abreaction," etc. The significant clinical fact here is that in ways which are as yet not quite clear there is some temporary advantage to the ego in the release found in this opportunity for expression. In residential practice with the severely ego-disturbed child, there is a clear-cut basis for trying to provide him with avenues through which he may achieve such experiences. This is found in the clinical fact that with these types of children there is such a severe underdevelopment in their ability to use language as a means of expression of emotion. Their veritable fixation on action-proneness as a means of expression is partly a function of this peculiar atrophy of verbal symbolization of feelings. Thus, any and all successful attempts that are made to assist the child in the use of words to express feelings are in themselves a form of direct support and repair to ego. Because this function of the interview, namely, its expressional value to the ego, is so important, it is especially necessary and desirable not to befog this prized channel with attempts at insight giving and interpretation to which may beckon so invitingly much of the material that may emerge in this kind of interview moment. This means that interpretation would be frowned upon, not in all interviews, but only in those where there is an obvious clinical advantage and usefulness to the ego in feeling drainage through its own words rather than insight through interpretation from the clinician's mouth, so to speak. The following illustration may clarify these points:

Danny was all puffed up with sullenness and hostility when he came home from school today, and acted quite aggressively to our housemother and other group members. I asked him quietly if something was wrong. First he ignored me and then suddenly said, "I want to talk to you private, Wineman." We went into the office. Here he sat down, propped his chin up on his fists and said, "I ain't gonna go back to that goddam school tomorrow. The guys all tease me about pissing the bed and they tell everybody in the school about it. Then they say my privates are small and I got a tiny dick and all of that." Here he began to cry, with large tears streaming down his cheeks. "I'll kill the dirty bastards, that's what I'll do. They can't keep teasing me that way." I listened with scarcely a word from me and he repeated the theme a few times. I said I was sorry to hear that, that I knew this was hard to stand. "I ain't the only one who pisses the bed around here and they know it." I agreed that this was so. A couple of the other guys had the same problem. At this he seemed to become more relaxed, as though simply reassuring him that the problem wasn't his alone somehow took the smart out of the public teasing the others were doing. (Entry: 10/13/47, David Wineman)

Obviously this interview has many elements in it that could be explored. For instance, the castration elements, concerning which there was corroborative material in other aspects of his behavior, could have been probed. Social problems could have been raised: "You know the guys are so mean to you partly because of the way you act toward them. Maybe if we could help you in that, they wouldn't have to try to embarrass you in school." Yet, it was felt that none of these approaches was as yet warranted and that, even if it was, the pure expressional element was so important at this moment that other manipulative attempts should be tried separately. For here Danny is seen using a verbal mode of conveying anger, hurt, confusion instead of brutal aggression, and this achievement should be granted maximal protection.

d. The "Counterdistortional" Interview. One of the striking features in the behavior of the youngsters we are dealing with is their uncanny skill in using alibi patterns against their own conscience, in defense of impulsivity.[9] This is especially fascinating when we contrast it with the spectacle of deficiency and helplessness in the way in which the ego performs in so many other areas which do not have to do with value demands against the primitive and impulsive in their behavior. In these former situations we are suddenly confronted with ego functions which seem to be hypertrophically developed. Far from being inefficient, in these moments the ego performs with amazing agility and nimbleness. The classical model for this type of defense is found in the typical alibi behavior of a delinquent suspected of stealing. Here, all kinds of argument acrobatics are resorted to in order to keep the interrogator from discovering, and the child from confessing, the truth. Our youngsters, however, act in this way not only when they are involved in a stealing incident, but on any item of impulsive behavior which they understand is ordinarily tabu but in which, nevertheless, they have indulged. Thus, therapy with this type of youngster, carried on in the residential scene, is dependent in part upon ways and means of actually coming to grips with the skill pattern involved in this protectiveness toward id impulses through what may be termed the

---

[9] See *Children Who Hate*, pp. 141-196.

"counterdistortional" interview session. In this type of interview the residential clinician initiates discussion with the child around actual issues which arise in the group life with him and which are produced from such outcroppings of well-protected impulsiveness as we have described. We try to lure him into a confession of misdeed or to confront him with a particularly untenable piece of behavior or to shock him into an admission of guilt, unfairness, or what not, depending upon the nature of the incident or incidents that have occurred in the group. For, unless one elicits some admission from the child that he is in fact involved in the very impulsivity that makes up such an important part of this symptom picture, the ego has no incentive toward any kind of educability in the direction of change. To avoid misunderstanding, it should be emphasized that the issue here is not that such clarification with the child is in itself therapy. The main point is that without it therapy could not really happen. The analogy of the delinquent who has stolen is a case in point. Unless one gets some clear-cut admission from a delinquent that he does in fact steal, one cannot even start working with him or this problem.

An element which usually operates as an asset in the application of the counterdistortional interview is that these youngsters actually seem to believe in something like a basically agreed upon duelling code.[10] This means, for instance, that if they catch the adult in an inconsistency or premature attempt to call their bluff before he can prove his point, or if he should make an insinuation as to a motive on their part for which he does not have enough evidence, they react as though he is totally in the wrong, as though from now on, since such a mistake was committed, the adult no longer has the right even to continue the discussion, no matter how obvious the real situation would be to them as well as to the interviewer. On the other hand, it could be observed by us that, if the interviewer learned to be skillful enough to avoid such traps and to work within the duelling code set by them, the mere fact of his allegiance to it seemed to melt away some of their resistance against surrender and they would finally admit their complicity in an issue, even though it might put them at a temporary disadvantage.

Taking an experience from the Pioneer House setting, a situation involving Bill might be considered as typical. Bill, like all of the other Pioneers, had consistent difficulty in the classroom situation,

10 See *Children Who Hate*, pp. 177-178.

in spite of the fact that the teacher and school worked very hard to meet the clinical demands of our group. On one occasion, he had to be taken home because of an aggressive episode and, as usual, was vehement in projecting all of the blame upon the teacher, cursing him out liberally and insisting that he was not going to go back to school because the teacher was mistreating him. In a counterdistortional interview the same day with the director of the Home the following happened:

Director: Well, Bill, I was sorry to learn that you had to be brought home from school today. How come?

Bill: (regarding me warily) That goddam teacher is not going to get away with pushing me around, shoving me in my seat, and things like that.

Director: What did he do to you?

Bill: Aw, he came up and grabbed me and took me out in the hall.

Director: Why did he do this?

Bill: How am I supposed to know why he did it?

Director: What I mean is, did he have some reason for acting this way toward you?

Bill: Hell, no.

Director: It is hard for me to understand why your teacher would just suddenly come up and grab you and take you out in the hall.

Bill: Well, he did.

Director: Bill, I am not saying that he didn't. All I am trying to find out is if he had some reason to do this. Can you think of anything that may have been happening at the time that might explain it?

Bill: No.

Director: Look, Bill, it just doesn't make sense that your teacher would just do that out of the blue. Something must have been going on.

Bill: That goddam Joe (a kid in class) started fussing around with my stuff. I just tell him to get the hell away and K. (teacher) comes up and puts me out in the hall.

Director: That's all that happened?

Bill: Yeah.

Director: Did Joe go away when you told him to?

Bill: What?

Director: Did Joe leave your stuff alone as soon as you told him to?

Bill: Hell, no. So I pushed him and he still came back. So I smacked his face in and he started to cry.

Director: And then what happened?

Bill: K. came over and told me to cut it out. He said to sit down.

Director: Did you?

Bill: I said I wasn't going to let that goddam Joe monkey with my stuff and K. said to sit down.

Director: Did you?

Bill: Did I what?

Director: Sit down.

Bill: Yes.

Director: Then why did you say before he put you in your seat?

Bill: He did.

Director: I thought you just said you cooperated and sat down when he asked you to. If you did, why did he have to put you in your seat?

Bill: (silence)

Director: Something here isn't making sense, Bill.

Bill: Well, when he came up he said to lay off Joe and I said I wasn't going to let him mess up my stuff.

Director: And then what happened?

Bill: He said, "Sit down and I'll attend to that." I said he better get the hell away from here.

Director: Where was Joe at this time?

Bill: Back in his seat.

Director: Then what was the fuss about?

Bill: I wanted to make sure.

Director: Sure about what?

Bill: That he wouldn't come back. K. said, "Sit down." So I said I wouldn't if that Joe wouldn't stay away from my stuff.

Director: Then what happened?

Bill: K. said, "Sit down."

Director: And then?

Bill: He sat me down.

Director: What happened then?

Bill: I said, "Leggo me, you sonofabitch."

Director: What happened then?

Bill: He took me out in the hall and said I couldn't talk like that to him. And then he called up here and the counselor came out to get me.

Director: In other words, you refused to sit down and end the fight.

Bill: Yes.

Director: And then when K. sat you down, you cussed him out right in front of everybody.

Bill: Yeah.

Director: How come?

Bill: Why should I let that goddam Joe mess with my stuff?
Director: Was he still doing it?
Bill: No.
Director: Then how come you cussed out the teacher because of that?
Bill: (silence)
Director: That wasn't the reason you were cussing him out, was
Bill: What do you mean?
Director: Well, how could it be if Joe wasn't doing it any more?
Bill: (silence)
Director: You really cussed out K. for insisting that you sit down; he
   wasn't saying it was O.K. for Joe to mess with your stuff, was he?
Bill: No.
Director: But you still let him have it right in front of everybody be-
   cause, when you wouldn't sit down, he sat you down.
Bill: That's right.
Director: But is it?
Bill: He don't have no right to put me in my seat. I don't have to
   sit down if I don't wanna.
Director: Tell me something. Where do you think you could get away
   with acting like that? In what classroom, anywhere, could you simply
   go after a kid when the teacher had just told you to stay in your
   seat?
Bill: (silence) (Entry: 9/28/47, Fritz Redl)

Finally, here, after detailed probing and checking, the director
has been able to confront Bill with what he has really done and in
so doing actually to promote an awareness in Bill of one of his real
problems: "You do what you want to do just because you want to
do it." We are aware, of course, of the clinical complexity of this
behavior in addition to the pure impulsivity issue and also that it
may lure us in two directions, neither of which would be valid
here. (1) It seems to hold such fertile possibilities for interpretive
probing into why he has to treat the teacher that way. (2) It is such
a perfect "set-up" for a value lesson right there and then. Yet both
of these possibilities should really be warded off until later in treatment when many preparatory interviews will have worked on the
problem of his poor functioning in total reality situations. All we
want to show him here is that he has exploited a situation to behave
impulsively and primitively toward his teacher. His initial caginess
in refusing to divulge all he has done, in pretending that his teacher
was the "mean" one, has to be broken through in the counterdis-

tortional style of interview before this confession will be forth-coming.[11]

e. THE INTERPRETATIONAL INTERVIEW. As its title suggests, the interpretational interview is aimed at interpreting mental mechanisms for the purpose of influencing the ego's functioning in a clinically desired direction. Its use with the ego-disturbed child presupposes the kind of mobility for selection of issue and interview moments already described in the section on "Focusing experiences through the interview." Within such a framework it is possible to spread interpretational coverage over a wide variety of issues relevant to the particular disturbance patterns of the child in residential therapy. Aside from the selection of issues to be approached through the interpretational interview, the time planning itself becomes a fascinating problem and basically a three-way breakdown is possible:

(1) Interpretation within short-range time proximity to the actual behavioral item under consideration.

This is really interpretation in almost direct time-context to a given item. In its favor is the obvious point that the issue is still "hot" and that this very vividness is a valuable asset when one considers the rapid rate of evaporation of awareness of his own contribution to behavioral items which typifies this kind of youngster. Against it is the fact that, just because the issue is still hot, what little positive functioning the ego of the child has normally at its behest is not usable because of the momentary liquidation of ego functioning. Thus, any interpretation in direct context with the problem-relevant issue which the interpretation is aimed at must allow enough time for minimal clearing away of "smoke from the battlefield" and some restitution of control and logical functioning.

Tonight Danny became quite upset in a fight with Bill and went into one of his rage tantrums. I took him into the office to cool off and he, as usual, began to insult me with all kinds of obscenities. I told him I would let him go back to the group after he quieted down and in about five minutes he did, saying that if I did not hold him he would stop trying to kick things over and at me and would just sit down. I said, "O.K.," and we sat there for a while. In the course of this, he began to talk and accused me of being unfair to him, said I didn't

[11] The reader will find a very interesting example of the point counterpoint style of interviewing in some of the recorded interviews in Edmund Bergler, M.D., *Neurotic Counterfeit-Sex* (New York: Grune & Stratton, Inc., 1951).

do anything to the others, just to him. I quietly counterargued this by showing him instances where I interfered with the others just as much and by reassuring him that I held him only when he got mad and couldn't control himself. He then said repeatedly, "I always swear like that when I get mad." I then suggested that maybe sometimes it was the other way around; sometimes I felt that he worked himself up to a fury so that he could hit and swear the way he liked. As soon as this interpretive attempt sank in, Danny got mad and yelled, "Don't say that. It isn't like that. No, I don't." (Entry: 12/16/46, Fritz Redl)

The very struggle Danny puts up against acceptance indicates that he is able to grasp the interpretation, that enough time has elapsed, in other words, between the acting out and the interpretive attempt to insure restitution of some inner cognitive functioning of the ego, even if it is displeased with what it perceives. Had the interpretation been made earlier, during the fit, while he was still disconnected, it would have fallen entirely by the wayside. The refusal to accept the interpretation is in itself a manifestation of deep-set resistances which themselves will require more pervasive and long-range handling than is envisaged in this attempt, which is only the beginning of such a process. Here only a single item in very close proximity to its emergence in the living situation is interpreted.

(2) Postsituational interpretation with protective isolation of the ego from the life scene in which the behavioral item which is to be interpreted has taken place.

Let us return to the same mechanism of Danny's that was interpreted in the above example, namely, his secondary gain pattern growing out of the temper tantrum. We found that in the classroom situation he was constantly producing tantrums, as a result of which he had to be taken back to Pioneer House for the day because it would have been too disruptive to the total classroom situation for him to remain. It soon became clear that he was engaged in a two-step process: (a) He was almost voluntarily abandoning control around petty issues having little real frustration value for him, and (b) once started, he actually lost control and produced a real tantrum against which his defenses were still quite weak. It was felt therefore that the strategic point at which to strike was the first step in this process, which actually was a kind of "malingering" against his nascent control pattern. This decision was supported by the fact that continuous observation within the Home itself indicated that he was beginning actually to develop controls against his symptom which were then being abandoned in the school situation. Interviews in the school situation around these upsets would have been very difficult because the high motivation to get "kicked out" right there on the spot would have defeated all attempts at showing him what he was doing. This seemed to be implied because, obviously, being sent home without any negative consequences was very pleasurable and constituted the main motive behind the self-regulated tantrums. Thus, it was important to let him go through with another one of these episodes, bring him home to the more gratifying and less issue-identified atmosphere, and make the interpretive attempt.

Exec. Dir.: Danny, could we talk a little about your troubles at school?
Danny: (ingenuously) Aw, you know how it is, Dave, those guys get me all upset and I can't help myself.
Exec. Dir.: How do they upset you?
Danny: Well, they make a lot of noise and I can't stand that, you know.
Exec. Dir.: Can't you go across the hall to the rest room? I know your teacher would be glad to let you do that.
Danny: I don't like to go there (lamely).
Exec. Dir.: You know, Danny, what I think is wrong?
Danny: What?
Exec. Dir.: Well, here at Pioneer House we've become quite familiar with your tantrums. Many times we know that you really can't help yourself. Yet it seems as though you have begun to improve quite a bit and you don't have so many any more. Still at school you don't try to control yourself at all. You just let yourself go. I wonder why.
Danny: I don't know.
Exec. Dir.: Well, I think you really want to get sent home. I know it's more pleasant here than in school and we like you and want to give you as much fun as possible. But it seems as though you still don't get enough even with all of the things we do together. Do you feel that way?
Danny: I do like it here.
Exec. Dir.: Maybe even enough to try to make sure that you will get sent home so that you can have an extra share of it?
Danny: Uh, uh. I don't think that's it.
Exec. Dir.: Well, I'll tell you what. Why don't we try it this way—whenever you feel you're in hot water at school, you call me. I'll arrange with the school so that they'll let you do that. Then I'll

come out there and talk with you right there. Maybe we can help
you get through the day that way.

Danny: (No comment, no "gripes.") (Entry: 1/12/47, David Wineman)

In this interview sequence, the interpretation involves a wider
slice than just pointing out the mechanism of "letting yourself go."
It also interprets a motive to Danny: "You really want to get sent
here because you want more gratifications." This is fused with a
substitute gratification of lesser satisfaction richness: "I will come
out to you." Through this, the adult shows that he is concerned,
wants to help Danny enough to make a special trip. It also sets the
stage for a restructuring of the interview situation as well as of the
gratification pattern. Interviews will now be held in school. It is felt
that with this kind of interpretive preparation, this shifting of scene
has more of a strategic chance. Thus, the interpretation has really
a double goal: (a) Increasing the insight of the ego as to what is
happening in this situation, and why, and (b) Through this, paving the way for an increased reality demand for control.

(3) Presituational or anticipatory interpretation of incipient breakdown of controls for the purpose of strengthening defenses
against sudden symptom onrush.

Most symptoms which involve a sudden reduction of control
against impulses more or less "advertise" their incipient invasion of
the ego through "storm warnings." Certain behavior manifestations
emerge that are always associated with the early developmental
stages of the particular upset involved. If sufficient interviewing has
gone on previously, in which the mechanism itself has been fairly
well identified for the child, then "tipping him off" that an episode
is on the way may help the ego to ward off a full-scale invasion.
This is especially true if the ego has already become positively identified with our therapeutic attempts in its behalf. Thus, for example,
considering Danny's temper tantrum symptom again, many times
during the later stages of treatment we could help him ward off
temper outbursts by pointing out to him that he was leading up
to one.

Tonight, Danny was displeased with the evening activity plan which
called for work in the craft shop. This was in contrast to the rest of
the group who were quite keen on carving out plaques to hang in

their rooms. Danny sat glowering for a while. Joel, who was on duty with the group, talked with him and tried to suggest some substitute activities, but Danny would not discuss it with him except to say that he wanted to go for a station wagon ride and that he never got to do what he wanted, etc. Joel patiently tried to show him that this was not true, that we had in fact gone out to a park last night. Nothing sufficed to cool Danny's anger. Finally, Joel had to join the rest of the group in the shop. I was in the living room at the time, watching the whole proceeding. When Joel left, Danny got up and walked through the kitchen, slamming the door viciously. He went into the wood shop, picked up a piece of wood, slammed it down and walked out again. At this point I joined him and said, "Danny, you know you are really going to work yourself up to a tantrum. This is just how you act before you go into one. I know you are disappointed in the program but what good will it do to 'blow your top?'" He paid no attention to me and stalked about the room angrily. He picked up a comic book and threw it down. Then I said, "Look, in about ten minutes you will really begin to feel angry. You're going to start throwing more stuff around and get really destructive. I will ask you to stop and you'll begin to swear at me. By that time you won't be able to stop but now you can. How about it?" He looked at me and sat down quite sullenly. I asked him if there was anything we might do together and he said, "Hell with you." I replied, "I'm sorry you feel bad but it's better than getting all upset, especially if you are really able to control yourself." About half an hour later he came to my office quite enthusiastically to report that he had made a project for himself: he cleaned out the book shelves of some unusable torn books and magazines. Would I help him throw them out in the alley? I praised him, and he and I carried out the debris and burned it in the alley. (Entry: 5/6/48, David Wineman)

Of course, this would have been totally impossible during the early stages of treatment. By this time, Danny had established some real controls over aggressive behavior and was in sufficiently positive rapport with the adult staff for it to use such an approach. Still, the ego needed this extra "quick power charge" to cope with the impending attack. In addition to ego gains for handling it, there already was, however, less need for the outbursts because of the increase in security and gratification of basic needs which had been made possible during the previous seventeen months.

f. THE PROMOTIONAL BUILD-UP INTERVIEW. Admittedly, our present knowledge about the dynamics of self-imagery on the ego level in children is rather scanty.[12] Yet, in normal and clasically neurotic children, the ego seems to have some basic ability to enter into two types of activity which are quite important in this process. First, the normal child usually is able to construct some kind of consistent image of the self as it exists at any given time. He knows "what kind of guy" he is. Second, the normal child has within his ego boundaries some kind of value-derived ego-ideal of what he would like to be or strive toward. If we follow the figure of speech already introduced, he knows what "kind of guy" he would like his total self to be. One of the original problems of "egos that cannot perform" is their serious impoverishment on both of these levels of activity. Very slowly and subtly, as the cumulative weight of the therapeutic design begins to hit the children, a faint beginning in the evolution of ego-ideal imagery manifests itself. For example, Mike, standing next to his teacher who is trying to cope with a classmate in a tantrum, is heard to say, "Gee, look at that guy. I used to be like that when I first came to Pioneer House." Such verbalizations are signs that some new ego imagery is being developed along lines of self-conceptualization stemming from adult-identified value schemes, which, for the first time, are beginning to register on the ego. Yet, because these ego images are so fragile and tender, there is need for direct nourishment through what could be termed the "promotional build-up" style of interviewing. For this purpose, special interview moments are constructed out of the total life scene.

Today, Andy, in a flashback to an old pattern, threw a book at Bette (counselor) in a fit of temper because his craft project fell on the floor and broke. I talked with him about it, pointing out that, while I could see him getting sore over his bad luck, there was no reason to take it out on Bette. Andy was silent on this score, and then I said, "Gee, Andy, I don't think you have to act this way any more when something happens like that." Andy laughed and said he used to do that all the time, and I said, "Yeah, that's just the point I'm making, too. You used to but you don't have to any more because you're getting smarter about things like that. You know it wasn't Bette's fault and that it's kind of mean to take revenge on her." (Entry: 1/2/48, David Wineman)

[12] See Percival M. Symonds, *The Ego and the Self* (New York: Appleton-Century-Crofts, Inc., 1951), and Jeanne Lampl-de Groot, "Neurotics, Delinquents and Ideal-Formation," in *Searchlights On Delinquency*, Editor, K. R. Eissler (New York: International Universities Press, Inc., 1949), for clinically oriented analyses of some of the problems involved in self-perception and behavior.

Of crucial and obvious importance, of course, in this interview approach is the fact that there must be reliable evidence that the new type of self-concept that is being appealed to already exists. This is an attempt not to create but rather to strengthen such an already tangible self-image as a tool for coping with impulsivity.[13]

g. GROUP INTERVIEWS. Any of the individual interview strategies we have been describing can be applied within the total group setting with some mechanical modifications necessitated by the group scene itself. The functions of the interview, however, can remain the same regardless of the mechanical changes. For example, rub-in sessions with groups and guilt-squeeze and counterdistortional sessions were quite common occurrences at Pioneer House as well as in the Group Project and Summer camp settings. The question of when to use the group as opposed to the individual interview or vice versa is a very fascinating one and depends, among other things, upon the amount of collective verbalization the group can be exposed to without being swamped by group psychological excitement which will eventually flood the whole interview design of the moment and make it unusable except for group mischief purposes. In addition to this factor, the question of the issue itself is of importance. Interviewing the group, for example, around an individual problem of one of the group members should be undertaken only if it is felt that the problem itself can be influenced in this way. This will be true even if the individual problem has group psychological dimensions such as bullying, stealing, etc. What impact the group psychological reaction will have on the given individual and his problem as a result of group interviewing is always of crucial significance. Without, however, going into a discussion of criteria for when and how, our point here is that group interviewing is a usable tool in work with this type of disturbance and that it can be broken down to serve the same clinical goals and functions as individual interviewing. The following is a digest of a group interview:

Following an outburst of some rather wild acting-out upon the occasion of the presence of some visitors to Pioneer House in which all

[13] A condensed theoretical treatment of some of the elements involved in the relation between self-imagery and behavior can be found in James Benjamins, "Changes in Performance in Relation to Influences Upon Self-Conceptulization," *The Jn. of Abnormal and Soc. Psych.*, Vol. 45, No. 3, July, 1950, pp. 473-480. See also G. Allport, *Personality: A Psychological Interpretation* (New York: Henry Holt, 1937), and G. Murphy, *Personality* (New York: Harper, 1947).

of the group members had participated, I had a talk with the group about their need to act up in this fashion. First everyone proudly boasted about how much "hell-raising" he had done. Danny was almost manic on the subject, arousing Andy's ire and need to prove that he had done more than anybody else. Mike, Bill, and Larry also chimed in with their own particular contributions. I made the point that we knew exactly what everyone had done, that was why I had asked them all to talk with me. This was a deliberate maneuver on my part, since they were beginning to relive so energetically their behavior of this morning that it could easily have built up to another wild spree of acting-out. I added, "I think that maybe if we can talk about why you guys have to act this way, it would help to prevent the same thing from happening again. How about it?" Danny came in with the comment that he knew why Andy did it—he just wanted to be a "big shit, that's all." Andy retorted with, "How about you, fat boy? Why do you do it?" Danny giggled and said he was always like that. Mike indicted Andy quite emphatically, saying that Andy had pretended that the counselor had hurt him and scratched his leg with a stone to prove it so that he could get even by acting up. I picked this up and asked Andy, "How about it? Was that what happened?" Andy angrily tried to refute the charge but finally was forced to accept the weakness of his argument. I then said that this was one of the things that Andy was doing right along: pulling stuff and then trying to get out from under by holding someone else responsible. Andy then said, "Sure, so what? I'm a show-off." When the rest of the group cackled derisively, I reminded them that they, too, had participated in this; it wasn't only Andy. Mike broke into one of his high-pitched wailing sounds. I pressed the point: Why when visitors were around? What did they think? Danny then said magnanimously, "I guess we all want to be big shits." There was group agreement on this. I reflected this sentiment: "So it boils down really to wanting to put on a show, getting them to notice you. Is that it?" Bill said, "We think that maybe they'll think we're special and come to a show we'll put on." I said, "You know, guys, there is nothing wrong with wanting to show off in front of visitors, but it's the way you guys do it that's kind of off the beam. Our visitors would be glad to watch you do some of the special things you can all do. Like Andy, for instance, who can sing. And Danny, too. If we even want to put on a program for visitors, it would be O.K. But not running around making funny sounds and saying swear words just to impress them. I don't think we have to do that any more. How about it? Can't we figure out ways with the counselors so you guys can have a really good time with our visitors?" They responded pretty favorably to this suggestion and even went so far as to make some fantasies about a big supershow they would put on, how they would invite all of the friends who came to visit us, charge admission, etc. I suggested that they could plan something like this with the counselor if they wished and ended the meeting on this note. (Entry: 8/28/47, David Wineman)

Here we see that there are quite a number of different elements in operation. To begin with, there is an obvious expressional note to their original group confession and reliving of their actions of the morning. Then, on the individual side of the picture, Andy's projective mechanisms are revealed and interpreted as well as his own need to "show off." The rest of the youngsters spontaneously yield on this point following Andy's lead and are able to admit to the show-off theme on a group-wide basis. From here there is a promotional build-up theme in the executive director's attempt to restructure their need for attention from visitors, giving it value support and acceptance, but making suggestions as to how this could be carried out in a more acceptable way. One of the most fascinating elements in this interview is the almost contagious process of the symptom-admission itself, i.e., of being show-offs, which in individual interviewing might be much more difficult to extract because of the absence of group emotional support and the initiatory act of admission by Andy, who was one of the high prestige members of the group. This is one of the reasons why, in moments of favorable group psychological transference to the adult, the group interview can be very effective. On the other hand, as indicated above, there are not only individual but also group psychological variables involved in the destiny of a specific group interview. A careful appraisal of indications as well as counterindications becomes, thus, an important part of clinical strategy.

Total Strategy and Clinical Movement

Total strategy around symptom behavior involves a collective action, distributed through clinical time, of the various techniques or substrategies already separately described and illustrated through cross-sectional flashes of behavior in section I of this chapter. The interweaving of these substrategies into a more perceptible whole, descriptively, may be achieved if we follow a single symptom through its various modes of expression in the life scene of the treatment home, emphasizing particular interactions between symptom and therapeutic strategy at different points in clinical time. For this purpose, the more detailed clinical records of some of the Pioneer House children will be drawn upon. However, this is not meant to represent a full-scale story about all of the clinical events of any particular case, nor will all of the children be used.

1. Giving Ego Support Around a Severe Sibling Confusion

From the case history of Bill, we know that among other severe problems is that of intensive and open sibling rivalry with a slightly older brother. In the treatment setting we observe, however, that, instead of a simple displacement of this hostility to other children, Bill first erects a defense against the hostility in being unusually generous, giving away possessions, food, etc., in an attempt to deny the hostility and to bind the other children to him on a "good or loving brother" basis. This pattern gradually undergoes changes in the direction that Bill finally centers all of his admiration and love on Andy, who is one of the most talented (in school, arts and crafts, sports, etc.) children in the group, much admired by the others and the undisputed child leader. This fact of Andy's high group status may well predispose Bill to select him as the prize sibling surrogate among the Pioneer House children. For Andy is really the "darling of the group," as Bill's brother may have been perceived by him to be the mother's favorite. The fact that the adults in the Home do not play favorites does not alter this possibility too much. Andy's superior performance may well feed fantasies in Bill that, even if the adults don't show it, they still regard him more highly because, in Bill's frame of reference, the superior child, the one who is better in school and more adept generally, would be preferred by his own parents. Thus, finally, it is against this hostility to Andy that his strongest defenses are retained. Bill's complete subjugation to Andy in the fulfillment of this need renders him incapable of following out many of his own impulses. In fact, he seems to have surrendered much of his ego autonomy to Andy, practically living through Andy's ego. Soon his preference tastes in food, clothing, and activites become identical with Andy's. Once in telling a dream at the table, he says, "What happened next, Andy?" Another time he is being urged to come to the table for dinner and he replies, "Why should I, Andy ain't hungry!" These tragi-comic notes are even more ironically emphasized when Andy, his own power drive stimulated by Bill's out-spoken self-abnegation, begins to behave quite sadistically toward Bill. Bill takes this without complaint, simply incorporating it as part of his adjustment to Andy. Interestingly enough, he even becomes angry when the staff interferes in some of these brutality episodes. "So what, so he smacked me, mind yer own goddam business," he tells a counselor in one such moment.

Bill during the first stage of symptom cultivation

In this initial unfolding of events, we are following a fairly consistent policy of strategic noninterference. We do not try to discuss Bill's self-abnegation to Andy or interfere in his relationship with any intention to break the tie which is clearly pathological on Bill's part. To begin with, we may readily understand that, even if such attempts are made, they will fail just as completely as our efforts to save Bill from Andy's sadistic exploitation of him are blasted by Bill's curses at us for even trying. It is this reaction, however, that leads to a form of *exploitative interference*. We speculate that eventually Bill will take a paranoid twist away from his masochism. He will see himself as persecuted, but not by Andy. It is rather against us, we speculate, that his hostility will go for all that is happening to him. So we begin deliberately to interfere in more and more of the milder sado-masochistic transactions between the two boys that we might otherwise let pass just so that Bill can become angry at us, call us names, tell us to "get the hell away from us, you bastards." In this way, we establish clear-cut emotionally vivid moments when we have tried to protect him and he has not let us, hoping thus to create a reserve of memory ties to these protective moments which we will then be able to use when he begins to accuse us of being to blame for Andy's aggression toward him. This style of interference has another and more subtle meaning. It also says, "Andy is being mean. We don't like that. We want him to stop." This acts as a stimulant upon Bill's own hidden aggression which will not be touched off so long as he can make his ego deny that this behavior of Andy's is in fact "mean."

Counterdelusional strategy in action

Today Andy was very mean to Bill, hitting him quite viciously with his hockey stick during a game in the backyard. Bill came into the house dissolved in tears. "This goddam Pioneer House. You can't do this to me. I'm gonna go home to my mother. I'm not staying here no more." And he went upstairs and started to pack his things. I went up with him and sat down in his room, whereupon the following interview sequence occurred:

Exec. Dir.: Bill, I'm sorry that Andy hurt you with his stick.

B: Yeah, everything happens around here. You're a bunch of mean bastards.

Exec. Dir.: How can you say that we're mean?

B: (silence)

Exec. Dir.: Do you really think we are doing something to you? Do we smack you around, make you do things for us, make you our slave? No, Andy is doing those things, not we. And you let him. Every time we tried to say something to stop it, you got mad at us. Now, all of a sudden, you're starting to blame us for it.

B: I'm getting the hell out of here. I'm going home to my mother.

Exec. Dir.: Really, Bill, if you are not happy here, you can go home. We like you and want you to stay but we won't force you. We are not a jail but, if you leave, you have to know that it is not because of what we have done to you. It's because of what you wanted Andy to do.

Challenged so sharply in his delusional argument against me, Bill quieted down and began to slow down his packing, finally giving it up altogether. As I saw he was beginning to fiddle around with his things, I left his room, saying I hoped he'd feel better, and terminated the talk in this way (Entry: 3/12/48, David Wineman)

The first level reaction in the wearing out of Bill's defense against his displaced sibling hatred has begun. Only, since he cannot express his aggression toward Andy openly, he diverts it to us. We are the ones who are abusing him. We are his persecutors. In this respect, he is doing two things: First, as mentioned, he is making us his attackers instead of Andy. Second, regarding us as parent images, he is saying to us: "You don't care what he is doing to me. You love him more." Through a magical trick he suddenly draws upon the good mother image as "dea ex machina." He will run home to the mother. He has thus completely reversed the clinical facts in his case history picture. The treatment home adults become the bad parents, his own parents the benign images. They will save him from us, from the brutality of his sibling. This is where our "record" as conveyed through this interpretive sequence speaks against the delusion. He is told that (a) he has wanted to have

Andy do these things to him, and (b) we have tried to protect him. He still remembers the names he called us for that. And this breaks the delusional bubble and distinguishes us from the real mother who may not have tried to protect him at all. Through the moments of exploitative interference we have made our protective attitude so vivid for him that the delusion cannot hold out long against the interview-supported memory tie to those moments. This is all we want to accomplish at this point. He is not ready for probing into why he has to believe these things, why he has to accuse us of being responsible for Andy's actions, or even why he wanted Andy to be "mean" to him. However, now that he cannot so easily place the blame on us and since he is still unable to discharge his aggression directly against Andy, a reshifting of symptom emphasis may be expected.

"Corraling" Bill's sibling aggression through a "squeeze play" combining interpretation and rule rub-in

Just before dinner tonight Andy perpetrated one of his little meannesses on Bill; he derided Bill's performance in a baseball game at school in front of most of the other kids and counselors. Bill immediately became angry but forced himself to smile foolishly, then, unable to master his aggression, danced up to Andy and began to tap him lightly. Andy immediately bristled up and Bill then pretended he was just joking and turned it into a kidding-around episode. During dinner Bill resorted to verbal sallies at Andy which were still on an ambivalent kidding level and nothing developed. After dinner, the kids were scattered around the living room with nothing definite going on. Andy was perched on the window ledge reading a comic book with one eye on what was going on in the room; Larry was lying on the floor with his rear perched way up in the air and his nose buried in a book; Bill was wandering around rather empty-handed and two others were listening to the phonograph records. Bill suddenly picked up an empty record album and, whispering over to Andy to watch, raised the record album high in the air over Larry's head. Then he gestured to Andy, asking him if he should smack Larry with the album; Andy shrugged his shoulders and said, "O.K." So Bill brought down the album with a crash on Larry's head; Larry let out a yowl of rage and Bill danced up and down with glee. I had been warning Bill as he held the album poised over Larry's head not to hit him with it but of course he had ignored me. Now I hustled him out of the living room and into the office where I sat him down for a talk. I was deliberately direct and to the point because of his own defiant attitude.

Exec. Dir.: What's the idea of smacking Larry that way? He wasn't doing anything to you.

Bill: I felt like it, ha ha.

Exec. Dir.: Listen, I know what's eating you. You're sore at Andy. I
saw before dinner that you wanted to take a poke at him but you
stopped yourself. So now you let it all out on Larry.

Bill: (surprised) That's right.

Exec. Dir.: Why don't you smack Andy if you're mad at him?

Bill: Because he's my "boss."

Exec. Dir.: What do you mean, "boss"?

Bill: He's my boss, that's all, and I wouldn't smack him.

Exec. Dir.: If there is some reason why you feel you need a boss who
can do everything to you without your defending yourself, that's your
own business. I think that it's kind of strange but since you feel that
way we'll let that part of it go. But we can't allow you to hit other
guys just because you get sore at your "boss" for the way he treats
you. That's out.

Bill: I won't hit him if he's my boss.

Exec. Dir.: O.K., but you can't hit other guys when you really are sore
at him. And another thing: I saw you ask *him* for permission to hit
Larry, as though he has to tell you it's O.K.

Bill: That's right, because he's my boss.

Exec. Dir.: Well, that's another part of it, isn't it Bill? He's your boss
so he tells you what's right and wrong. If you want him to do that,
then we won't stop you. We think that's a problem, too, because it
would be much better if you could make up your own mind about
what is the right or wrong thing to do. Still, we can't let you do
something just because Andy says it's right if we really know it's
wrong. Do you think that is clear?

Bill: (Silence. Says little after this point.) (Entry: 4/8/48, David
Wineman)

In this sequence of events we are trying to corral Bill's sibling
aggression. For, in the first place, we make a rule rub-in to the effect
that he cannot mistreat another child who has done nothing to him.
This means that we remove from his path the scapegoat against
whom the displaced aggression is directed: "What's the idea of
smacking Larry? He wasn't doing anything to you. We can't allow
that." Woven in with this we have also interpreted the displacement
of hostility *per se:* "You are sore at Andy. Instead of hitting him,
you hit Larry. How come?" Here the corralling effect becomes even
clearer for we are saying: "Your aggression is not really against
Larry. It is against Andy." We go a step further in the interpre-

tational maneuver in pointing out to him that he not only displaces his aggression from Andy onto Larry, but he also projects his superego onto Andy: "I saw you ask him for permission to hit Larry, as though he has to tell you it's O.K."

Throughout, too, we try to create an interpretive challenge to the ego: "I think that it's kind of strange that you need a boss who can do everything to you without your defending yourself. I think it's strange but we'll let that part of it go." What we are saying here on Bill's own level is: "How come you need a boss? We think there is something screwy in all of this." But we go no further on this theme. We want only to label it for future reference because eventually we will want to use it. With respect to this aspect of his behavior we want to make our handling vivid enough to guarantee a memory link. This link, "There is something fishy about needing a boss," will be fitted into a future interpretive chain when his ego is sufficiently improved to face the original case history pattern at its deeper levels. Then the need to create a "good" brother out of Andy, to lure him into brutality through masochistic surrender, can be explored. We look forward to the time when his aggression will flare directly against Andy. At this time he will displace all of the responsibility onto Andy. Then we will unpack the "record" again and "play" it for him. The record will say: "You created this. Remember the time when you used to live for Andy only. Anything he wanted was O.K. with you. If he beat you, then that was O.K. too. And if we tried to stop him, you called us dirty bastards. Remember? And then, do you remember when you began to get fed up with it? You tried to pin the blame on us then. We were doing it to you. Remember? And we told you that was the bunk—we weren't doing it, you were. And, if you wanted to, we told you that you could go home to your mother as you threatened to but that you couldn't get away with the idea that we wanted Andy to beat up on you. Then you began to beat up the other guys —like Larry—who couldn't fight you back. You started hitting them because you were mad at Andy. He was still your boss so you couldn't hit him. Remember? And we said that was out. You couldn't hit other guys just because you were sore at Andy. And now you are finally getting around to hitting Andy and fighting with him all the time." This will be the "invitation to the dance." From here, banking on our painfully constructed memory bridges to the past in which his own behavior in relation to Andy is revealed in its full pathological sway, we can begin to dig away at the implications of his behavior. "Why did you have to hold back so long?" "Isn't this a lot like what used to go on at home between you and your brother?" Unfortunately, we must here record a dismal epilogue to our clinical story on Bill. For this last stage never materialized because of the premature closing of the Home. We would have needed another six months to a year with him to build in sufficient ego strength in terms of all the major functions of the ego in order for him to be able to use interviewing of this type. This may sound strangely exaggerated to the reader. And yet, the part of the story we have been able to talk about took fourteen months to develop. We cannot pre-shrink psychological processes to meet the demands of human energy, time, or money any more than we could command a tuberculous lesion to heal because the sanitorium was closing down.

2. Extricating the Ego from a Nighttime Phobia

The ego responses of the severely ego-disturbed child to anxiety, fear, and insecurity deviate greatly from those of more normal and classically neurotic children.[14] Anxiety attacks, for example, in the neurotic child may be structured through the acquisition of a phobia about the dark, fear of attackers, etc., among a rich variety of other types of ego defenses against danger from within to which such children are prey. By contrast, the severely ego-disturbed child with whom we are dealing in this study is able to make very little use of fantasy structure to work out inner problems. Even where his ego is organized enough to build up a phobia in which the aggression stemming from inner conflict becomes projected outward, so much of the ego becomes involved in this fantasy that no part of it is left over to cope with the effects of the phobia itself. A more intact child who builds up this kind of symptom is able to use his environment and relationships to balance some of the fear element. He may run to the adult for protection from his fantasy attackers. Or he may insist on sleeping only in a room with a small lamp on or with the door open. With our children, no part of the ego seemed to be able to function in this way. If they developed a fear fantasy of any kind, their only way of coping with it was to escape into severe action blow-ups in which fierce aggression burst forth.

The acute trouble the ego finds itself in under such circumstances

[14] Cf. *Children Who Hate*, p. 78.

is exemplified in the case of Mike. He had nightly attacks of extreme wildness and varied forms of diffused aggression in connection with a classical nighttime phobia in which he fantasied people who were coming into his room to attack him. Now here we might say is his ego engaged in a rather complex fantasy task of coping with inner case-history-loaded conflicts. Which particular conflicts they are cannot be determined until his ego is prepared to cope with the phobia itself more peacefully. This means that it must learn how to tolerate the existence of the fear, to use the surrounding environment in such a way that the aggressive reaction does not wash away the very implications of fear which are the reason for the violent behavior in the first place. Thus, all of our treatment strategy is devoted to helping the ego to reach this stage where the child can even begin to talk with us about the phobic fears. This means that we must, as we did, nightly interfere protectively in the attacks themselves. We remove him from the scene (the dark bedroom), sit with him, soothe him, and control him at the same time. At this point, a few more details on the kinds of behavior that these nighttime attacks revealed and the pattern of our interference tactics will be helpful.

"I'll kill ya, ya fucker, whee whee (high banshee wails), yah yah." All of this is accompanied by lunging and hitting at the pillow, bed, blankets, etc. At the same time Mike may be laughing wildly and reaching over and smacking Larry, whose bed is near his, or sticking his big toe or whole foot erotically onto any part of Larry's exposed anatomy. If Larry should protest, then Mike may suddenly and violently perceive him as he does one of his imaginary attackers and attack him viciously. At this point we usually have to remove him from the room. Invariably, during the first ten or fifteen minutes after his removal he continues the same style of behavior with us as he uses toward his "attackers" or Larry. Gradually we soothe him with appropriate phrases like "O.K., Mike," or "Come on now, quiet down," etc., and he begins to "come to" and grow quieter. From this point on we just sit quietly while he gets sleepy, and then we are able to say, "Ready to go back now?" and he will reply, "O.K., Dave," or "Fritz," whoever is with him . . .

Counterdelusional action strategy against Mike's "attackers"

On the one hand, this type of protective interference is not specifically oriented towards the removal of problems in the sense that through it we could expect his nighttime phobias to change or go away. It is really designed to offer direct support to that ego area which is reacting toward the very existence of the phobia through almost total loss of function. On the other hand, the fact that we do interfere, in the way that we do, brings us into the "ego neighborhood" of the phobia characters—the attackers. For we can see that we enter into the fantasy. Mike behaves toward us for a brief while after the interference maneuver as though we were the attackers. Only, we do not attack. Instead we comfort and soothe, and thus behave counterdelusionally toward the implications of the phobia. Here we are really engaged on two levels at one and the same time: (1) We support his ego by taking over for its lost controls so that he does not have to react to his fears in such a wild and uncontrolled way, and (2) We challenge the projected characters in the fantasy through our opposite behavior from what Mike momentarily transfers to us out of the fantasy at the incidence of interference. This goes on for some twelve months with some modulation in rhythm and intensity before we can say that Mike is anywhere near ready for someone to talk with him about the phobia itself, which, incidentally, does not yield in its hold over his nightly fantasies. What does seem to change slowly is the violence with which Mike reacts to the fantasy production itself. However, the phobic structure *per se* has been influenced through our counterdelusional behavior in such a way that we have reduced some of its panic potential. And, as we begin to observe that Mike does not require such strenuous efforts on our part to tide him over the impact of the fears themselves, we also see other indications that he may be approaching the time when we can begin to "talk about it." For Mike begins to show a brand new skill in conceptualizing feelings instead of acting them out. In other words, he begins to be able to develop and manipulate ideas pertaining to the emotional self.

Thus, on one occasion, there was an incident in the station wagon in which one of the boys became angry with a counselor and insisted on walking home in the rain. It was bitterly cold and the boy (Danny) was getting soaked to the skin. He had recently recovered from a bronchial infection and there was real danger of new trouble. Under these conditions, the counselor wisely inspired an anxiety reaction in Danny by stressing that, if he continued in this way, he was actually running the risk of catching pneumonia, which brought about the desired response and he returned to the wagon. Mike, together with the rest of the group, became infected with this anxiety and began to talk about dying. A fascinating group discussion took place in which all of the boys participated and in which each one brought out his fantasies and fears about death and "things" that bothered him when he woke up in the middle of the night. This marked an ego gain on a group-wide basis, for the earlier Pioneer would never have been able to cope with such an anxiety threat in such a typically structured way. The whole discussion is too long to reproduce at this point but Mike's participation, in excerpt, follows:

Mike: I dream that I turn into a monkey. A gorilla attacks me and swings me around by my tail. He hits me against the wall and things. When I wake up, I say, "I hope my brother Pat never dies." Man, he's the best brother a guy ever had. When kids in the neighborhood used to beat me up, Pat would beat them up for picking on someone smaller than they. He could beat their big brothers too. Just before I die I'm going to cut a hole in my chest (makes appropriate motions), pull out my heart, and put a new one in. That way I'll keep on living. I'll live forever . . . (Entry: 2/13/48, Betty Braun)

Here Mike is showing a decidedly new approach as compared to his earlier pattern around the phobia. We see him caught in a contagiously spread deep-level anxiety reaction around fears of dying and destruction of the self. His ego in this situation acquires a magical power fantasy as a means of coping with this threat. He will prevent himself from dying by pulling out his heart and putting a new one in. This fantasy acts as a total protection against the anxiety. By contrast, the earlier ego reaction to such a threat would have sought to prove in a literal way his power to resist destruction. He would have become hyperactive, personally assaultive upon the adults around, or perhaps upon the other children. Thus, we speculate that improvement in ego functioning has occurred which tends to eliminate the strong need for action-denial of anxiety which has characterized Mike's previous attempts to cope with such problems.

Once this kind of material began to emerge freely in the presence of group-identified adults, it became usable for more focused individual interviewing. Especially the phobic difficulties seemed approachable. One evening, about two weeks after the incident leading to the omnipotence fantasy occurred, he had to be taken out of his room again at night. As was already customary during this phase, he quieted down quickly without the long period of waiting and soothing. It was felt that, in view of both developments, his quieter reaction to the phobia itself plus the emergence of new skills for coping with anxiety, an attempt at an interview might be made.

Exec. Dir.: Say Mike, how come you are so upset tonight?

Mike: (Doesn't answer. Begins usual resistance tactics like picking up different things on my desk—paper clips, pencils, etc.—and playing with them.)

Exec. Dir.: (Stressing the issue.) Come on, Mike. This has been going on now for quite a while and quite often you have to be taken out of your room. Surely, you must have some idea of what's bothering you.

Mike: (Still fools around with the different items mentioned; makes no comment.)

Exec. Dir.: You know what, Mike, remember that time in the station wagon about two weeks ago when everybody was talking about things that bothered them at night, remember what you said?

Mike: (Looks intrigued.) No, what?

Exec. Dir.: Well, you said that sometimes at night you dream that you are a monkey and a gorilla swings you by the tail.

Mike: (Responding beautifully, drops all of the "resistance tools," and begins talking seriously.) Yeah, Dave, you know why I get upset at night?

Exec. Dir.: Why?

Mike: Because I'm afraid of the dark.

Exec. Dir.: I knew that a long time ago.

Mike: How?

Exec. Dir.: Because I saw that you would never stay in your room at night when the other two guys weren't there. But I never spoke about it to you. Know why?

Mike: Why?

Exec. Dir.: Because you weren't as smart as you are now. Now you can better put into words how you feel about things. That's why I think it's time to start talking things over.

Mike: (Taking the cue, drops all manifestation of disinterest.) I'm not only scared when the other guys *aren't* there but even when they *are* (emphasis his). I try to pull the covers up over my head and everything but it doesn't help. I wouldn't be scared if my mother and father were sleeping there with me but I am if they're not. I want to be where there are lights and people.

Exec. Dir.: That's why you get wild, isn't it? When you're *scared*, you get *wild* (emphasis mine). So then you make a lot of noise and either I or Bob (head counselor) come into your room and tell you to quiet down. But you really don't want to stay in your room because you're scared, so you make even more noise and make us take you out. You really don't care even if we have to hold you to quiet you down as long as you are with us.

Mike: (Nodding.) And the dark isn't the only thing I'm scared of either.

Exec. Dir.: No?

Mike: (Enumerating on fingers.) I'm scared to cross the street because maybe I'll get hit by a car. I'm afraid to walk in the woods alone. I'm afraid to ring the doorbell. You know why? Because a kid I knew came to the door of his own house one day and you know what happened? His own mother came to the door and an ax fell on his head and split it open.

Exec. Dir. (No comment.)

Mike: The other night I dreamed that Hank Greenberg hit me with a great big bat and crushed my chest in. Then I dreamed that I was magic and changed myself into a lion and a gorilla and they chased me through the woods and caught me.

Exec. Dir.: Who were "they" in the dream?

Mike: The guys that catch wild animals—they caught me and put me in a cage.

Exec. Dir.: Looks like you have two kinds of dreams: in one kind, big, powerful things attack you and in the other you make yourself big and strong like two wild animals so that nobody can hurt you.

Mike: (Smiles, but no comment.)

Exec. Dir.: Well, when you're scared you get wild; I guess we know that for sure now.

Mike: (Nods, no comment.)

Following this, there was a complicated story of how Mike and his father once went into the woods and were chased by a bear. He drew drawings of the bear—where they were, where the bear was, etc. Finally after this petered out, he went off to bed very quietly. (Entry: 2/23/48, David Wineman)

Preparing Mike through the strategically timed interview for new ways of handling his fears

In this interview we are first of all making what might be called a mechanism interpretation. The mechanism here is the tendency for the ego to react to anxiety with aggression. We do not interpret or seek to clarify in any way the basis for the fantasies. It is still much too early for that. Instead we interpret the ego's behavior in relation to the fantasy: "When you're scared you get wild." While it is true that Mike doesn't get so "wild" any more, we must take a stand with respect to this strong potentiality in his ego functioning. We want to cement in the gain that has taken place by labeling it clearly for him for two reasons: (1) We know that in this stage of nascent ego change there is a tremendous potential for regression back to earlier defense patterns. If these occur, having already made a clear-cut statement of this mechanism to him with his acceptance and understanding, we have a basis for future appeal to the improved cognitive perception of himself which may dissolve in a moment of real danger from within. We can say then, "Oh, come on, Mike, you know darn well that you're scared again or you wouldn't be getting this wild. Let's talk it over, huh?" (2) This mechanism cuts across all of his responses to inner and outer anxiety-raising stimuli. Clarifying it in relation to the phobias gives us the chance to use it in an ever-widening circle of appeals in relation to other ego emergency situations in which he finds himself. We want "wildness" now to acquire symptomatic meaning for him in connection with whatever it occurs. In future instances when we observe aggression in connection with other well-known threats such as the situation of entering a new schoolroom, meeting a new teacher, playing a new game, or whatever may crop up which has this meaning for him, we may try for a strategic toehold in this manner: "Well, Mike, you're acting wild again. Remember how that always happens when something is scaring you? What do you suppose is going on this time, what's doing it, etc.?" Thus, with respect to a variety of situations where it can be diagnostically deduced that the aggressive response is a denial of or escape from anxiety, this interview marks the beginning of a long-range attack on this mechanism. Through future interviews from this point on, we will be trying to "fasten in" more and more securely this particular piece of insight: "Being scared makes you wild." Only much later will we dare to probe into questions like "Why do you think these things may be scaring you so much?" In addition to the insight aim basis of these talks, a new way is created to handle fear situations *per se*: namely, to talk about them. These interviews have clear-cut expressional as well as interpretive significance and, hopefully, will in time replace the pattern of acting out. It is interesting to note that, in the interview of 2/23/48 quoted from, Mike's verbal style resembles that of a more classically neurotic child who might within the first two or three months of treatment give such material as this. Yet, with Mike, it took twelve months to achieve this and only after the most

intensive support to his ego through the nightly protective interference.

A final point that should be made in connection with this particular interview is the implication it raises for strategic timing. It is
clear that Mike will be more productive and motivated to talk about
this particular problem around the bedtime routine simply on the
count that he is then more anxious and more consciously accepting
of his dependency needs toward the adult than at other times during the twenty-four-hour period. This is related to the acute occurrence of the phobia at this time every night. This does not imply
that one would necessarily talk with him every night but rather
that, if interviews were contemplated about this problem at this
stage of treatment, then they should most logically happen in this
way. At a later stage, when more consolidation of ego functioning
and relationship pattern occurs, the interview may be more reasonably detached from the natural time setting in which the symptom
occurs.

3. *Ego Troubles under the Impact of Liberation from Fear*

With some of our Pioneers our main clinical task was to
stem the torrential aggression which ran so rampant through their behavior. With still others, however, we had just the reverse problem.
In their case, aggression could not be liberated until adequate guarantees were given from the surrounding environment that loss of
love and counterbrutality would not follow upon the heels of such
daring behavior against the adult. Larry, for the first eight months
of treatment, was docile and passive and scarcely once showed more
serious aggressiveness than being peevish and stubbornly mulish
around issues where he didn't want to give in. He would show rage
reactions abundantly around game and activity areas where he was
threatened by failure but these were of the most infantile type,
mainly characterized by loud wailing and stamping of his foot. He
never, during this time, destroyed materials, smashed furniture, or
participated in an aggressive attack against the adult, acts which,
with the other children, were a daily occurrence. His main interest was in passive oral reception of libidinal supplies from the
adult, of such "sucking" intensity that he was positively parasitic
upon the clinical environment. Yet we knew that such a deeply
rejected child as Larry, with six years of ill-fated boarding placement in his life and a final experience of two and one-half years

with a primitive stepfather, who, in his drunken rages, treated him with all of the unrefined barbarousness of a concentration camp guard, even to the point of threatening to kill him with a shot gun, would have stored up a hatred of the adult which must some day show its hand. That Larry, in what it would not be too much of an imaginative stretch to call a daily fear of his life, learned well how to repress even the faintest flickers of aggressiveness we knew from our very earliest contact.

During the course of our drive from his home to Pioneer House, to which I was taking him for the first time, Larry expressed some curiosity about the different gadgets in my car. He was surprised when I explained them to him and even encouraged him to try the lighter which he had correctly recognized. I also encouraged him to turn the radio on, but he hesitated, and then said he had better not fool with it: it might be "dangerous" if he pushed the wrong button. He then maintained that the ignition key in his father's car was on the other side (the one he was sitting on), and it was apparent that he did not allow himself to know too much about the car because such knowledge was dangerous and might lead to disobedient behavior. (Entry: 11/29/46, Fritz Redl)

Knowing the terrifying experience with the stepfather, little speculation is required to deduce what Larry meant by "dangerous." Part of treatment strategy with a child whose aggressive impulses have been so traumatized is to expect and support trends toward the liberation of these masses of aggression that have been pushed back into the unconscious. Without the unbinding of some of this aggression, Larry could not be expected to give up the passive oral relationship to the adult. While this pattern satisfies primary infantile needs never before worked through, it also acts as a barrier against further maturation and the expression of the aggression itself. Nowhere except in a residential setting could such a goal have been visualized because we had ample reason to believe that, once the aggression burst forth, it would be torrential and primitive to such a degree that only clinical personnel could put up with it and handle it. At the same time, nowhere will a traumatized child like Larry be free enough to surrender his defenses against aggression except in a climate where complete freedom from adult counterbrutality is guaranteed. Thus, the period of time in which we provide Larry with long overdue gratification, in which we declare most openly our policy with respect to how we will treat children, is at the same time counterdelusional toward his whole fear-loaded ideology about the adult world as well as nutritional toward his satisfaction starvation. From the point of view that we are expecting a behavioral turn sooner or later in which his feelings toward the stepfather will emerge, we can say that we are engaged in an operation of strategic waiting or strategic noninterference. The big difference between Larry and both Bill and Mike, whom we described in our first two case examples under this section, is, of course, that in their cases it was a manifest piece of problem-relevant behavior that we were pinning strategy around, while in Larry's case it was a latent or missing item from his manifest behavioral scheme that we knew should be there that we were trying to nurture into existence so that then we could handle it. In a child with Larry's defenses, the experience of being loved brings with it a certain unbinding of basic fear involvements. This is shown in the following sequence occurring during the eighth month at the Home.

During our walk this evening, Larry and I passed a beer garden a couple of blocks from the Home. Larry began to talk about men who drink. When he got big he was never going to drink. From here he plunged directly into the story, never before even remotely touched on during his stay with us, of his stepfather, whom he called, by the way, "My dad." "Ya see, it was something like this. He would get mad at his boss'n then he'd get drunk, real bad drunk. Then he'd come home and he'd be so mean. He would yell at me for nothing at all. Once I forgot to feed my dog Queenie and he hit me and kicked me and screamed at me. That's why I'm afraid to go home. I hate my dad. My mother, she's all right and I like my house but I just hate my dad especially when he gets drunk. I never can sleep at home. My father, he gets drunk and all night long they argument (his usage) and make so much noise that I can't sleep and I'm afraid of what he's gonna do. That's why I like to stay with you." He repeated this story at least four times, each time anxiously and pleadingly asking me as he clung to my hand, "You understand that, Emmy?" I assured him that I did and when we arrived at the Home told him, "We're really glad to have you here with us, Larry." (Entry: 8/3/47, Emily Kener)

Here, after he has been associatively stimulated by passing the bar, we can see the loosening up of the repressive forces around painful memories. The ego, now more nimble, copes with its distress on a level of maturity that is surprising and gratifying when one remembers that this is the child whose approach to the adult has been along the most deeply infantile lines—clutching, clinging, merging body surfaces in a blind, mute endeavor to collect long overdue love payments. Of course, dependency and continued need for the adult loom large behind this behavior, but the new ability of the ego to articulate its feeling in word symbols represents a tremendous increase in its ability to push up its communication levels from previously more primitive modes.

Larry finds new channels for communication in the expressional interview

We may note here that our housemother, sensitive to the newness and deep significance of this material engages in little, if any, verbal manipulation. She is there as therapeutic listener, as a powerful agent for reassurance, comfort, and continued acceptance. In this type of interview sequence nothing more is demanded. The ego is not here looking for, or able to take, insight probes, case-history-aimed remarks of any kind. It wants only to unloose feelings and through these to restitute control over anxiety. It is of vast importance for clinical personnel to be able to make instantaneous diagnoses of the meaning of verbal material and of their specific situational function with regard to it. It is not merely a consideration of role. Our housemother was clinically experienced and able to handle casework process. While it is true that we might have wished to channelize interpretational interviews to the casework person at the Home and not load our housemother with too much casework interpretational significance for the child, the strategic issue here was not so much one of role distribution but rather of the ego's needs at this particular moment. If the Home caseworker or even our consultant psychiatrist had been with Larry, he would have behaved in the same way as did the housemother in this instance (although it is doubtful if Larry would have had the same ability to use them as he did the housemother, for very obvious reasons). Here we respect the need of the ego to share a disturbed thought with another, recognizing this as an important item in human experience, and indeed one which our children have not learned to use in their previous life patterns at all.

Ego change in its relation to acting out

At this point in our clinical story of Larry we come upon what seems at first glance to constitute a paradox in our clinical reasoning. For soon on the heels of this new freedom to verbalize feelings, signifying a growth in ego functioning, Larry begins to act out terrifically severe aggressive fantasies toward the counselor.

On a marshmallow roast this evening with the group, Bill suddenly grabbed at my genitals while he, Larry, and I were walking down the path leading to our fire. I sternly forbade this and then to my pure amazement the docile Larry suddenly jumped on me from the rear and did the same thing. When I again, with him, repeated my "Verbot," he began skipping around and poking at me and ducking out of reach, and then ran into the bushes and began to throw stones at me and the rest of the group near the fire. Joel (co-counselor) called out to him to stop and said we were ready to roast our marshmallows now and he could come over if he agreed to quiet down. This infuriated him even further, and he picked up a brick, came within three feet of Joel, and just heaved it at him. Joel ducked and came over to Larry, saying that this was "out," and he'd have to quiet down now. We couldn't permit that kind of action toward anybody. At this point, Larry went into a screaming, kicking, biting tantrum, trying to inflict injury at any cost on Joel. This extreme wildness continued, with Joel having all he could do to hold him, for about twenty-five minutes. (Entry: 8/18/47, John Haddad)

The seeming paradox this behavior raises is this: power to conceptualize feelings in Mike, our previous example, releases him from the need to act out, whereas the same kind of ego development in Larry is only the precursor toward extremely primitive acting out. First, let us deal briefly with the suspicion that this was only a contagiously stimulated act based on Bill's first setting the stage through his sexual attack on the counselor. It is true that this is a contagion sequence in which Bill performs the initiatory act (grabbing genitalia of counselor) and Larry then becomes the recipient, repeating the same behavior. However, Bill did not set the stage for the aggressive reaction to counselor interference, only the grabbing *per se*. Second, Larry had been exposed to similar behavior at different times during the previous eight months, never once showing anything else than shock effect, marked through withdrawal and even more intensive clinging to the adult as insurance against being criticized for even being around when such things were done. So the implication can be ruled out that this was merely a contagiously derived piece of behavior. Rather, at this particular time, Larry, instead of having a shock reaction, had quite the reverse: his ego, identified with the act, carried it out, broke into aggressive display because there was a preconsciously set ego tolerance already guaranteed through the emancipation from fear. And this strikes at the heart of the apparent paradox: Mike, unable to cope with fear, denies its very existence through aggression. Larry, unable to cope with aggression, denies it out of fear of destruction. Thus, ego improvement in Mike enables him to recognize and accept fear without aggressive breakdown. Similarly, ego improvement in Larry allows him to express destructive wishes toward the adult without fear of total counterdestruction even though these attacks are not totally anxiety-free.

Our handling of this new ability to liberate previously repressed massive quantities of aggressiveness is built around three important clinical considerations. First, we recognize the need for limit stressing on the individual level. We cannot permit Larry literally to mangle us to pieces in his retroactively eruptive effort to take revenge on his stepfather, the feelings toward whom he now transfers to the male personnel of the Home. Allowing him this much leeway for total regression along destructive lines is hardly therapeutic. Second, we recognize the need for group psychological protection against the simultaneous anxiety and seduction towards aggression which Larry's primitive system of sudden revolt against adult controls creates. Thus we are committed, as is already obvious in the incident reported upon, to action interference with the fits themselves. At the same time, Larry must be given every reassurance that our basic attitude of love toward him has not changed. To effect this we must religiously follow all basic rules for antiseptic interference. Third, we recognize the possibility of handling some of this with him on an interview level since he now has the freedom for verbal as well as action expression. We want to avail ourselves of this new ego skill in moments strategically related to the fits themselves. Shortly after the incident of 8/18/47 reported above, which is followed by some minor but qualitatively similar incidents, we find a moment in our "clinical time clock" with Larry which seems favorable for some interview of this new development.

Larry was in the office this evening after dinner, having asked me to help him count some money which he had retrieved from the now defunct flag fund of last year. (This was a fund to get a flag for the Pioneer House front yard which the boys started on their own and then gave up.) He was in a pretty even, good mood, and I felt that maybe it would be possible to exploit this for a chat about some of his recent upsets. Having finished with the money counting, I brought out that I had been thinking about talking with him about "those times you got so upset during the last week or so, remember? Like that time you and the guys went out to the park with Joel for the marshmallow cook-out?" He immediately said, "Yes," and then "clammed up," taking on a stubborn, defiant look. I went on to say that I hadn't said anything about it afterward because I thought he might be too upset to talk about it. But now, when everything was all quieted down, didn't he think we might try to figure out why he got so mad? Larry then tried to minimize by saying that it was a "little" thing. I gently countered this by saying, "Well, I don't know if I'd call it exactly little. You heaved some pretty chunky rocks at Joel and got so mad when he said to stop that he had to really hold you for about twenty minutes. Isn't that so?" To which he admitted with a kind of triumphant chuckle that he guessed I was right. I then asked him why he thought he had been getting so upset at the counselors lately. Was anything bothering him? He remained vague so I continued by asking, "Isn't this the way you would act if someone were being real mean to you?" He said he guessed so and I went on saying, "Was it that you felt this was so—was Joel being mean?" To which he replied by saying that he didn't think so. "That makes it more of a mystery than ever, then, doesn't it?" I said. "Here you have a big blow-up but at the same time you can't quite figure out why you went to such extremes." Larry did not answer; he just sat there and stared straight ahead. I then took another whack, asking, "Larry, I wonder if you could tell me if you have ever really been treated in such a mean way that you might want to act like that in return?" His response to this was really amazing. His facial cast changed to infantile and whiney from stubborn and resistive, his eyes filled with tears and, with considerable difficulty in speaking, he said, "There's one person I'm always mad at. That's my father. He was very mean for the least little thing. He would get drunk and then he wouldn't know what he was doing and then he would be terrible. The least little thing you'd do wrong, he'd get mean." At this point Larry became absolutely quiet so I waited, and, after a minute or so, he said, "There's one thing I'll never forget. That was when he pointed a loaded shotgun at me and said he was going to kill me. He did that a couple of times. I only wish he was the one who had to do all the chores and that he would make mistakes and somebody could get mad at him like he did at me." I said I could see how things had been quite bad for Larry. "Here at Pioneer House," I continued, "things are different. Everybody likes you. You can see that now after you've been with us so long. Maybe when those thoughts and memories of your stepfather come into your mind, it bothers you quite a bit. We could have some more talks about it any time you want." Larry nodded but didn't say anything and soon afterward he left to join the rest of the group. (Entry: 8/18/47, David Wineman)

Preparing Larry to cope with case history confusions

Initially, in the interview, Larry is confronted with the disproportionate quality of his behavior: "This is the way you might act if someone were real mean to you." From here the cognitive and selective functions of the ego are worked with: "Was someone that mean to you?" is a cognitive issue which it is possible to clarify with Larry, who finally admits that no one was mistreating him. Secondly, the selective function of the ego is then approached: "Why did you get so angry then?" Here we want to emphasize his lack of realism in selection of reaction techniques. From this point on the interview builds up to a climax and presents Larry with an opportunity for restructuring the case history confusion deriving from his relationship to the stepfather. This is brought about through the flashback question: "Have you ever been treated in such a way that you might want to act like that?" This gives Larry the chance to express the original affect which belongs to the acting out but this is now done within the structural framework of the interview and on the level of ideation and verbalized feeling rather than action *per se*. Sympathetic reassurance is given in the form: "I understand how you must have felt. There must have been many things you wished might happen so that your stepfather would know how it felt." Next, in the interview, comes a theme which is elliptically interpretive as well as a form of reassurance. "Here at Pioneer House things are different. Everybody likes you." This means (1) this is not the place where such affect belongs, and (2) no one is going to hurt you like that here even if you have acted in this way. The next and final step in the interview involves an attempt to create an anticipatory pattern or promotional build-up for future talks around this problem: "Maybe these memories bother you. We could have some talks about it any time." This last theme is quite important, since we hope to tackle the increased desire and need to act out the hostility toward the stepfather through the interview medium as much as we can. In summary this interview can be seen to combine the following functions:

(1) Its main function is expressional, i.e., it provides a restructuriza-
tion for the ventilative discharge of affect originating in the
relationship to the stepfather.

(2) Auxiliary to the expressional function there are three noticeable subfunctions:

   (a) A challenge to the ego through almost a "rub-in" approach to evaluate behavior.

   (b) Transference interpretation, elliptically expressed, in
the comparison of past and present reality situations
and their differential meaning in relation to hostility.

   (c) Promotional build-up to create anticipatory pattern for
future interviewing.

The description offered gives a view of steps involved in working
through some of Larry's most infantile need patterns and in the
initial establishment of healthier ego functioning. Space forbids
continuing this description of the clinical events in Larry's case.
From about this time onward, however, a definite decrease in infantilism plus a growing awareness of inner problems with respect
to hostility and its case history bases were achieved.

4. First round with a "delinquent ego"

We have stressed in *Children Who Hate* the fact that the ego
pathology of the children with whom we are concerned presents a
baffling dualism: on the one hand a serious atrophy plunging them
into devastating failure in meeting the daily task challenges confronting any child, and on the other an enigmatic hypertrophy
which places in their hands an aggressive, manipulative mastery
over the outside world and their own conscience whenever they are
faced with the challenge of defending their freedom for impulse
expression. The atrophy we captioned under the title, "The Ego
That Cannot Perform"; the hypertrophy under "The Delinquent
Ego and Its Techniques." [15] Of course, we never meant to imply
that these two patterns of ego functioning are ever reflected as
totally separate packages of behavior in the child with the clarity of
time discreteness which one might see in the two phases of a manic-
depressive psychosis. Rather they are inextricably interwoven in the
behavioral scheme of the child and what we see in the day-to-day
scene is a combination of both patterns functioning as an entity. In

[15] See *Children Who Hate*, Chapters III and IV.

particular moments and situations, however, we do see unmistakable accenting of one or the other of the patterns to such a heavy degree that, for all operational purposes, we must devote ourselves to coping with it as a separate clinical challenge, never losing our awareness that the other face of this Janus monster may be confronting us at the next moment. In this section it is our purpose to present in an abridged clinical-time perspective some highlights of our therapeutic encounters with the "delinquent ego" of Andy, who by now should be well known to the readers of either of our two books from the many times he has been flashed onto the scene for short moments in our previous illustrations.[16]

Who—me?

If we had never had a single case history note on Andy, the first night at Pioneer House should have presaged for us some of the significant forces at work within him. As we expected, the first night with our group was sheer mayhem. Bedtime was simply a word in a dictionary that somebody wrote once and then lost. The children were all over and a pitch of group psychological excitement was produced which required our combined staff energies to calm down. The behavior of Andy was most striking for the clarity with which it showed what proved to be a serious linkage of pathologies: infantilism and delinquent impulses wrapped up in one explosive package. He was the rioteer par excellence. Chasing madly through the house, he encouraged the others to hide and evade counselors who sought to get them back into the sleeping rooms. He originated a battle cry, "Hee-haw!" which seemed to free the others for defiant action. His "hee-haw" was the clarion call in the melee of confusion and frantic hyperkinetic behavior of the others.

Finally, he and Joe tore down into the basement and scrambled in the coal pile, throwing pieces of coal at anyone who came near. Then Joe darted upstairs but Andy, in taking off from the bin, caught his foot on a shovel and fell. Immediately he began to cry with a howling wail and I picked him up and carried him upstairs crosswise in my arms. His foot was bleeding and I laid him down on the couch in the living room. Then Emily (housemother) and I examined the cut. Meanwhile, Andy continued to cry as though his heart were breaking. The cut was superficial. We cleaned it and dressed it. Emily continued to cradle Andy's

[16] *Children Who Hate*, pp. 49, 52, 55, 149; this book, see pp. 105, 110, 157, 194, 196, 201-202, 229, 247, 277-278, 308, 310, 313, 312-318.

head in her lap while I worked on the cut and finally he stopped crying and sat there in a rather numb silence. I told Andy I was sorry he had hurt himself and made the point, too, that it was risky running around in the dark basement whose room arrangement he didn't even know. He glared at me and shouted, "I didn't do nothing!" I said, "What do you mean you didn't do anything? You were chasing around down there, weren't you, and up here too, for that matter?" He pulled away from Emily, the baby in him suddenly erased, and in a fury said, "You son-ofabitch—why don't you talk to the other guys? Why blame me for everything?" "Andy," I said gently, "I'm not blaming you for what they did; as a matter of fact, I'm not blaming you for anything. I'm just saying that it's too bad you got hurt." "I didn't do nothing. My foot hurts and all you kin do is talk to me. I wanna go to bed." And he continued to glare at me with irritation and hostility, yawning and refusing to say another single word. I took him up to bed where, ex-hausted, he soon fell asleep. (Entry: 12/1/46, David Wineman)

Here we have Andy cutting his toe and exploiting the ensuing scene where the executive director and housemother baby and bandage him. He doesn't mind being carried, handled, and fon-dled until—until when? Until the executive director seems to im-ply through his sympathetically worded statement about the injury that Andy "was doing something." Then swiftly, his delinquent ego becoming suddenly powerfully aware of the danger in which this infantilization scene places him, he is catapulted into *defiance and delinquent argumentation*. Brazenly, with the not quite dried tears and the throbbing toe ruthlessly banned from the scene of battle operations, he proceeds to extricate himself from the possi-bility of regret for his actions: "Why blame me—I didn't do nothing —sonofabitch . . . ?"

Our conjecture on the basis of the first night's operations is not misleading. For, as we go through the first chaotic weeks and months with our Pioneers, we see that Andy continues to treat us as though we were some immense enemy against whom he must take elaborate precautions. Our willingness to give him affection and protective handling is dangerous to his delinquent impulse life. Especially is this noticeable in precisely those moments which epitomize the problem: in the direct act of giving, of extending gratifications to him.

At the Christmas party, Andy appeared depressed, especially at the time of the distribution of gifts. It was strange to see him not even open his packages at first and then, slowly, careful to register no change of expression at all, open each one and set it aside with no comment. They were gifts he had finally been willing to ask for after careful interviewing on the part of the housemother as to what he would like for Christmas. And now he acted as casually, as if he were being given a stick of gum. The depression passed quickly enough, however, and a wave of irritability and hostility emerged to take its place as we tried to move the boys into the sleeping routine some one hour later, after they had had a chance to play with their new things and mutually inspect and compare them. If anything, he was even more unmanageable than he has ever been and especially nasty and aggressive to Emily (housemother) and Fritz (Director). (Entry: 12/21/46, David Wineman)

The excerpt from our record of the Christmas party seems clear enough without elaboration except that we should add that Andy's increased hostility toward the housemother and the director of the Home, who certainly filled the father role, is more than mere accident: these are the central parent images who now particularly play the role of filling love needs and are thus the greatest threats to the delinquent ego.

"Surgery" for strangulated love needs

We might well assert that Andy is in a process of strangulating his love needs just so that he can maintain his anti-adult outlook, which in turn makes it possible for him to retain the right for aggressive exploitation of his environment.[17] So long as he can continue to do this he will successfully ward off any implications of change. As if this were not serious enough, secondary complications arise because the success with which he manages this makes him even sicker, for he "starves" himself but accuses us of doing it. In other words, it is not only that his impulse system emerges the easy victor, but his frustration over the very love which he deprives himself of is, so to speak, charged up against us. Thus, our first unavoidable clinical challenge lies in finding ways in which, despite his determined efforts to the contrary, we can "unsnarl" his twisted and tortured love demands so that some peaceful gratification is possible.

Of course. in part, this will be accomplished through the exposure to the treatment milieu, per se, with its intense concentra-

[17] See Children Who Hate, p. 173, "Strangulation of Love, Dependency, and Activity Needs."

tion on hygienic handling, as well as through the generally ego-supportive aspects of programming.

Still, how about the special things we can do for Andy to help him drop some of this savage warfare against us? Which moments are available for specific clinical exploitation of the kind we wish to focus upon in this section? To make it unmistakably clear to the reader what it is that faces us here—that it is not merely a child who has episodic flare-ups of resentment, irritation, and hostility— let us quote from our record at the end of the first month.

Andy has definitely built himself into the role of central figure in what we might term "group excitement and orgiastic outbursts." His chief weapon seems to be his own lack of embarrassment about anything primitive. He can engage in the most open sex antics (exhibitionistic masturbation or displaying himself nude at the window of the front room or sex wrestling with the other kids) without even a glimmer of embarrassment or shame. As far as the other group members are concerned, whatever vestiges of guilt they might have are swept aside by the "exculpation magics" of Andy's "initiatory" act. He has invented a cue word, expressive enough for the behavior which follows it, "hootchy kootchy," which now has only to be said to induce any group member into open sex play. And it is not only sex play for which Andy functions as such a contagion center. His constant throwing of any object at hand, for example, done with such sang-froid, has infected the group seriously. If anyone in the group has the chief function of keeping a corrupt group code alive, it is Andy with his chronic defiance, "rabble rousing," and rioteering, and his frank and shameless interest in what might be generally termed "instinctual" behavior. (Entry: 12/30/46, Fritz Redl)

And yet, coupled with this brutally clear emergence of the "delinquent ego" in operation, is a distorted representation in Andy's behavior of other strivings that he does not dare as yet to let us (or himself) take seriously. For not infrequently, in the midst of a raucous, primitive group scene, Andy will suddenly fall to the ground as though he has hurt himself (twisting his ankle is the chief "act"), bury his head in his arms, and cry sobbingly with his face to the floor. When we approach to help him, he jumps up and shouts triumphantly, "Hee-haw." How much this reminds us of the first night already described! For even if these are "fakes," the same exploitation of (and need to have us perform) our affectional and protective interests is there. So, taking our cue from Andy's unconscious, we always follow through on these "malingering" invitations for infantile experience with us, instead of warding him off and telling him to stop kidding us, which perhaps he even hopes we will do so that he can indict us in some dark and bitter part of his ego. On the other hand, just so that he will not continue to believe that we do not see through him, we indicate our awareness that we know he is fooling us about the hurt, but in these moments put our arms around him affectionately even while laughing with him at the joke he has played on us. And we look for other "safe" moments (i.e., safe for him) in which he can allow us to express our affection toward him without fighting us.

Tonight, Andy came to me and asked to be rubbed down with liniment after his wrestling match with Mike in the evening program. His muscles needed it, he said, and I complied, mindful of the rare moments which this scrupulously aloof child presents for positive body contact. (Entry: 2/1/47, Emily Kener)

And if Andy likes to fool us, why shouldn't we help him through the type of gift we select for him? When the director of the Home returns from an out-of-town trip during this period, his gift to Andy is a magician's set, which pleases him immensely.

Other such moments are possible, the principle followed being that we must respect the limits which Andy himself imposes and operate within the peculiar structure he sets for adult love-taking. For unlike Larry, who is only too eager to cuddle and sit on our laps, Andy must even be helped at first to find moments when affection looks like something else than what it is: we have to help him "smuggle" love past his own vigilant delinquent ego. This is the first step in our "surgery" for strangulated love needs. Andy needs some protective coating over the "love" pills: they must not taste too much like love, otherwise he must refuse or regurgitate. Once they are "down," they have the desired effect, however.

The reality rub-in interview as an auxiliary tool

In part, however, we can approach the problem more directly. The protective coating has to apply only to love dosage *per se*. As far as challenging, in strategic moments, some of the anti-adult ideology which Andy believes and uses in his defamatory campaign against the adult world, let us look at the record.

Andy was very prone to a bitter and contemptuous accusation against any and all staff: "Yeah," he would snarl, "the counselors! They git to do anythin' they want. Us kids—we can't do nothin'.'" At first, of course, we followed the policy of strategic noninterference as far as verbal handling of this was concerned. Not a single time would come up around a rule issue, or a decision on perhaps having to postpone some particular piece of programming that he wanted until next week (not that this happened too often), but that Andy would incitefully hurl out this acid denunciation. Finally, during the fifth month, we began to take this up with him in individual interview:

Exec. Dir.: I notice that whenever you don't like something, Andy, you accuse us of always having or doing anything we want and never letting you kids do anything.

Andy: (Just looks at me and then sarcastically parrots what I have just said.)

Exec. Dir.: (Hoping to appeal to Andy's vanity) Oh, come on, Andy. Surely you have more to say than that. You're smart enough to use your own words.

Andy: (Sullenly) Well, it's true. We never can do what we want.

Exec. Dir.: Can you really sit there after five months at Pioneer House and say that in this place the kids don't ever get a chance to do what they would like to do?

Andy: Yeah.

Exec. Dir.: With the program we plan with you guys, and all the places you get to go, and the things we do? Let me ask you: Where can you remember any place where you lived where you had more fun?

Andy: Say, I lived with my grandma once and she let me do anything I wanted and gave me candy all the time, too.

Exec. Dir.: (Remembering Andy's case history and his unsupervised experience with his grandmother) I never said we let you do whatever you wanted. I only said you do a lot of things that are fun. Do you still pretend that that isn't so?

Andy: Maybe not.

Exec. Dir.: (Closes interview with interpretive question.) Well, I wonder, then, why you keep saying that all the time . . .

Here in the fifth month we begin to counterpose reality against Andy's "delusional" propaganda. And we put "delusional" in quotes for a reason: we mean to imply by this that in part he believes in what he says and in part he doesn't, that he just uses it. It is to both parts of him that we are talking here. Backed up by five months of carefully reshuffled reality experience, we are trying to pit the reasonable part of his ego against the delusional and the delinquent, as if to say, "Listen, how can you believe that stuff any longer, and if you don't, is it really fair to keep saying it?" Not that we expect Andy to give it up as easily as all that. But the next time he erupts, the next time he falls back on this in a special issue about rules or routines or what he wants to do in programming, we want to have established a small clinically usable wedge which we can apply. We want to short cut the amount of time it takes to "pull him out of it," to be able to say, "Listen, Andy, come on now—we've been through this already: you *know* it isn't like that, you've already *admitted* that in that talk we had." In a very significant way this is *real exploitation of life events* that can take place only in a residential milieu, for where else will we be able to count upon a probable meeting of the necessary variables that are crucial to such an approach? These are:

(1) a reshuffled, counterdelusional reality scheme, in operation twenty-four hours a day, to begin with.
(2) a chance to use it when the ego appears to be moved up the slightest notch.
(3) a chance for us to follow the ego from the moment of initial clinical attack on a piece of pathology through vicissitudes around that particular particle, to help the child recapture past experience (an interview, in this instance) just at that moment when the memory tie to the past needs to be enlivened with either humor, cajolery, reality-firmness, or what not.

And so, with many tricky but discoverable moments of "love dosage" combined with selective interviewing and direct challenge to the delinquent defenses, we manage to tame down the delinquent ego a few degrees. There is, however, a fascinating and complex corollary to coping with the delinquent ego, closely allied to it in the clinical scene and one that we should try to include shortly in our clinical sound track on Andy: how far must we go with the ego before we can talk about *superego repair*?

Exploitation of the group scene as a bridge for increasing value sensitivities: implications for superego repair.[18]

We have indicated in *Children Who Hate* that superego repair cannot really be envisaged without prior ego repair to the point where the ego can at least cope with a guilt feeling without breakdown. This means repair on the side of the atrophy as well as the hypertrophy. Here, in the case of Andy, we simply want to include a few clinical notes which show the beginnings of such at-

[18] See *Children Who Hate*, "The Complexity of Superego Repair," p. 208.

tempts with him. These occurred late in the history of his stay at the Home and for good reason: it took this long before we could be sure that he was in good enough ego shape for these to begin to work at all. What we say here can be taken as a part of the clinical piece on Andy, the reader remembering—or taking note of dates of recordings—that we take about an eight- to ten-month jump with Andy into the clinical future from the time we last saw him in an entry, and that during this time much more interviewing of the kind mentioned has taken place and gradual overcoming of delinquent ego defenses has been made possible.

From what we have said about Andy, it may appear obvious to the reader that he was one of the children in the group who had the highest status. At first, this was attached to his "freedom" for delinquent behavior, as our prior recording indicated. Along with this, and continuing after it faded, his status was derived from a certain superiority in achievement (arts and crafts, school, athletics, etc.). This made of Andy, for many months, the actual "indigenous" child leader of the group. This was of great use in approaching value issues with him directly. The reader may remember that in the case of Bill (p. 280) it was necessary to tell him directly that we observed him using Andy as a superego representative. Conversely, the same thing was necessary and desirable with Andy, namely, we made it clear to him that we knew that not only Bill but the group at large was using him this way and that many times undesirable things happened because of this. At first he fought hard against even admitting that he had influence over the others but gradually, step by step, we got him to admit it. The next crucial element was to have such interviews with him and make the main issue not the fact that he did or did not have such an influence (which after all was not a moral issue *per se*) but to challenge him in connection with *what* he was supporting in the other kids.

Exec. Dir.: Look, Andy, I know you gave Mike the go-ahead sign and encouraged him to heave his sandwich from his lunch at Tom (station wagon driver on way to school).

Andy: So what? Can I help it if he asks me?

Exec. Dir.: No, you can't. But how about whether what he's asking you to okay is fair or not? Or, in this case, even safe? After all, it was pretty dopey of Mike to heave that sandwich at Tom. Suppose he lost control of the wheel?

Andy: Why don't you talk to Mike?

Exec. Dir.: You know I will. But let's not pretend to each other it's that simple. You know you have some influence over the other guys. And I'm not saying that's bad. In fact, every gang of guys has some one guy they look up to. O.K. All I'm bringing up is, how about thinking a little bit about what is going on out there in front of your nose, about what you're getting mixed up with when the guys do something like that? (Entry: 2/12/48, David Wineman)

Of course, it would have been foolish even to begin such interviewing with Andy before we were fairly certain that our earlier attempts to bring about some repair in relationship had taken root. Otherwise all we would have accomplished would have been to sharpen Andy's perception of a dangerous and powerful tool which he could use against us. Also, as we have tried to make clear, no such interview could even imply that we were in any way opposed to, or critical of, the fact that Andy was in fact a leader. Rather, his leader role was merely the basis on which value issues were approached with him in the interview in an extremely practical and realistic way.

And we soon had some hint that we had not been unsuccessful in our spadework for superego repair, for shortly afterwards things like this began to happen. One day on the way home from school, Andy took the initiative in supporting a new counselor against whom the group was directing a good deal of "station wagon behavior" by actually doing a "rub-in" interview with them: "If Bob (regular counselor who used to be with them before reassignment) was here, you guys wouldn't be acting this way." And now, perhaps it is time to say "cut" on our synopsis of Andy, content that we may have been able to convey to the reader some elements in his gradual movement through clinical time from delinquency and primitive impulsivity to greater libidinal and value proximity to the adult. His last months at Pioneer House were marked by a much more intensive interest in the adult, with scarcely a shadow of the old reserved, bitter, and surly Andy. Yet there was a curious in-betweenness about him which really seemed to constitute a kind of half-way point between his former intense egocentrism and a not quite developed ability to enter with complete freedom into object relationships with the adult. For let us remember this was only a "first round." And thus, for Andy in his way, too, the closing of the Home was a tragedy, because the complexity of finding his way farther along the pathways of maturity would have still required a long clinical trail with many vicissitudes which only a total therapeutic milieu could have hoped to meet.

Summary

We have attempted to describe specific strategies within the total treatment design for directly influencing pathology in the child. The treatment environment is conceived of as a shaping tool which can be manipulated either to soften or lure out symptomatic behavior. Which is done will depend upon the clinical usefulness of such behavior and the life scene into which it will emerge. Symptoms are thus subjected to a kind of cultivation procedure in order to bring them into contact with attempts on the part of the clinician to cope with them. This will give him relatively greater strategic power than if the whole question is simply left to chance. While shaping or cultivating clinically fertile issues is of vast importance, it must be carried to its logical strategic conclusion by creating a highly mobile interview design in which the residential clinician is enabled to focus his interview strategies selectively upon such ongoing behavioral trends as are visualized as having high clinical usefulness at the moment of their occurrence. This means that in the residential setting the usual "interview by appointment" pattern which is applicable to the classical neurotic in the office interview style of therapy must be changed drastically to protect this strategic need. Further, interviewing with the ego-disturbed child visualizes a number of functions with respect to ego support and repair which are distinguishable from the straight interpretational interview. In addition to insight about inner mental issues, interviews can help the ego to gain more insight about issues of outer reality or about its own ways of coping with guilt. It can focus, on the other hand, in certain specific instances, upon the ego's intricately developed skills against surrendering impulsivity and waywardness. Some interviews function to provide the ego with chances for feeling-ventilation and for overcoming the traumatic impact of past life situations. In still other instances the interview is used as a tool for promotional building up and strengthening of healthier images of the self which have already accrued from therapy and which, with special support, can be gainfully exploited to integrate further the response of the child to various challenges from his life scene. This

specific breakdown of the goal functions of the interview is predi-
cated upon the disturbed ego functioning of the child himself and
seeks to give concrete special help in the specific areas of ego need
as they seem to become visible in the life situation.

Therapeutic Gains, Closure of Pioneer House, and Follow-Up

QUITE naturally, the reader may want to know something about the plans made for the five children we had in treatment at the time of the premature closing of Pioneer House.

We want to preface any remarks that are made about this period by emphasizing that any clinician would have recognized that the children were not as yet ready to return to a full-blown community setting. Certainly, in the field of medicine proper, not only the clinician but the average layman as well would be aghast if an analogous event occurred. Think of a group of surgeons who are contemplating a delicate and dangerous operation. They build up their patient's bodily resources to cope with the physiological strain of such an operation. The patient rallies and, perhaps after months of patient building up, is ready for surgery. The operation is begun —and at this point, imagine, they are told, "Call it all off, stuff it all back, sew him up, you can't continue. For this is too costly, not enough people are being served, the per capita costs are so high!" In the realm of psychotherapeutic endeavor, every bit as delicate and dangerous as the medical situation which we have hypothesized, this is what happened at Pioneer House. There were no clinical grounds whatsoever for discharging these children at that time and, if we had been able to procure funds for their continued treatment, they would not have been. Ironically enough, the time of our closing coincided with a period of treatment which was producing some of the most promising implications for actual change. While we knew at the same time that real treatment had barely begun, we also had ample evidence that important personality changes had demonstrably taken place. Among these, without attempting to go into detail, the following might be mentioned:

Increased ability to use verbal modes of communication

To begin with, as we have stated in a number of places in this book as well as in *Children Who Hate,* our children were extremely blocked in the whole area of word symbolization of feelings, conflicts, etc. Their very action-proneness was a function, in part, of this area of pathology. We began to see changes in this area. A new feeling for language developed, bringing with it an ability to formulate ideas with respect to themselves, their social relations, and the world around them.

Increased ability to relate meaningfully to image symbols

The children began to demonstrate an increased capacity to form meaningful images of places and people. The term Pioneer House popped up more and more frequently in their conversations and its use varied from rather sentimental nostalgia for when they first came, "Boy, remember when us guys came to Pioneer House—hey, how long ago was that?—boy, did we have fun making the counselors chase us" to "Hey, cut it out you guys, you'll get Pioneer House in trouble" (if one of them was cursing out of doors, etc.). The positive image of the Home remained a constant while the image of themselves had changed: they had more consciousness of amenities and better controls, and both the negative and positive features of their behavior were referred to the Pioneer House image.

Diminished suspiciousness of the adult: ability to take affection

This was one of the most marked areas of change. Comparison between their reactions to receiving gifts, as one instance of the pathology in this area, at the beginning and ending of the Pioneer House period was quite revealing. While in the beginning we were cursed and abused even in the face of lavish display, toward the end they really showed appreciation and gratitude approaching in some of its dimensions the behavior of normal children. When we compared this with their former unreasonableness in the face of gratification offerings, we were especially impressed. The keynote here seemed to be a significant reduction in their total defensive warfare against the adult.

Increased ability to cope with rules and routines

In keeping with the improved rapport with the adult world, the children's reaction toward rules and routines became more realistic. There was not so much perception of these items as instances of "meanness" on the part of the adult, and there was more realization of their necessity in the social or group setting.

Diminution of major symptomatology

All therapy, while not being satisfied by symptom disappearance alone, is concerned with what happens to the symptom. Certainly successful therapy is attended by the lessening of symptoms. At Pioneer House we did observe a definite symptom diminution in most of our children. Temper tantrums, stealing, social blindness, and hair-trigger frustration tolerances abated. Especially the frustration tolerance problem was fascinating in its eventual tone-down since it opened so many more programming chances with our group. Thus, for example, programming with much longer time perspectives became possible. Interrelated with their improved ability to use program structures was their gain in sublimative capacity and ability to use previous satisfaction images as resources. Also, because they were better able to cope with insecurity, fear, and anxiety as well as newness, the challenge of new activities was better handled, and the general organization and control of impulse strivings was raised. Perhaps one of the more fascinating improvements in terms of major symptomatology was the gain in insight among the children of their "own contribution to the behavioral chain" as compared to the high "evaporation rate" in reference to this item in their earlier behavior pattern. What we have referred to in *Children Who Hate* as "the wisdom of tool appraisal"—figuring out which of a number of ways to cope with situations is more reasonable—improved considerably as did their ability to cope with failure, mistakes, and success. The emergence of new value sensitivities seemed well on the way and certainly the increased ability to cope with guilt without aggressive disorganization was promising.

Quick fade-out of delusional attacks

One aspect of change in symptom or ego ability to cope with disturbance is this: what happens during a set-back or reversal? In this respect we noted that even when our children would be revisited by their old delusional symptomatology, it did not have the same intensity as formerly. They were more easily brought back to reality-oriented ego behavior, especially with respect to some of their paranoid charges against the adult. Counterdelusional handling became less necessary and, when necessary, more quickly effective. Most encouraging, under this item, was the improved capacity of the children to deal with sudden "case history flooding" of particular situations. To begin with they became more intact in this respect —fewer situations reminded them of the unpleasant past, and those that did were handled better.

Increased ability to make use of community program resources

Diminished impulsivity, increased awareness of social reality, and increased reasonableness made it possible for us to make use of community program resources much more than during the earlier and more disturbed days of the group. For example, toward the end of placement, they could, for short periods of time, handle themselves adequately by themselves at the YMCA. Of course such programming had to be carefully dosed along with more supportive activities in close proximity to the Pioneer House-identified adult but the emergence of the possibility alone showed a great area of change. Because the children improved considerably in their reaction to competitive challenge we began, some time before closure, to be able to schedule baseball games and other events with some of the surrounding settlements, thus adding to our total program mobility in this way as well.

These, then, were some of the changes that occurred. Since adequate institutional facilities which might continue the clinical work with the children were not available elsewhere than at Pioneer House, we were faced with one of two alternatives: either the children had to be returned to their own homes or they had to be placed in foster homes. Review of the home situations revealed that, in no case, had a sufficient degree of change taken place during the child's period of residence at Pioneer House to warrant return of the child to his own home with anywhere near the possibility of a favorable prognosis. Therefore, the only remaining alternative was to place them in as carefully selected foster homes as possible, in combination with as much supervision of the placement and other supportive aids as we could offer. This plan was actually adopted in the case of four out of the five youngsters after thorough discussion with and final consent of parents and children themselves. The fifth child was returned to his own home on the basis that his disturbance pattern, especially in the sphere of adult relationships, was of such intensity that, even in the best of foster homes and with the greatest support that could be given, it was obvious that his behavior would not be acceptable. Thus, during the last three months of Pioneer House, financial sponsorship for the follow-up plan for a period of one year having been obtained from the Junior League, we studied a number of foster homes, of which four were finally selected as offering the best potentialities. In addition to the selection of optimum foster homes, the follow-up program utilized a combination of treatment and diagnostic tools as follows:

1. Continual casework supervision of the entire placement by the former executive director of Pioneer House, a trained caseworker. This provided the advantage of continuity of contact with the children through previous Pioneer House affiliation of the caseworker. On this basis, close consultation and casework help was given to children and foster or real parents.

2. Testing and consultation services to meet new developments as they came along.

3. Continuation of some personalized form of contact with the previous Pioneer House personnel (occasional parties, individual trips, etc.).

4. Continuation of symbols of affection and interest of the type that any family would show a child that moved out of its boundaries, in terms of presents at Christmas, on birthdays, and on other occasions.

5. Additional support in school difficulties which were to be expected, especially during the transitional months (school contacts through caseworker, tutoring in certain areas).

6. Continued group experience in the form of a Pioneer Club

to provide a transitional group exposure during the readjustment period under the leadership of a group worker trained in clinical group work with this type of child.

The follow-up program concerned itself, too, with the maintenance of adequate recording of all individual and group contacts for the purpose of action planning, as well as total research.

It is not our purpose here to make a detailed evaluation of the trends shown by the children during the follow-up period. It would be much too space-consuming and extensive for the few pages we have left. We hope at some future time to prepare some of these observations for publication. But a few comments about basic findings are possible. To begin with, the various improvement areas described were well enough established to remain intact over a period of approximately eight months following closing. All but one of our placed children, however, had to be returned to their own homes from within one to three months after the closing of Pioneer House. This was due primarily to two factors. First, as we have emphasized, these children were not ready to interrupt treatment and to move into foster home placement to begin with. Second, even the best foster homes that we could locate, after careful search and appraisal, were still not adequate to deal with our children with the clinical wisdom which they required.

Moving back to their own homes re-exposed them to traumatic life situations ranging all the way from the amazing to the unbelievable. Even so, the changes mentioned held up pretty well at first. Their use of relationship with us, their ability to make themselves available for interviewing in connection with some of the grim reality problems imposed upon them by their own environments, with a subsequent readiness to use interpretive handling, were quite impressive.

Danny, who had been traumatized by a brutal alcoholic father whom his mother had divorced just before he came to Pioneer House, "walked into" an incredible repetition of this original situation; his mother was married again to almost exactly the same type of man, apparently driven by her own neurosis into re-establishing a sado-masochistic arrangement. Violent quarrels between the parents, knifing attacks by the stepfather, quickly restored the same mechanisms which had been involved in Danny's initial attacks of berserk temper at Pioneer House. Yet, before any outbursts on his part occurred, he was able to come to the caseworker, bring out this material, and, for a short time, even use the interpretive suggestion, "Yes, Danny, I guess we both know how upset this makes you. It's just what happened when your own father was still living with your mother. You are going to want to blow your top again. But it won't help anything. I want you to call me any time you get upset. You can blow off to me as much as you like. If you start up around home or in school, it will only be worse for you."

The amazing thing was that Danny could really do this for a while. Our Danny, who originally at Pioneer House was, in some moments, so delusional that, even after he had stuffed himself full of food, he would accuse us of not wanting to feed him! But the irony in this situation transcends our amazement: for what child, no matter how excellent the condition of his ego (and Danny's was far from excellent), could indefinitely cope with such a destructive environment? Desperately wandering around to avoid being in the home, he drifted into a wider range of stealing episodes. Finally he was picked up by the police and sent to an institution for delinquents.

Not all of our children fared as Danny did. Because of the fact that the environmental factors in their individual lives became so complex, the question of why some broke down while others did not cannot at this time be satisfactorily answered. However, except in the case of Larry for whom it was possible to find a promising treatment arrangement, most of the sharp improvements that we had noted were slowly erased, confirming almost precisely our conviction as to their total lack of readiness for adjustment to anything else but residential therapy.

Thus our "children who hate" went back into the limbo of "the children that nobody wants." The spectacle of their retraumatization, of strengths that had been so painfully, if incompletely, implanted in their personalities being literally wasted in a battle with a hostile environment, is one that fades slowly, if at all, from our minds. Even our scientific satisfaction in having somehow scratched the surface of the mysteries of their ego pathology does not help the process of erasure.

And we are still having trouble in recovering from our amazement that, in one of the richest cities in the United States, with its pride and world-wide fame in the nonhuman aspects of engineering, it would remain impossible to create adequate treatment channels to rescue these five lives.

ACKNOWLEDGMENTS

IN our book *Children Who Hate* we had the opportunity to thank a great number of people who made the existence of Pioneer House possible—the Pioneer House Board of the Junior League, Inc., of Detroit, our advisory board, and our numerous friends and helpers in the community. We are now happy, at last, to express our thanks and great appreciation to those who carried the main burden of the treatment process itself.

First we think of those who shared with us the daily challenge of life in the foxholes of childhood aggression at the Home itself. Emily Kener, the Housemother, Bob Case, our Head Counselor, and Joel Vernick, Vera Kare, and Barbara Smith, our resident student counselors, displayed a degree of skill in handling the children, a quality of morale and devotion with which they bore the brunt of life in a treatment home, which will remain unforgettable for us. They merged into a solid team with their nonresident colleagues, Betty Braun, Pearl Bruce, Shirley Danto, Paul Deutschberger, and Lucietta Irwin, at that time Field Work Students at the School of Social Work, Wayne University. Their work was supplemented during one summer by John Haddad, Betty Kalichman, Henry Maier, and Marion Nassau, and by Norman Ferin and Wade McBride at other times.

Treatment in a residential setting rests as heavily on those people who are in charge of the physical comfort as on the direct therapeutic staff. The affection which our cook, Cleo Tuggle, threw into the job was as important and admirable as the cheerful patience of those primarily responsible for our maintenance problems: Tom Tuggle, and Etta and Sue Ware.

For a treatment home with as heavy recording and research tasks as ours had set itself, it is important that those in secretarial functions mold harmoniously into the total treatment strategy and into the direct life with the children. Barbara Simonds and Jean Meldrum earned our great admiration in this respect. They were helped at times by Mrs. Joan Hall and Mrs. Catherine Flannery, of the Junior League of Detroit, who served us as volunteers.

A program which fans out into the larger community, as ours did, needs many additional services and supplementations beyond the immediate scope of the Home itself. In this respect we are especially obliged to Miss Mary Barker of the Detroit Girl Scouts, who gave us invaluable help on special programs and became a real friend of the children, and Miss Joyce Jopling of the Detroit Public Library, whose exceptional understanding of our children's problems opened up vistas for books and stories way beyond what a library otherwise could have done for us. The invaluable services of the Detroit Public Schools, the Canfield Police Station, the Boys Club of Detroit, the Department of Art Education of Wayne University, and others, we have already mentioned in *Children Who Hate*.

When the time came to close Pioneer House because of financial reasons, we were faced with the grim task of returning our children to the community while they were literally in the middle of treatment. We could not even have begun this job without the help of a host of interested and sympathetic friends from many different walks of life and professional disciplines. We think here of our follow-up Board, especially of the invaluable services of Mrs. John W. Blanchard, of the Junior League; Mrs. Abigail Bosworth of the Children's Division of the State Child Welfare Department; Mesdames Theodore R. Buttrick, John C. Garlinghouse, and Daniel Goodenough of the Junior League; Miss Sara Kerr of the Detroit Visiting Teachers; Dr. W. Mason Mathews of the Merrill-Palmer School, our gracious and immensely interested Board chairman; Mrs. Annie McCormick of the Family Service of Oakland County, Michigan; and Miss Doris Reuel, formerly of the Lutheran Charities, Inc.

To Dr. William C. Morse, Director, Walter Zach, Program Director, and counsellors Glen Core, John Maturo, Edward Norris, and Lee Salk of the University of Michigan Fresh Air Camp we owe an unpayable debt for making possible for our children a camp experience in the summers of 1948 and 1949. Only their deep belief in and identification with the clinical task made it possible to cope with the massive disorganization which the children produced following their premature release from residential therapy. For help in planning recreational and group experience at other times we wish to thank Dr. Esther McGinnis, formerly director of the Merrill-Palmer School, who made it possible to obtain club space and the use of the Merrill-Palmer camp site in the summer of 1950 for a camping trip in which Joel Vernick and Edward Holmberg merged their skills to provide an excellent experience for the Pioneer boys.

One of the most challenging tasks of the follow-up period consisted of finding suitable foster homes for the ex-Pioneers. For their spirited and loyal help in ways too numerous to mention we are indebted in this phase of our operations to Mr. Albert A. Ball and Mr. A. E. Ramsay of the Michigan Children's Institute; Miss Zoe Gross of the Children's Division of the State Child Welfare Department; and Mrs. Ella Zwerdling, formerly of the Jewish Social Service Bureau in Detroit.

To the various schools to which our Pioneers were sent, once they were back in the community, they brought behavioral disturbances which needed ingenious, tireless handling and a real devotion to children. For their zeal and courage in working with our children we wish to thank Mrs. Mildred Konstanzer, Mr. Richard Kulka, Mr. Delmar Pardonnet, Miss Hattie M. Smith, and Miss Caroline Smith.

Dr. Martha Ericson Dale, formerly of the Psychology Department of the Merrill-Palmer School, deserves our thanks for her Rorschach analyses of some of our children during the follow-up period. Dr. Mathews, too, extended his services beyond those of Board chairman to guide this phase of the work.

Quite naturally, once the children were beyond the reach of our own residential approach, the efforts of other clinicians who worked with them and with us became of paramount importance. In this respect we are appreciative of the services of Mrs. Mordecai Falick, remedial reading therapist, Mr. David Faigenbaum, psychologist at the Oakland County Michigan Juvenile Court, and Ralph D. Rabinovitch, M.D., Chief of Children's Services, Neuropsychiatric

Institute, University of Michigan Hospital, and Dr. Marie I. Rasey of Wayne University.

As in *Children Who Hate,* so in this book we wish to express our appreciation to Mr. Seymour Riklin of the Department of Philosophy, Wayne University, who helped us in the preparation of the whole manuscript. To Mrs. Jean Schnaar we are indebted for help in the laborious job of editing. Nor would our roster be complete unless we took this opportunity to thank again for their numerous services and their invaluable guidance of our thinking in many phases of operation both during and after Pioneer House Dr. Bruno Bettelheim of the Orthogenic School, Chicago, Illinois; Dr. Norman Polansky and Miss Mary Lee Nicholson of the School of Social Work at Wayne University; and Dr. Editha Sterba of the Detroit Psychoanalytic Society.

The preparation of this book was partially aided by a research grant from the Division of Mental Hygiene, United States Public Health Service (Research Grant MH 94).

APPENDIX [1]

Background Information on Projects Mentioned in the Text

TO round out the picture for those of our readers who may not have read *Children Who Hate*, we would like to give a short sketch of the various projects which provided the clinical background for both books.

Pioneer House, a residential treatment setting for severely disturbed preadolescent boys, was organized in September of 1946. A three-month period was consumed in organizational and staff orientational work and, in December, 1946, our first children came to live at the Home. It was located in the neighborhood of Wayne University in Detroit where the Junior League, the financial sponsors of our program, had bought a small home to be used for this purpose.[2] Pioneer House remained in operation until June, 1948, when we had to close since it turned out to be impossible to find guarantees of continued financial support.

[1] Material in this section represents a condensation from Fritz Redl and David Wineman, *Children Who Hate* (Glencoe, Illinois: The Free Press, 1951) Chapter I, "Pioneer House: Experimentation with a New Design."

[2] Pioneer House was exclusively financed, throughout its period of operation, by the Junior League of Detroit, Inc. None of the parents of any of the children who were referred to us were able to make any appreciable contribution toward the expense of keeping them in the Home. The per capita costs were naturally high in spite of the fact that the Director of the Home contributed his services free of charge, as did a number of special consultants.

The Staff

Our professional staff, including full-time and part-time personnel, numbered at any given time approximately ten individuals. There were the director and executive director (the co-authors). In addition, we had a housemother and, in the second year of operations, a full-time boys' worker. Also, there were usually five field work students from the Wayne University School of Public Affairs and Social Work, placed at the Home by the School as part of their training in casework, group work, and group therapy. In addition, a group work consultant, the then executive director of the Detroit Group Project, figured very prominently in consultation for and direct participation in programming with our youngsters. Finally, there were a resident cook, a housemaid, two part-time maids, and a secretary.

Recording

Three types of records were kept at Pioneer House: (1) group records, maintained by the counselor staff, which preserved each day's significant events in the life of the group, (2) individual behavior logs on each child maintained both by the housemother and executive director, and (3) a special daily program analysis log which gave a detailed picture of the reactions of the children to each phase of the activity program. These were also maintained by the counselors.

Final Selection and Population Shifts

We first selected an initial group of six children from among some thirty to thirty-five referrals to our Home from the various social agencies. Our selection, the criteria for which cannot be gone into in detail in this short description, was weighted in the direction of youngsters from lower socio-economic, "open-door-style neighborhood" community settings. These children had what might be commonly referred to as "predelinquent or delinquent" behavior patterns. This involved such symptoms as: hyper-aggression, stealing, lying, truancy, temper tantrums, sassiness to adults, and most of the rough and tumble behavior that goes into the pattern of a "tough guy" in the making. The age range was between eight and eleven. Other factors that were evaluated were, in very brief summary: I.Q., health and physique, known group

allergies and sensitivities, intensity of problem behavior, and tough-
ness-shyness range. There were still others of a more complexly
group psychological nature which we cannot merely mention without a chance to discuss them more thoroughly. Of this group of six,
only three children were able to be absorbed permanently into the
Home, the other three proving too advanced in their disturbance
pattern to be helped in an open institution of the Pioneer House
type. These latter three left Pioneer House within three months
from the time the clinical work began. At about this point we added
a new child who became one of the permanent members of the
group and, two months later, still another who also remained with
us. These five children were then our stable population during the
entire period of operation. We admitted two other children after we
had added our fifth permanent member, both of whom remained
with us for approximately two months. It was our experience that it
took from one and a half to three months to determine if a given
child could be contained within our particular design. The following table shows the number of children, date of admission, date of
discharge, and length of stay.

TABLE A

Name (PSEUDONYMS)	Age	Date of Admission	Date of Discharge	Length of Stay
"Danny"	10	12/1/46	6/23/48	19 mos.
"Larry"	8	12/1/46	6/23/48	19 mos.
"Andy"	9	12/1/46	6/23/48	19 mos.
"Mike"	9	12/1/47	6/23/48	17 mos.
"Bill"	9	4/1/47	6/23/48	15 mos.
"Henry"	10	12/1/46	12/30/46	1 mo.
"Joe"	9	12/1/46	2/5/47	3 mos.
"Sam"	9	12/1/46	2/5/47	3 mos.
"Harry"	9	4/5/47	5/20/47	1½ mos.
"Donald"	10	4/15/47	6/20/47	2 mos.

Total—10

In our record illustrations all of these boys appear but most fre
quently the first five youngsters, since they were our stable, long-
range population.

In the case of the children who left us before the Home closed
we have some follow-up information available. Three are in detention homes or state reformatories, one has made a fairly adequate

adjustment in the community, and a fifth has left town with his family, thus removing any chance for follow-up appraisal.

The Children: This Is What Happened to Them before They Came

Children do not come into treatment out of a vacuum. The following is intended to provide the reader with some of the significant features of the mode of existence, the interweaving of symptom and milieu, of the Pioneer House youngsters.

The adults in their lives. Almost uniformly, we observed that what the psychiatric clinician calls the "adult-child relationship" was severely damaged. Broken homes, the chain reaction style of foster home placement and institutional storage, a rapidly shifting galaxy of neglectful, disinterested, sometimes cruel and brutal adults formed a basic theme in the background histories of the youngsters before they came to us. Once the children were with us, the parents seemed to lose interest in them almost entirely. Their main, unconcealed reaction was: "We're glad you've got them, not us. Life is so peaceful without them." And rare was the time, after they were with us at the Home, that we would hear the youngsters say, "Gee, it was fun when I was with so-and-so once." There were no uncles, aunts, cousins, or friends who seemed to have taken any interest in them sufficient to provide gratifications of significant enough richness to be stored in their memories. This whole vacuum in adult relationship cannot possibly be overestimated in terms of how impoverished these children felt or how much hatred and suspicion they had toward the adult world.

The siblings in their lives. In the relationships of the brothers and sisters of our children there was open, naked rivalry and tension, quarreling and bickering. Most of their siblings presented emotional problems in their own right. However, our Pioneers were felt by the parent to be the "worst one." Usually there was some selective psychological factor which predisposed the parent to hold this discriminatory position.

Danny's mother felt that he resembled her divorced husband whom she hated for his brutality toward her, his promiscuity, and his total neglect of all family responsibilities. To her Danny was "a chip off the old block," this remark being reiterated by her in many contacts we had with her. She constantly reminded him of this, would tell him she wished he had been born a girl, maintained a constant critical, un-giving, and punitive mode of behavior toward him.

In other cases it was clear that step-parents who became involved in the children's lives had behaved toward them with typical story book step-parent psychology, setting up severe sibling hatred because they openly favored their own offspring.

Andy came to live with his father when he was six after having spent the first five years being shuttled from one home to the other. His step-mother was cold and unfeeling, overprotected three half siblings, loaded Andy with household chores, criticized and nagged him chronically. He in turn released all of his hostility against his siblings quite sadistically, and was openly and interminably jealous.

Generally, we felt that little or no incentive had been given the children who had come to Pioneer House for adequate sibling adjustments in their own homes. In each family, on one psychological basis or another, the placed child was the most severely mistreated and unwanted of the total sibling group.

Life in the school and community. School adjustments of the "children who hate" were uniformly precarious. Dogged on the one hand by their extreme weakness of ego functioning which created severe obstacles along the lines of even remotely modest achievements in any phase of activity within the school, and on the other hand by their peculiar gift for aggressive exploitation of their environment along delinquent lines, their total behavior pattern was earmarked by severe social disorganization and apathy. Pseudo-stupidity about school matters went side by side with lying, bully-ing, stealing, sassiness, obscenity, truancy—the familiar gamut of traits of the "children who hate." Community-wise, one of two patterns was found. Either they were "communityless" because of the rapidly shifting life scenes forced upon them by a quick succession of placements, or, in the rare cases where they had lived in one community most of their lives, their behavior had become part of neigh-borhood legend. In the latter case, of course, any security that might have been expected on the basis of the permanency of their residence was destroyed because of their status as "social lepers."

Traumatic life events. Instances of destructive experiences were so numerous in the case histories of our children that we could say that benign experience was the exception, trauma the rule. Seldom, in ordinary clinical experiences with more typically neurotic children, is there seen such gross and continuous exposure to traumatization on so many different levels as in the cases of "the children who hate."

The missing links in their lives. A bird's-eye peek into the past of the children who hate shows some serious gaps among the things in life that are ordinarily regarded as "good" or "lucky" or "happy." A list of some of the basic "missing links in their lives" looks something like this:

1. Factors leading to identification with adults, feeling of being loved and wanted, and encouragement to accept values and standards of the adult world.

2. Opportunities for and help in achieving a gratifying recreational pattern.

3. Opportunities for adequate peer relationship.

4. Opportunities for making community ties, establishing a feeling of being rooted somewhere where one belongs, where other people besides your parents know you and like you.

5. Ongoing family structures which are not in some phase of basic disintegration at almost any given time in their lives.

6. Adequate economic security for some of the basic needs and necessities of life.

The Detroit Group Project and its Summer Camp

The Detroit Group Project was founded in 1942 by Fritz Redl as an "agency to serve other agencies" by offering group therapy to the children they refer. It is financed by the Council of Social Agencies of Metropolitan Detroit, and is co-sponsored by the School of Social Work, Wayne University. It owes its development primarily to Mrs. Selma Fraiberg, Mrs. Marabel Beck, Miss Mary Lee Nicholson, who have assumed leadership over the project in succession, and to Mr. Paul Deutschberger, who is its present director, and of course to its staff and the wonderful cooperation of the agencies whom it serves. It is now operating with three full-time staff members, one full-time secretary, and usually a few Field Work students from Wayne University. The project also enjoys the devoted services of a most enlightened Board, consisting of prominent citizens of the community, of lay as well as professional members. It operates, at the time of this writing, about eight clubs in various areas of Detroit, serving a total of about eighty children, of the age range between eight and thirteen. It is run, of course, on an intercultural and interracial basis. It operates both "straight" therapy groups and so-called "protected groups," both closely tied to the group work agencies on whose premises they meet.

The Detroit Group Project Summer Camp, developed as an extended service of the Detroit Group Project, was in operation during the summers 1944–1947. It had the use of the camp site "Chief Noonday," situated near Middleville, Michigan, and owned by the Michigan State Department of Conservation. It had to discontinue its existence for lack of financial support by the Council of Social Agencies, primarily caused by the need to develop a camp site of its own after the lease of the State site had been terminated. Besides the Group Project budget, the camp was supported by Charitable Relief, Inc., whose presidents, Mr. and Mrs. Fred Johnson, deserve our great gratitude for their enthusiastic participation. It also received help from the McGregor Foundation, the Mendelsohn Fund, the Tribute Fund, and other Foundations, at times. The Camp combined service to children with an opportunity for the training of graduate students in social work, clinical psychology, and education from all over the United States. A full-time Field Work Supervisor in case work as well as in Group Work supplemented the training which the student counselors received in classes and seminars. The Camp was also co-sponsored by the School of Social Work of Wayne University, which offered credit for training received there and furnished Fritz Redl as director and instructor at the Camp. There were many people who left their impact on the development of these efforts in "clinical group work with disturbed children." Our thanks go especially to: Miss Estelle Allston, Mrs. Marabel Beck, Mrs. Selma Fraiberg, Miss Mary Lee Nicholson, Mr. Robert Rosema, Mr. Benjamin Rubenstein, and Miss Dorothea Sullivan, and, of course, to all the members of our staff, whose names are too numerous to list here. The Camp served about eighty children at a time over a six- to eight-week period and had an adult staff of a total of fifty-four. All clinics and social agencies referring children to the camp had ample contact before and after the camp session, and reports on individual as well as group psychological development of the children were exchanged between the camp and the referring agencies. The children were usually between seven and fifteen years of age. The camp was co-educational and, of course, interracial.

INDEX